I'm Okay you're a brat

I'm Okay you're a brat

SETTING THE PRIORITIES STRAIGHT AND FREEING YOU FROM THE GUILT AND MAD MYTHS OF PARENTHOOD

SUSAN JEFFERS, Ph.D.

ST. MARTIN'S GRIFFIN
NEW YORK

Every effort has been made to ensure that proper credit has been given for all sources used in this book. The author and publisher would be grateful for notification of any corrections that need to be made. Sources not given appropriate credit will be included in future printings.

Library of Congress Catalog Card Number: 00-102823

ISBN 1-58063-202-5

P1

Published by Renaissance Books
Distributed by St. Martin's Press
Manufactured in the United States of America
First Edition

Previously published in England by Hodder & Stoughton and in Australia by Hodder Headline Australia Pty Limited

To my wonderful ones!
My children, Gerry and Leslie . . .
My children-by-marriage, Alice and Guy . . .
and my daughter-in-law, Meredith

May this book show you the way

And to my loving husband,
Mark Shelmerdine

Who always shows me the way

I love you all!

Acknowledgments

There are so many beautiful people to thank who have made the writing of this book such an exciting adventure . . .

Joe McNeely and the people at Renaissance Books, who made this book possible in the U. S. market. Your unwavering support is truly appreciated. Thank you!

Dominick Abel, my wonderful agent, a very caring human being who believes in my work and always lets me know it. He also, thank goodness, keeps the ball rolling and rolling and rolling. Thank you!

Gerry Gershman, my loving son, whose interest and support of this book continues. He gave the book its humorous title and made many suggestions along the way, all of which were invaluable. Thank you!

Donna Gradstein, my dear friend, who, in the middle of a hectic life (including five children!), proofread the manuscript, checked all the footnotes, and gave me so much feedback, love, and support. Friends don't get any better than that . . . *and* . . . we have such a good time together. Thank you!

More dear friends (in alphabetical order): Francesca Beale, Mary Becker, Matt Bombeck, Trevor Chenery, Nancy Erickson, Susan Forward, Wendy Forward, Henry Gradstein, Miranda Holden, Robert Holden, John Levoff, Lois Luger, Renata Mihalic, Wayne Muller, Melissa Oberon, Alejandro Ortiz, Beverly Raymond, Matt Walton, DC Walton, Diana Von Welanetz Wentworth, and my loyal and caring sister, Marcia . . . who all contributed in some form or another . . . reading the manuscript, giving me back helpful suggestions, sharing stories, sending me books and articles, giving me wonderful leads and information, cheering me on, always letting me know that I was on the right track . . . or all of the above! Thank you!

And a very special thank you to the men and women I interviewed, whose privacy will be honored. They truly are very giving people whose sometimes painful and sometimes joyful truths greatly added to the richness and honesty of this book. They've contributed to the lives of everyone who reads it. Thank you!

I can never say "thank you" enough to my amazing husband, Mark Shelmerdine, for the incredible love and support he gives me every day of my life. How blessed I am for his joyous presence in my life. Thank you! Thank you! Thank you!

And the biggest thank you of all to my two wonderful parents, Jeanne and Leon Gildenberg, who sacrificed so much to raise the brat who wrote this book! Even though they are now in Heaven, I always feel their loving presence in my life and I am grateful. Thank you, Mom! Thank you, Dad!

Contents

I'm Okay you're a brat

INTRODUCTION

IT'S ABOUT TIME!

It was our original idea to write and to illustrate a volume on teenagers that was not a put-down, but would be filled with love, humor and poignancy. How does aggravation, hostility and pain grab you?

Erma Bombeck to her co-creator Bil Keane.[1]

My son, Gerry, gave me the title for this book and I loved it the minute I heard it. It makes me laugh, as it does most people who hear it . . . which is a very good thing. It also expresses in a nutshell the frustration that all parents, even those who adore parenting, feel during those very difficult times that are an inevitable part of the raising of children.

One day we will look back and realize what crazy times we now live in when it comes to issues relating to parenthood. Whether we are conscious of it or not, we are presently drowning in a sea of crazy-making myths that are mercilessly taking away our peace of mind. For those of us who are parents, these myths have filled us with guilt, fear, and confusion and they have ripped away our sacred trust in ourselves. For those of us who are would-be parents, they have misled us by painting a distorted picture of what having a child is truly about. It's definitely time for these destructive myths to be exposed so that the critical decisions we have to make, either as a parent or a would-be parent, are based on fact rather than fiction.

Before I go any further, let me give you my definition of "myth"as I'm using it here: *A myth is an unproven collective belief that is accepted by society-at-large as truth.* "If everyone believes it, it must be so." Need I remind you that everyone once believed that the earth was flat? Many of the decrees passed down by our society in recent years belong in "the earth is flat" category of erroneous (or at least, questionable) beliefs that we've accepted as truth.

My goal in writing this book was to expose these harmful myths and, in the process, end the unnecessary suffering they have caused for so many of us. My deepest hope is that in the midst of the humor and honesty within these pages, you will find a wonderful sense of comfort, understanding, lightness, and inner wisdom that has eluded you before.

And there's more: For many reasons, which will become evident as you read, few people feel comfortable telling the whole truth about their parenting experience. As a result, we have, in Western society, a phenomenon that's been called the conspiracy of silence. This conspiracy has caused a lopsided picture of parenting in which the rewards are hugely magnified and the woes are glaringly absent. Again, this discrepancy affects not only parents, but also those who are thinking about becoming parents. It is so important for the well-being of all concerned that the whole truth be known. To this end, you will find on these pages the de-glorified, de-sanctified, and de-romanticized side of the story that you may never have heard before. My gratitude goes to the many beautiful people who were generous enough to share their closely held secrets. You will be moved by their willingness to tell you what is true for them. You will also notice that I have written this book with a great deal of compassion for the feelings of parents; certainly, too many books dwell only on the feelings of the child . . . another sign of our lopsided view of the parenting picture.

I'm Okay . . . You're a Brat!

I'm Okay . . . You're a Brat! is written for a very broad audience of both men and women:

- Parents of all ages who experience guilt and confusion relative to the job they did or are doing in the raising of their children
- Would-be-parents who need to see all sides of the big picture before they decide to take the big step
- Those who want to remain childfree and need to know that this can be a very healthy and sound choice, contrary to what society has told them
- Those who can't have children and need to know that their happiness and fulfillment does not depend on their becoming parents.

There are too few books about parenthood written with the honesty you will find within these pages. Most of you will thank me profusely for questioning long-held ideologies that have kept parents imprisoned in a web of guilt. Others will criticize me for going against the grain of their beliefs. But I'm willing to take that chance. In fact, controversy is a good thing. For when diverse feelings are exposed and understood, and when the illusions are smashed, we have ALL been set free. Then and only then is it possible to live our lives in an authentic way—which is good for everyone involved, including the children. In the pages that follow you will learn:

- Why parenthood is a joy for some and a headache for others
- Why many relationships suffer when you, me, and baby makes three
- Why our life changes so drastically when a child is born
- Why the "myths of motherhood" are destroying our peace of mind and taking away the joy of parenting for both men and women

- Why what you put in doesn't necessarily come out
- Why there is little reason to feel guilt
- Why many childcare experts need to be sent back to school
- Why one can love one's kids and hate parenthood
- Why one can have great fulfillment in life with—or without—children
- and much more.

Even if you are in general agreement with the ideas I present, you will no doubt find many points throughout the chapters with which to disagree—sometimes strongly. This is the nature of a subject that is as individual and controversial as this. As I always suggest to those reading my books, *take what works for you and let the rest go.* Most of all, let go of your resistance—then have a good time reading it.

I've written many books of a very different nature, but none has generated as much enthusiasm as this one. At the time I was writing it, I told a colleague the subject matter as he was driving us to a business meeting. This was a mistake, as he almost drove his car into a tree! He was the parent of a teenager . . . need I say more? "At last!" he exclaimed with great excitement in his voice, "Now, the truth will be known." A student of mine started shrieking, crying, and hugging me ecstatically. I thought she'd lost her mind! "Oh, Susan, you've released me! I have lived with such guilt because, while I love my kids, I *hated* so many aspects of raising them! Now, I feel free!" And I could go on with the roars of laughter and faces filled with delight as I talked about the nature of *I'm Okay . . . You're a Brat!*

All of these bizarrely animated and joyous reactions convinced me that both men and women definitely needed to hear what I was saying. In fact, I will guarantee that as parents of children—young and old—read this book, you will hear a loud collective sigh of relief reverberating throughout the Western world! I sincerely hope that this book brings you a sense of relief as well. I invite you to laugh, cry, ponder, agree, disagree, and most of all . . .

Enjoy!

A special note to men: *While a few of the chapters appear to be written for women,* read them anyway. *The myths of motherhood, by definition, are tightly entwined with the myths of fatherhood. Both men and women need to understand the societal imbalance when it comes to parenting and both men and women need to be involved in correcting this imbalance. So, men, read it all and absorb it all. You will be glad you did.*

Endnote

[1]Bombeck, Erma, and Bil Keane. *Just Wait Till You Have Children of Your Own!* Ballantine Books, New York, 1971, p. vi. Written by Erma Bombeck in a letter to her co-creator Bil Keane.

PART I

ANOTHER SIDE OF THE PICTURE

1

WHY DIDN'T ANYONE TELL ME?

In acknowledging that parenting is not only a profound experience, but an exceptionally difficult job, it will be possible to capture a fuller appreciation of the experience and of the problems. It is hardly an exaggeration to assert that flying to the moon is nothing in comparison with raising a child.

Irwin Matus[1]

If anyone told me I'd be writing a book on parenting a few years ago, I would have laughed hysterically. I believed the raising of children was happily a thing of the past for me since my children and stepchildren are all grown up. But when my son and daughter-in-law stated that they were thinking of having a child, a whole flood of conflicting emotions poured into my being.

"Caring Me" thought, "I don't want you to have to go through the pain and worry and suffering that are an inevitable part of parenting."

"Vengeful Me" thought, "Ha! *Now* you'll understand how unbelievably hard it was!"

"Loving Me" thought, "I hope your children bring you astonishing moments of wonder and joy."

"Self-Defensive Me" thought, "Don't expect me to baby-sit!"

"Sensible Me" thought, "Oh, don't do it! It will complicate your life in more ways than you can ever imagine."

"Cautious Me" thought, "How are you going to afford the huge financial commitment of raising and educating children?"

"Healthy Me" thought, "I know you will learn and grow from whatever choices you make in life (and . . . don't expect me to baby-sit)."

There were so many things I wanted to tell them, things that had been on my mind for a long, long time—ever since I, myself, became a parent many years ago.

When my first child was born, I was filled with fairy-tale expectations about the joys of parenting. It was a time of great celebration. But the party soon ended, all the revelers went home . . . and reality set in. And as my days as a parent turned into weeks, into months, into years and into decades, the question never left my mind . . .

Why didn't anyone ever tell me how shockingly hard it was going to be?

My mother didn't tell me. My friends who were parents before me didn't tell me. The famous childcare experts who I relied on and trusted didn't tell me. *Nobody* ever told me. To this day, many years later, the world-at-large still glorifies, sanctifies, and romanticizes the longest and most difficult project in the world called PARENTHOOD, which has been justifiably described by comedian, Rick Reynolds, as "life-drainingly, wretchedly, miserably hard."[2] It truly does feel that on this subject, a conspiracy of silence pervades our society.

Before I go any further let me make it absolutely clear that . . .

There are those individuals who have found the raising of children to be the biggest joy and sense of accomplishment in their lives.

Yes, there really are! In later chapters you will read my theories as to *why* these men and women love parenting so much and why many of us don't. There are logical reasons for both. And if you are one of the former, I ask that you have compassion for the rest of us who must have been sleeping or in the bathroom when what I call the "Loving-Being-a-Parent (LBP) genes" were being handed out by the powers that be. Remember those LBP genes. I shall be talking about them throughout the book.

Trust me when I tell you, *we all wish we had these LBP genes . . .* but we don't. Yes, there are wonderful times when those of us without LBP genes also experience profound moments of joy and fulfillment as we raise our children; but, on balance, our experience lies in the "life-death-drainingly, wretchedly, miserably hard" category.

As I searched my own heart and as I interviewed the men and women who opened up their hearts to me, I saw that too many of today's parents—*even those whose children are long gone from the nest*—are discouraged by many aspects of parenting. They are tired of feeling guilty. They are tired of worrying. They are tired of being blamed for all the ills in their children's lives when they tried so hard to do their very best. They love their children, but for a whole list of reasons, many bear hidden hurts, anguish, and resentment. Some are very angry or live with the biggest secret of all . . . they wish they never had children to begin with. And they hold this secret painfully within the depths of their being.

Given that women are still the primary care-givers (and, thankfully, this is slowly changing), one would think that they would find solace in sharing their honest feelings with each other instead of holding them inside. This usually is not the case. One woman put it this way:

> I wish women could be honest and say, "God, isn't this tough? Isn't this the toughest thing you've ever done? Isn't it the worst thing when your babies are sick? Isn't it the worst thing when your baby wakes up twenty times a night? Isn't this awful?" Nobody talks about it with this level of truth.

While, of course, there are some people out there telling the truth, they are few and far between. And from what I have learned from my interviews, it is rare that parents warn unsuspecting friends who are considering having a child about the perils of parenthood. In fact, the underlying message our society as a whole sends is that . . . *in order to feel fulfilled as human beings, we must have children.* And so we have children. After all, who does not want to be fulfilled as a human being? Unfortunately, most of us are not at all prepared for the task at hand.

Not only are we not prepared, we are filled with illusions and expectations about the joy and wholeness we will feel. Yes, as I stated earlier, for some of us with the LBP genes these expectations are definitely fulfilled . . . in fact, overflowing! But for many of us, they are not . . . and as you traverse this book, you will understand why. Barry Stevens talks of the painful breaking of her bubble of illusion surrounding her children:

> I felt slaughtered, over and over, and I didn't see that what had been slaughtered was nothing but an idea—a fantasy—an illusion—although it hurt like a knife in my chest. I had made a picture in my head—it existed nowhere else—and then screamed when it was ripped apart.[3]

That's telling the truth! And for many like Barry Stevens, parenting is a huge disappointment, or a horrendous responsibility, or an unappreciated sacrifice, or an anger-producing, guilt-producing, worry-producing, sadness-producing activity . . . or all of the above. Of course, those with the LBP genes mentioned earlier will wonder what I am talking about!

While there are undeniably some wonderful aspects of parenting, why is there such a suppression of the "other side" of the coin? Why do we hold our secrets painfully within? Why can't we shout them out and console each other when our hearts are being ripped apart? Let me suggest a few reasons:

1. WE HIDE THE TRUTH FROM OURSELVES

Many of us are invested in seeing ourselves as A Good Parent. When we are invested in this Good Parent role, as defined by our society, the mind simply cannot accept the fact that there are many aspects of parenting that we really don't like. A Good Parent would love it all . . . or so it seems. Also, having a child is an *irreversible* act. It is simply too hard to admit to ourselves that we have created a situation in our lives that we may find difficult to accept . . . that we have given ourselves a life sentence of responsibility. Instead of admitting something so unacceptable, many of us "lie" to ourselves and others about how grand it all is.

It is interesting that some of those who are in denial about their negative feelings unconsciously go overboard on the side of praise to compensate. In psychology, this is called *reaction formation*. Every time I hear someone going on and on and on about the glories of parenthood, I say to myself, "Methinks they praiseth too much." And I wonder what thoughts lurk beneath the murky surface. Is their adoration of parenthood real—which, of course, it may be—or simply an inability to admit their possible dislike of the whole parenting situation? For many, it is the former; for many others, it is the latter.

If everyone understood that The Good Parent can have realistic conflicting feelings about parenthood, this self-denial would not be necessary. Instead, there would be greater peace of mind and a general lightening up about the whole situation. Perhaps as the conspiracy of silence breaks down within our culture, those who previously were not able to accept the truth of their feelings will be liberated at last.

2. WE ARE TOO ASHAMED TO ADMIT OUR FEELINGS TO OTHERS

While some are in denial about their negative feelings, others are very much aware of them. Horrors! This, in the midst of a conspiracy of silence, creates a great deal of shame. Society says women are supposed to be in a state of maternal bliss once a child is born; it is very hard to admit they are often in maternal hell. One woman talked about The Bad Thoughts she sometimes feels about her child. These Bad Thoughts include everything from mild annoyance to wanting to kill her child . . . or herself. A whole range of these Bad Thoughts consume the minds of many parents and they truly feel themselves to be Bad People. As a result, they hide their "shameful" feelings from others, sometimes even their spouses

In Western society, those who love the experience tell the truth. Those who don't love the experience *pretend* to love it. In her excellent book, *The Mask of Motherhood,* Susan Maushart says that women are "still in the closet on the subject of motherhood. And 'faking it' in our public behavior and public discourse has become a way of life."[4] She feels our inability to talk about it or failure to do so diminishes us as parents and people. She says that, for the present generation of women, the myth of motherhood is among the most deeply repressed and destructive of all female deceptions. We deceive each other and we deceive ourselves.

Our "faking motherhood" is understandable in today's social climate. This is a time when children are pampered and glorified as innocent little angels with very delicate feelings who need constant love, assurance, nurturing, and all good things. In such a world, how can you admit to other people that there are those moments that you truly want to give them a smack? Or even that you're sorry you had them to begin with? It's hard, isn't it?

Alone with your agonizing thoughts, you are convinced that you are an evil person. Your society has taught you that parenthood, particularly motherhood, is the ultimate privilege and joy in the world. And you are feeling a great deal of misery. The only question on your lips, is "What is wrong with me?" My answer to that question is, "Nothing is wrong with you!" You are not A Bad Person if you have bad thoughts about your children or your role as a parent. You are a human being feeling the effect of a colossal change in your lifestyle.

It is interesting that a number of parents began our interviews raving about the experience of parenting. I would then inject, "Gee, while I loved my kids, I didn't like the process of parenting."

Once they heard my honesty, the floodgates lifted for some and their true emotions came pouring forth. For example, one young mother was raving about how wonderful it was being home with her six-month-old child. As I "confessed" my experiences, she was soon revealing, slowly at first and then in a steady stream of words, how trapped she really felt and how she resented her husband for going off to work each morning leaving her with the baby and on and on and on. It sounded very familiar. I assured her she was not alone; nor was she A Bad Person. She expressed her relief at finally being able to get it all off her chest.

Yes, *all* parents have The Bad Thoughts many times in their parenting experience, even if they are among the fortunate who love being a parent—those with the LBP genes. That's just the way it is and it is nothing to be ashamed of.

While I have spoken mostly of mothers, fathers also feel deep shame at their distress at how a child changes their lives. They wear the mask of fatherhood. For them, the huge responsibility they feel for the well-being of their wives and children causes many of them to hide their true feelings. Most distressing is the changing relationship with their wives, which I will talk about in a later chapter. But to admit to such inner thoughts would be, in a loving father and husband's mind, a huge betrayal of those he holds so dear in his heart.

3. WE ARE VERY CONFUSED

The strangest thing happens to both men and women after our children are born. From deep within our being, a "responsibility-response" is unleashed, the power of which is enormous. From where it comes, I do not know. Perhaps it's instinctual. Perhaps it's the only humane response one can have holding this helpless little being who is desperately in need of our love, care, and protection. There and then, we make a conscious or unconscious pledge to love, care for, and protect our child as best we can. And isn't that the primary role of parenthood?

But here's the problem: at the same time they are loving, caring for, and protecting their children, many mothers and fathers are discovering a very painful truth: *they are disliking—or worse, detesting—almost every moment of it!* They are learning that the Parenting Role simply does not fit who they are as human beings. They learn that they were not born with the LBP genes. One mother expressed this conundrum beautifully. She said:

My child is my life, but he has ruined my life!

She went on to say that all she loved about adulthood disappeared as she began catering to the needs of her son. Others confessed very similar thoughts.

Confusing isn't it? Even though "I love my children" and "I hate parenting" are two very separate issues, they are mixed-up in our minds. This love/hate confusion can't help but make us feel we are being disloyal and subversive toward the very child we have pledged to protect. What results is a deep sense of inner guilt. It is this inner guilt that makes it very difficult to tell our truth to others. Hence, we remain silent about our negative feelings, expressing only one side of the picture—the very real love we feel for our child.

It is this same confusion factor that explains why the few articles truthfully decrying the horrors of parenting seem to always end with a one-liner about how "it's all worth it." Have you noticed that? It is simply too difficult for the author to simply end with "I hate what the raising of this child is doing to my life." Period. End of story. Rather, we read, "I hate what the raising of this child is doing to my life . . . but it's all worth it." Maybe it is worth it to the author; maybe it isn't. Unfortunately, the reader doesn't take in the essential message of the article; he or she takes in only the "but it's all worth it" part that was thrown in at the end, perhaps as a way of relieving the author's guilt.

More and more people are withstanding the intense pressure they feel from family and friends, and deciding that while they might indeed love any children they would have, they doubt whether they would love the Parenthood role. And they are deciding not to have children. It makes sense that understanding both the up side and the down side of parenting will help people make much wiser choices.

4. WE DON'T WANT TO HURT OUR CHILDREN

Another reason there seems to be a conspiracy of silence is that we fear that the truth, which can be very ugly at times, will be hurtful to our children. Have you considered the possibility that *lying may be cruel to our children?* One of the contributors to a beautiful book, *Child of Mine,* wrote this about revealing the down side of her parenting experience:

> I worry about what my son will think when he reads this. But I have to believe it's better to tell the truth, in all its complication, than to perpetuate a myth. Someday, I think, he'll be better for knowing.[5]

Exploding the myths and offering a healthy dose of reality can't help but allow our children to make more intelligent choices as they consider becoming parents. We need to stop glorifying parenthood and teach them in a balanced fashion what we all wish we had known before we took the big step.

As I write this, I know some of you may be wondering what my children are feeling about their mother writing a book that reveals the down side of parenting. As I told you earlier, my son came up with the catchy title; needless to say, he has a vested interest in the success of this book. On a few occasions, he has opened our phone conversations with, "Hi, it's your brat calling" and we have a good laugh. My daughter jokes that I'm the only mother she knows who isn't pressuring her children to make her a grandparent. I take this as a compliment. As author Jason Salzman laments:

> Too many vulnerable childfree adults are being ruthlessly manipulated into parenthood by their parents, who think that happiness among older people depends on having a grandchild to spoil.[6]

Obviously, I am not in that category of parent! As I stated earlier, part of my motivation for writing this book was to help my extended family of children who are now all adults make an educated decision as to whether or not they should have children. They welcome my input and are carefully considering the pros and cons. If they decide in the affirmative, they will not have their bubble of unrealistic expectations burst; rather they will enter the experience with open eyes and an open heart.

5. WE WANT TO ELUDE "THE GUILT-PEDDLERS"

Even if you don't think of yourself as A Bad Person, "the guilt-peddlers" are around trying to convince you that you are. "How can you say that about your child?" they query. The guilt-peddlers try to make you feel bad and will succeed, *if you let them.* And who are the guilt-peddlers? Your parents, your friends, acquaintances, strangers, journalists, and childcare experts—all of whom have been indoctrinated by the romanticized myths of parenthood and are, as a result, part of the conspiracy of silence. (More about the guilt-peddlers later.)

I encountered a number of guilt-peddlers in the writing of this book. For example, I wanted to interview a woman who conducts therapy sessions with teenagers and their parents. I phoned explaining my mission and told her that the title of my book was *I'm Okay . . . You're a Brat!* I expected the familiar peals of laughter I usually get, even from those who love parenting, when mentioning the title. Instead I got a sound of horror followed by an admonishment: "Children are never brats!" Talk about denial! Is she blind? Even the best of children (and certainly teenagers brought into therapy sessions, for Heaven's sake!) often belong in the brat category! I assuredly was a certifiable brat when I was young. I wanted to say to her, "Lady, lighten up!" but it would have fallen on deaf ears. Needless to say, she didn't want to be interviewed by someone who even jokingly referred to children as brats.

As I thought about her attitude, I felt sorry for the parents she worked with. Can you imagine how much her clients conceal from her for fear of being castigated by the "doctor of denial?" Can you imagine the amount of guilt they feel when they really *do* think of their kids as brats . . . or worse? You can see why there is much about parenting that needs to be said that has not been said!

This is a time where parents, particularly mothers, are blamed for anything that goes wrong with their children. So given the large number of guilt-peddlers lurking around, how do you reveal to anyone that you really don't (or didn't) like the process of raising kids? Or for that matter, how do you admit to anyone if you are childfree, that you really want to stay childfree? Ultimately we need to feel safe within ourselves to be able to tell the truth of our situation, despite the put-downs by those who have no compassion for who we are as human beings, nor tolerance for a different point of view.

6. MISERY LOVES COMPANY

Notice the look of delight in the eyes of your friends who are already parents as you announce your "wonderful news" about becoming pregnant. You may think it's because they are sharing your joy. Maybe it is; maybe it isn't. Their look of delight may reflect the fact that they no longer have to be so envious of your freedom. Some people are only happy when everyone else is as miserable as they are! Not a pretty picture.

Our friends are not our friends when they accentuate only the positive and forget to tell us about the negative. As the saying goes, "With friends like this, we don't need any enemies." It is infuriating when we call our friends telling them of our woes after a child is born and they respond, "Oh, yes, the first six months are a nightmare." Your reaction has to be, "*Now* you tell me! Why didn't you tell me before?" This is probably the same friend who convinced you that you must have a child, as parenthood is the most wonderful experience one can have in life. As I said earlier, for many, this is true, but some of us can think of a hundred life experiences we would prefer to have!

These are just a few reasons why the wall of silence exists. Thankfully, there are quite a few cracks finally appearing in this seemingly indestructible wall. People are becoming more and more truthful in a variety of areas.

The comedy arena takes the lead. Humorists have been joking about the horrors of raising a child for a very long time. The problem is we don't believe them. We think to ourselves, "Oh, they don't really mean it. They're only joking." I'm here to tell you, "No, they are not 'only joking.'" Most are revealing their truth in a way that you and I and even the guilt-peddlers find acceptable. But I implore you:

Listen carefully to the voice of truth that whispers loudly within the humor. Funny or serious, truth is truth.

A case in point is the late Erma Bombeck who wrote many best-selling books with such titles as *I Lost Everything in the Post-Natal Depression, At Wit's End,* and *Just Wait 'Till You Have Children of Your Own.* After her death, I interviewed her son, Matt, and I asked if his mother was really joking or if there was any truth in her humor. He answered that her writing was, in fact, her way out of the doldrums and the morass of boredom and frustration she felt being a stay-at-home mom. I found this same sentiment "jokingly" expressed in one of her books as follows:

> There seemed to be several avenues open to me: (a) take myself seriously and end up drinking gin just after the school bus left; (b) take the children seriously and end up drinking gin before the school bus left; (c) admit to the fear and frustration and have a good time with it.[7]

Yes, she did admit to the fear and frustration and, through her writing, she learned how to have a good time with it. I believe her incredible popularity derived from the fact that, beneath it all, she assured mothers in distress that there was another mother out there who was going through the same thing that they were. If you have never read the words of Erma Bombeck, I suggest you do. If you are someone who never took her seriously, I suggest you re-read her books, this time finding the truth behind her humor.

Bill Cosby is another wonderful example. In his very funny book *Fatherhood*, he wrote:

> I guess the real reason that my wife and I had children is the same reason that Napoleon had for invading Russia: it seemed like a good idea at the time. Since then, however, I've had some doubts, primarily about my intelligence.[8]

All of us are thankful for the likes of Erma Bombeck and Bill Cosby for they allow us to break the fairy-tale myths in a very enjoyable way. Our task now is to believe them.

Cartoonists have also helped crack open the wall of silence. For example, one of Mel Lazarus' cartoons depicted workmen changing a mother's club motto prominently displayed in the lobby. The original motto reads, "MOTHERHOOD IS THE MOST BLESSED STATION IN LIFE;" the new motto reads, "IT'S A DIRTY JOB, BUT SOMEBODY HAS TO DO IT." The woman in charge is explaining this change to an onlooker: "Ah! We're finally catching up with reality."

The truth about parenting is also appearing in other arenas as well. For example, I discovered magazine and newspaper articles with titles such as "Motherhood: the Big Lie,"[9] "I Don't Want Kids. Period,"[10] and "Honey, I didn't kill the kids today . . ."[11] The writers of these articles deserve medals for their honesty.

Hester Lacey, the author of "Motherhood: the Big Lie," stated she wrote her article because, "There's a great conspiracy of silence between women not to tell each other how hideous motherhood is."[12] That's honest! Lacey lamented that, indeed, we love our children, but "if we had a crystal ball to see life a year after the baby was born, we probably wouldn't do it." She speculated that if motherhood were advertised in a job column, there would be no applicants. In this same article, Kathy Lette, a wonderful author and mother of a six-year-old and a four-year-old, made the courageous admission that she is at the stage of "putting the kids in the cupboard under the sink with the poisonous substances within reach." Even though she is, of course, joking, some of you may be gasping, but . . . *that's really how many parents feel at various times in the parenting process, but never have the courage to admit.* Thank goodness, the great majority of us don't act on our feelings. But the feelings are definitely there!

Books are entering the truth arena as well. For example, the wonderful book *Child of Mine* talks about the first year of parenting through the eyes of a number of authors. Both those with and those without the LBP genes are beautifully represented. Amy Herrick, who is one of the latter, admits to us all:

> And often I wonder, if it had been given to me to know beforehand what I now know about motherhood—the swift and merciless loss of innocence, how you are transformed overnight from being someone's child to being someone's parent, handed summarily a love so incandescent and irrevocable that you have to stay awake twenty-four hours a day to protect it from all the dark dangers out of left field—if I had known all this beforehand, would I have agreed to have a child?[13]

This is a question many have asked themselves.

You might be puzzled as to why, even with the erupting sources of truth, the wall of silence remains standing. One explanation is that hard-held cultural beliefs are very difficult to change. It takes a "critical mass," that is, enough accumulated voices to be heard, in order for a societal shift in consciousness to occur. Each of our voices adds to the critical mass needed to break the conspiracy of silence. Each time we tell the truth of our experience, we will be doing our part in exposing the emperor with his clothes . . . or in this case, the baby without its diapers.

With enough people telling their truth, the critical mass will be reached, and the crucial shift needed to break the conspiracy of silence will occur. When this finally happens, instead of the guilt-peddlers admonishing us for telling the truth of our feelings, they will admonish us for *not* telling the truth of our feelings. (Unfortunately, we can't get rid of the guilt-peddlers!) If we live with our lies and don't share the truth of our experiences, we are simply helping to perpetuate the very unhealthy situation called the conspiracy of silence which hurts all of us. As Susan Maushart so beautifully states:

> The Mask of Motherhood is what mutes our rage into murmurs, and softens our sorrow into resignation.[14]

A painful and profound statement. As long ago as 1973, Shirley Radl wrote a wonderfully revealing book entitled *Mother's Day is Over* in which she talked about the conspiracy of silence surrounding motherhood.[15] Nothing much has changed since then; in fact, the conspiracy has become more entrenched. It's time for both mothers and fathers to take off the masks, break the cruel silence, and destroy the destructive belief system that keeps so many of us prisoners of our unbearable thoughts.

With that immensely important goal in mind, let's move on to the multitude of truths that need to be shouted from the rooftops . . . and let's begin shouting!

Endnotes

[1]Matus, Irwin. *Wrestling with Parenthood: Contemporary Dilemmas*. Gylantic Publishing, Littleton, Colorado, 1995, p. ix.

[2]Reynolds, Rick. From the theatrical stage production of Rick Reynolds' wonderful one-man show, *All Grown Up . . . and No Place to Go*. Written and directed by Rick Reynolds. Originally produced in San Francisco, 1995.

[3]Stevens, Barry. *Burst Out Laughing*. Celestial Arts, Berkeley, California, 1984, p. 127.

[4]Maushart, Susan. *The Mask of Motherhood*. Random House, Australia, NSW Australia, 1997, p. 3.

[5]An unidentified contributor in *Child of Mine: Writers Talk About the First Year of Motherhood*. Edited by Christina Baker Kline, Hyperion, New York, 1997, p. xii.

[6]Salzman, Jason. "A Cautionary Campaign" in *Newsweek*, in My Turn, January 19, 1998, page 14.

[7]Bombeck, Erma. *Forever, Erma*. Andrews and McMeel, Kansas City, 1996, p. 18.

[8]Cosby, Bill. *Fatherhood*. Bantam Books, New York, 1986, p. 38.

[9]Lacey, Hester. "Motherhood: The Big Lie," in the *Independent on Sunday* (British), 1998, p. 1.

[10]Castanon, Denise. "I Don't Want Kids. Period," community essay in the *Los Angeles Times*, May 3, 1997, p. B7.

[11]Appleyard, Diana. "Honey, I Didn't Kill the Kids Today . . ." in the *Independent* (British), 1996, p. 10.

[12]Lacey, Hester. Ibid.

[13]Herrick, Amy. "Mortal Terrors and Motherhood," in *Child of Mine: Writers Talk About the First Year of Motherhood*. Edited by Christina Baker Kline, Hyperion, New York, 1997, p. 82.

[14]Maushart, Susan. Ibid., p. 25.

[15]Radl, Shirley L. *Mother's Day Is Over*. Charterhouse, New York, 1973.

2

I WANT MY LIFE BACK!

How can something provide you with the missing piece of your life . . . and then rob you of all your other pieces?

Rick Reynolds[1]

I have heard expectant parents saying with great assurance that having a child won't change their lives. They are humorously, yet pitifully, misinformed. The truth is that:

Everything changes once a child is born!

There is not one iota, not one speck of your life, that remains the same—physically, psychologically, financially, emotionally, spiritually, intellectually, experientially. Name it, and it changes. It's as though we've traded one life for another and the big shock hits for many of us when we realize:

There is no going back!

Of course, those of us with the wonderful Loving-Being-a-Parent (LBP) genes genuinely and understandably feel we have made a fair trade; those of us without those wonderful genes genuinely and understandably feel we have been hoodwinked!

Yes, we are adding something to our lives when we have children; *but many of us feel we are subtracting a lot more than we are adding!* Those of you who don't have children may not understand how this is possible; those of you who do have children know *exactly* how this is possible!

Some parents don't mind the "losses" in their lifestyle; in fact they feel they have gained so much. Others can't believe the sacrifices they need to make in order to raise their children. Stay-at-home mothers are affected the most, but all of us trade in a great deal of the quality of our lives when our children are born. Let me run through a few of the obvious and not-so-obvious areas where we are "robbed." And you might also take note that *this is the longest chapter in the book!*

FREEDOM

It does not take us very long—about two minutes after we leave the hospital—to realize that the chains of parenthood are stronger than the chains of servitude. And, for better or worse, the ties that bind are never broken. On a physical level and on a very deep emotional level, we have relinquished much of our freedom. One mother, obviously without the LBP genes, expressed the following which mirrors the often-hidden thoughts of many others:

> I can't believe I traded in my old life for this. I voluntarily traded heaven for misery. I made a bad decision and I have to find a way to live with it.

And that's what many parents do . . . they learn to live with it.

One father said he felt totally cramped in terms of the new lifestyle the birth of his child mandated. He had always loved the freedom of calling his wife at the last minute and saying, "Let's take in a movie." And off they'd go. This kind of spontaneity is now a thing of the past. One couple fondly remembered going for long walks on summer evenings, hanging out in their favorite café, and lying in bed on a Sunday morning, making love and reading the papers. Times long gone and sorely missed. As you will see throughout this chapter and beyond, this loss of freedom pervades every aspect of our lives.

I have spoken to women who laughingly confess that they thought having children was a good excuse to quit their job and have more freedom. They now realize that, when children are involved, in many ways working is much freer than *not* working. As you will see in a later chapter, they miss simple things like calling in sick when they had the flu. Hard to do when caring for a child. Also, if you don't like your job, you can quit; but if you don't like being a parent, you can't quit! You are there "until death do you part." Parenting is, in fact, one of the toughest, longest, and most demanding "jobs" one can ever have.

It is the emotional bonds of parenting that are most difficult to deal with. Even with a caregiver, whose presence allows us more physical freedom to work or travel, the thought "I hope Joey is okay" never leaves our hearts and minds. We are mentally "on duty" twenty-four hours a day. And at some level, you "hope Joey is okay" for the rest of your life. Goodbye, freedom.

SLEEP, PRECIOUS SLEEP

Have you ever noticed the look of fatigue on the faces of new parents? No, it isn't because they are out partying every night, celebrating their new arrival. It is because of a new physical condition they've acquired called "sleep deprivation." Most parents of newborn infants don't sleep when they need to or want to—*they sleep when their infant lets them*. Yes, the child is in control here. If an infant needs to be fed every two hours, she doesn't care if you are tired. Honest!

And God forbid if the baby has colic! For the uninformed, colic is an inconsolable bout of crying, screaming, and shrieking that lasts for many hours a day, often all night. It usually begins when the baby is three weeks old, and (are you ready?) may not stop until the baby is *five* months old.

My son had colic for six weeks between the hours of 10P.M. and 3A.M. During this time, he cried and screamed and shrieked without end as I walked and walked in circles, carrying him in my arms in my desperate attempt to comfort him. Soon I was crying uncontrollably. I felt so badly for his pain; I also felt so badly for mine. I was a walking zombie, yearning for a full night's sleep. That's all I wanted . . . uninterrupted sleep.

My son's colic lasted *only* six long, long weeks. It could have been worse. One woman I interviewed told me that her child had colic for four months. The baby cried all night, every night, and most of every day. Nothing she did could console him. She and her husband had wanted this child so badly, but during these four months they lost sight of the reasons why. (Four years later, they still haven't figured it out.)

What does it feel like to be sleep deprived with a colicky baby? Here is one answer to that question:

> After the first few weeks of sleep deprivation, I began to lose control of my faculties. My initial worry about his health turned quickly into disbelief that anything can be such a huge intrusion in my life. This of course creates guilt. How can I feel so heartless when my child is in pain? But I was in pain of another sort. You feel like you are under some sort of strange exotic torture that someone's devised to torment you.

Even if a child blessedly doesn't have colic, chances are you still won't have a full night's sleep for many months to come. Infants don't understand what every medical textbook tells us—that we need seven or eight *consecutive* hours of sleep every night or there is a mental and physical price to pay. I have heard it said that "Sleep is the life blood of our sanity!" Depression, irritability, reduced attention, reduced memory, more frequent illness, lost productivity, accidents, rage, and resentment are documented effects of sleep deprivation. Not good!

Unfortunately, our little ones don't understand our need for eight hours of consecutive sleep. They need to sleep also, but they want it in two-hour stretches. Sleep two hours, eat two hours, sleep two hours, eat two hours. And so it goes, leaving us all in a state of semi-consciousness as three parents attest:

> I remember one night he was sick and he woke me up between ten and twenty times between 11 P.M. and 2 A.M. Another night, we had flown back across the country after visiting my parents and I was up almost 24 hours. When we got home, he was crying and wouldn't go to sleep. There is my husband, asleep with earplugs and a pillow over his head. I'm tossing the baby around on the bed trying to get him to fall asleep. I had to try very hard not to be violent with him. Anything to shut him up. I felt so stressed out.

> When my daughter was newborn, she was up every two hours and then she'd feed for an hour and fall asleep for half an hour and wake me up again. I kept waking up and thinking, "I am in hell." I had to sleep on a different floor than my husband because he didn't want to have anything to do with us. He had to go to work the next day. So I am on the main floor sofa bed watching all the late night shows. It was really bad. I kept saying. "I'm in hell. I'm in hell." After my daughter was born, other mothers told me that the first nine months usually are hell. But they didn't tell me before. It's like a con job. We're conned about babies.

> I had to go to the hospital for an operation. Do you know, I welcomed it? Finally, I would get some sleep. Surgery was better than caring for my baby. It's sad when you welcome surgery over taking care of your child.

You may think that once the colic disappears and a normal sleep pattern is established, all is well. Wrong! Now it's time for teething problems. Will this merriment never cease? "Yes, little one, I know your gums hurt. But *I am tired.*" Eventually the teething problems disappear and you sleep more peacefully throughout the night until the early, very early, morning at which time that playful, cuter-than-cute face is in your tired face wanting her breakfast and demanding your attention. Oh, boy. Does she demand your attention!

When they finally reach school age, you are still up early, dressing them, feeding them breakfast and waiting for the school bus to arrive. It's all early, early, early. No respite here. You may be someone who always saw the weekend as a time of rest and restoration. But children don't recognize it as such. They just see it as one more day of eating, drinking, playing, and running to all sorts of activities . . . all of which demand your participation. One father commented that even though his kids are all grown up, he always loses sleep on those nights when his kids are out partying. He said, "I never go to sleep until they are home safe. And that could be the wee hours of the morning."

And for heaven's sake, don't get sick. I remember catching the flu when my son was very little. All I wanted to do was sleep. He didn't think this was a good idea. Torture! At that moment in time, I decided I would never be sick again until I had someone to care for him or until he was all grown up . . . whichever came first. I became the healthiest mother in history. I clearly remember the day when I was once again free to "take to my bed," and for the first time in many years, I *allowed* myself the flu and all the heavenly time in bed my recovery required. I must say I enjoyed every moment of it! You see how warped you can become when a child enters your life?

MOBILITY

The pathetically naïve among us believe that a child needn't hamper mobility; you can just take the little one with you wherever you want to go. Obviously, these unsuspecting souls are not observers of human behavior. In the first place, *it's not that easy*. In the second place, *who wants your child there anyway?* Not me, nor most people I know . . . even those who have their own young children! Let's talk about the "not that easy" part first.

When the baby is an infant, who has the energy to be out and about? Janet Maloney Franze tells it like it is:

> You don't go out much, because by the time you feed the baby, clothe the baby, change the baby, change your baby-stained shirt, and slick back your still unwashed hair, it's time for the baby's nap. I don't know a single stay-at-home mother who will willingly screw up nap time.[2]

As children get a little older, mobility doesn't get any easier. Just going to the supermarket to pick up a few groceries becomes a big deal. Getting the child dressed, especially in the throes of winter, getting her into her car seat (which she resists every time), getting her out of her car seat, getting her into the grocery cart (which she resists every time), controlling her grabbing hands or putting up with her tantrums as you pass all the goodies along the way . . . and then reversing the whole process on the way home. With a child, "a few groceries" is a big production!

I once read a book encouraging people to see the world with child-in-tow. *Most of us would get tired just reading the book!* Taking children on your travels requires a huge amount of planning, buying, and "schlepping." As we learn about back-packs, slings, strollers, mobile beds, playground survival skills, taxi tantrums, in-the-air survival skills, nappy wipes, car seats, and other realities of traveling with children, surely we know we are better off staying home until they are at least 18!

One father reported that he will never, never, never (he was very adamant about it) go on a trip with his child again. "Too much hassle!" He concluded that if they didn't get someone to take care of the kids when he and his wife wanted to go away, he would rather stay home. Traveling with children for most parents (even those with the LBP genes) is not necessarily a great experience.

This very same "see the world" book suggested taking children to a beach where they could run around and play in the sand while you kicked-back and read a good book. It's hard to believe the author has a child, which she claims she does. I don't know of a responsible parent who would let a child run around and play in the sand—*without eyes focused on him or her at all times.* With children, freedom to read peacefully on the beach is a thing of the past.

I frequently walk the beach which lies gloriously at my back door. I walk with a feeling of peace and freedom. As I pass families with young children, they are not having the same experience I am having. Trust me on this one. They are feeding, changing, appeasing, and trailing behind their little ones to protect them from sand and sea. I remember it well. *They are "on duty" all the time.*

This being "on duty" is a constant pressure. And it is easier to be on duty at home where all is familiar than in a strange place with strange people and strange potential dangers enticing your child. As an adult, it is just this "strangeness" that makes travel wonderful. But as a parent with children in tow, it's what makes travel ominous.

Of course, there are no guarantees of safety at home either. One woman I interviewed told me that one summer afternoon, two mothers, two nannies, and two children were playing around a swimming pool. Her son went under the water and no one noticed until he had been submerged for quite a few moments. Thank goodness, no damage was done. She said that it's chilling when you think how much responsibility lies on your shoulders. We are their guardians and we are responsible for their safety. That's simply the way it is.

Now to the second point. "Who wants your child there anyway?" One of the myths we have been fed is that everyone just *loves* children. *Wrong*! I read a letter to the editor of a popular woman's magazine that asks why so many parents can't stay at home with their children instead of annoying others with the crying, whining, and everything else that goes along with young children. Hear! Hear!

For my husband (who doesn't have a vicious bone in his body) and me, a screaming baby at the next table in a nice restaurant brings up hostile tendencies. We're debased to the lowest part of our being as we jokingly murmur to each other under our breath, "GET RID OF THE KID." Most of the time, the parent is considerate enough to take a screaming child away from the table, but sometimes the child is just left to annoy the rest of us until someone complains. Not so strangely, those who are most offended at bratty children in a nice restaurant are *those with children at home.* They came to get away from their own kids and have no desire to be annoyed by someone else's!

Some parents I interviewed are sensitive to other people's feelings, but it comes with a price—never eating at "grown-up" restaurants. One woman said:

> We don't take him to nice restaurants. We don't want to disturb the other customers. It's selfish of us to do that, so we don't. We'll go to a child-place like McDonald's where there are masses of other kids around and our child doesn't stick out like a sore thumb. But I can't say I enjoy it.

Most parents have experienced the chill of entering a restaurant with their young child. Brutal! And if their child misbehaves, they remember the chill of *exiting* a restaurant with their young child! I once took my two-year-old son to a restaurant where "ladies lunch." He must have disliked the color of his soup or something equally illogical, because when it arrived, it precipitated a massive temper tantrum. As he screamed his heart out, his spoon went into the gooey mixture and, with a sudden flick of his wrist, a blob of the sticky substance was hurled backwards, landing on a lady-who-lunches' much-prized mink coat. I knew it was much-prized because of the woman's reaction. Need I say more?

I was certain it was my time to exit. Easier said than done. Did you ever try to 1) apologize, 2) "clean" a mink coat, 3) pay the bill, 4) put on a snow-suit, 5) hat, and 6) boots 7) on a child 8) having a tantrum—all at the same time? There wasn't a friendly eye in the place. Not that I blame them. Needless to say, that was the last time, for a very long time, I ate in that restaurant.

Actually there are very few adult places where children are welcome. Not even the homes of friends. One woman commented:

> I used to take my child to other people's houses when we were invited to dinner. I noticed that we were never invited back.

Another woman recounted an evening when she and her husband decided to take their son to a new friend's house for dinner:

> My son likes to bang on the floor with his toys, which is what kids do. I thought my friends would understand as they also have children. The mother finally said to me with an obvious edge to her voice, "My son doesn't bang toys on the floor." Naturally, I took all his toys away hoping he wouldn't become hysterical. But he did. We weren't invited back.

Still another woman reports her experience of visiting the home of a new acquaintance:

> My son likes to scream with excitement and exuberance. He really enjoyed the other little boy, so he would scream every five minutes and the other little boy got scared and started crying. We weren't invited back, needless to say.

I have some wonderful, younger friends with small kids. A great way for them to tease me is to threaten to arrive at my house with their children in tow. In truth, they seldom do it. They truly understand why we don't enjoy their children around . . . or any children around. The reason they understand it is because *they don't enjoy other people bringing children to their house either!* A very common statement among parents, is "I like my kids, but I don't like anyone else's." And certainly, at times, they don't even like their own!

The reality is, once a child enters the picture, our lives get smaller and smaller and smaller in more ways than our minds can possibly conceive. There is no question that we are better off sticking very close to home with our little ones, which for some is heaven and, for others, is very, very confining.

For those who can afford caregivers, there is relief in sight; for those who can't, their options for a social life are greatly and painfully diminished.

PRIVACY

From the minute a child is born to the time he flies from the nest, privacy is a thing of the past. Remember this:

Privacy *never* resides where a child resides.

Even when they are infants asleep in their crib, their presence is always sensed; we are forever alert for their cries telling us when we are needed. As they get older, one practically has to hide in a closet to have a little sense of privacy. In fact, I do remember hiding in the closet on a few occasions.

What does privacy mean?

- Privacy means being able to have sex with your mate for as long as you want . . . without a baby crying in the background.
- Privacy means being able to go to the bathroom . . . without someone shouting and hammering at the door to come in or bursting in unannounced.
- Privacy is reading a book . . . knowing there will be no interruptions.
- Privacy is being able to be in your own space and have your own thoughts . . . without loud music blaring in the background.
- Privacy is being able to have a phone conversation . . . without constant interruptions.

You get the picture. For those of us with the LBP genes, the lack of privacy is okay as we truly enjoy the presence of children in the house. For those of us without the LBP genes, having the house to ourselves when the children finally fly away feels as though we've died and gone to heaven. Privacy at last!

MONEY

The cost of children in today's world is staggering! How could such little people cost so much? Well, they do. And as they grow, the cost increases exponentially. I've seen estimates in the United States that it costs somewhere between $761,871 and $1,455,581 to raise a child to the age of 21. These costs include food, housing, transportation, clothing, health care, and college. They don't include toys to delight their insatiable senses, and all the perks of being a child. Nor do these costs include the wages a parent forfeits if he or she decides to stop working and take care of the child. Even if you think these estimates are ridiculously high, and I must say child-care has gotten much more expensive since I raised my children, don't underestimate the difference in your lifestyle that the cost of raising a child creates (unless, of course, you have a great deal of money).

Needing to provide so much for our little ones makes it necessary for many men and women to give up their dreams or put them on hold—sometimes permanently. Did you know there was actually a time when children were a financial asset? That's why people had such large families. At a very early age, the children became part of the work force, whether on the farm or in a factory or wherever else money could be earned. Of course, I am not condoning the horrible way children were sometimes treated before protective child labor laws were introduced; I am simply pointing out that times have greatly changed. Children today are definitely not a financial asset.

Most of us work our hearts out and sacrifice much in terms of material things to give our children the advantages we think they should have. When they are appreciative, our hearts sing and it seems to be worth it all. But appreciation isn't on the lips of too many children today. Instead, we incessantly hear the words, "More, More, More!" And more is never enough. As you may have already noticed, we live in a culture where spoiled brats abound!

CAREER OPPORTUNITIES

A parent's timetable is very much dependent on her or his child's timetable. This creates a great loss of flexibility which, in turn, creates a big roadblock when one is on the career track. Joyce Purnick got into a lot of hot water for speaking out to graduates of Barnard College in a commencement address:

> I am absolutely convinced I would not be the metro editor of the *Times* if I had had a family.[3]

The guilt-peddlers had a field day with that one! Here is one blatant example of someone courageously breaking the conspiracy of silence and being severely castigated for telling the truth as she sees it. But let's look at it rationally:

By definition, a working mother (or father, if he is the primary caregiver) cannot have the same kind of focus, freedom, flexibility and mobility as does a woman without children. Ironically, the majority of women work, but compromises have to made. And any woman wanting a booming and satisfying career will experience much frustration.

I remember a popular talk-show host telling her audience that the reason she does not have children is that she truly values her career and would not give children the time they deserve. Another important break in the conspiracy of silence. It was beautiful to hear such clarity and understanding. (I will elaborate on this in a later chapter.)

Men's careers are also affected, even if they aren't the primary caregivers. For example, a lawyer revealed to me the following:

> I would love to change careers and be a writer. But with my two kids, I'm stuck doing what I'm doing. My wife doesn't work. She felt it was important to be home with the kids. This leaves me with a huge responsibility. I guess that's one of the prices I have to pay. But each morning that I go off to work, I know that this is not what I want to be doing with my life. And it makes me very sad . . . and a bit resentful.

A bit resentful? I suspect that he would like to sit down and cry and/or put his fist through a wall . . . as would so many women stymied in their careers! As our conversation continued, he said that his wife is very threatened when he talks of becoming a writer So after dinner, he goes down to the basement and pretends to work on his legal briefs; in fact, he is working on his computer long into the night, trying to write a book. Needless to say, most of the time, he walks around in an exhausted and frustrated state.

He feels his wife is doing what she wants, but *he* certainly is not. One can understand his resentment. Of course what he doesn't know is that many stay-at-home mothers feel resentment watching their men go off to the "freedom" of the workplace. How little the conspiracy of silence allows us to really know about each other's hopes and dreams. Tragic!

CAMARADERIE

In today's world, parenting can be a very lonely endeavor, particularly for the stay-at-home mom. Children aren't great conversationalists. Have you ever spent a few hours talking to a four-year-old? Also, they can't sympathize with our needs. We are their caretakers, not their friends.

In today's world, mothers are very isolated if they stop work and lose the companionship of other adults. A long time ago, raising a child took place in the middle of an extended family—mothers, fathers, brothers, sisters, aunts, uncles, neighbors, friends—all there to lend a hand and teach us a lesson or two. No loneliness there. But this sense of community is a dying reality in Western society. One woman said longingly:

> I just wish there were arms who want to hold my baby. The only arms my child has are mine. And I sometimes just don't have the strength or the desire.

Some couples, who can't afford baby sitters, haven't been out with friends for *years*. Yes, *years*! Astounding, but true. As I said earlier, few people are eager for you to bring your children with you for a movie or a meal. And you are wise enough to know that true socialization is not possible with demanding children in tow. And so you just stay home.

Camaraderie is absent for other reasons. In today's world marked by much competitiveness, one discerns a strange "one-upmanship" mentality in other mothers, everyone trying to outdo the others in terms of better parenting and better children. "Your child can't wave yet? Pity!" One woman tells this story:

> I was president of the Parent Teacher's Association last year. And every time I would go to a function or a meeting, I would come home and my husband would find me in bed, covers over my head, literally. I felt devastated by the interactions I would have with the women. I guess it was my own fault. I was very sensitive to their back-biting and I felt no support. The only support I felt was from a male who was on my PTA board. He was a stay-at-home father. He was a loving, supportive, wonderful guy. But the women created for me an emotional instability and a sense of crisis. It was devastating for me. It really was. And supposedly, as an at-home mom and PTA president, you're in a supportive environment. But it wasn't that way at all.

She felt the problems arose from the fact that being a PTA president was an accomplishment and was threatening to other stay-at-home women who feel an intense sense of worthlessness. She said that in her circle, the only time she has seen women in a state of togetherness was when they were united *against* another woman or men in general.

This certainly matches my experience so many years ago. When I finally decided to leave the state of full-time motherhood and go back to school, which was a no-no at the time, *it was only the women, not the men, who loudly criticized my decision.* I always believed that their criticism wasn't about my "bad mothering," but rather about their jealousy that I was doing something that, deep within their hearts, they were all yearning to do.

This lack of camaraderie, and resulting loneliness, was a frequent complaint of the stay-at-home moms that I interviewed, who more than at any other time of their lives, really need good friends.

"SANITY"

It is unbelievable how an exuberant and healthy woman, joyously looking forward to her new baby, can turn into a totally depressed, irrational, and sometimes dangerous human being once the baby comes. It is certainly something that needs our attention. Some blame this unhealthy mental state on *postpartum depression* which can last longer than is reported. Erma Bombeck "jokes":

> My postnatal depression was longer than most. I went into it seven months before the baby came, and it lasted until the kid was 17. Then it began to taper off.[4]

Yes, postpartum depression can last a long time, given the entire lifestyle change a woman has to make if she chooses to be a stay-at-home mom.

Research has not yet identified a specific cause for postpartum depression, but it has been associated with a number of conditions: hormonal changes, a let-down after all the excitement, exhaustion, shock that the "old life" is gone forever, a feeling of isolation, and a sense that our dreams are on hold and life is passing us by as we cater to the needs of our little one. As Vivien Dai reports:

> We'd had this wonderful water birth and the whole house felt just like a big, warm womb. I hadn't even stepped out of the house all week. So there I was, standing at the door with Brandon in my arms, waving goodbye to Jay. The screen door was between me and the outside world, and all of a sudden I had a nervous breakdown. I felt like I was waving goodbye to my old self. I mean, I was a dancer, an artist, I'm supposed to be out there in the world, and all of a sudden I'm here with this little being who's totally dependent on me, and I didn't know who I was or what I was supposed to do next.[5]

This kind of loss of self is a huge blow to the rational mind. We are in never-never-land and we seem to be unable to find our way back.

And then there is the sleep deprivation I spoke about earlier. The kind of sleep deprivation new mothers experience is a very dangerous thing. This condition is certainly not taken seriously enough. When sleep deprived, we do things we would never do in a more rested state of mind. The lives of both the mother and the baby are at risk when mothers don't get enough sleep. Yet, we expect mothers to be the only caregivers to their children and then wonder why there is so much child abuse . . . and as you will see in a later chapter, the actual statistics on violence are quite shocking. Those who return to the workplace or pursue other personal interests usually possess a much healthier state of mind.

ADULTHOOD (THE BEST PARTS)

"Adulthood" is a strange loss because, if you think about it, parenting is such an adult activity. After all, you become the guardian of a totally helpless little being, a role not for the faint-hearted! You have to grow up. And yet many other parts of adulthood seem to disappear. As one stay-at-home mother told me with tears in her eyes:

> I've lost so much of what's wonderful and worthwhile about being an adult. I've lost all my loves. I can't read. I can't go to films. I have very little time to talk to others about any intellectual topic. And the only way I get by is to say to myself, "He's not going to need you so much forever. Next year, he'll give you a little more freedom and the year after that." That's the only way I can get through it.

This is a woman who decided to give up her job to properly "bond" with her child as ordained by certain childcare experts who I believe are sadly uninformed . . . to say the least. (You will discover more about my thoughts on this important subject in a later chapter.) This poor woman still hasn't figured out what "bonding" means and she is definitely re-thinking her decision to leave the workplace.

A mother of two adult children looked back at her life and said:

> My kids demanded so much from me. It seemed I gave up most of the things I considered pleasurable as an adult. Including my sex life, frankly. I was just too exhausted to want to have sex. I was always so jealous of my childless friends. The irony is, they were probably jealous of me. Little did they know.

(There's that old conspiracy of silence again.) One mother was very discomfited by the fact that she had read only two books in two years when she used to read three books a week! And so it goes.

Adulthood is lost in another way. One woman said:

> Not only do I lose my adult *activities*, I also lose my adult behavior. I can't remember ever behaving so badly. I know the title of your book is *I'm Okay . . . You're a Brat!* I

> wonder if I'm okay when I'm behaving like a brat! But I can't seem to help it. I was waiting in line to register my child in kindergarten. I'm so "anal", I got there really early—of course so did everyone else. So we had to wait in line for about one hour and 45 minutes. We all started to talk about our lives. Many of the mothers agreed that morning was the most difficult time, getting the kids dressed and out the door—all of us screaming like lunatics. It felt so good to know everyone else "loses it" too. I love these children and I'm screaming for no apparent reason. I actually have temper tantrums!

This was an intelligent, elegant, and wealthy woman who had full-time help. She said she doesn't understand how anyone does it all on their own. At least she can get out to the local university to take a class or two, so she doesn't feel totally stupid!

One father took care of his child for a month while his wife went to care for her ailing mother. He had this to say:

> I couldn't believe how difficult it was. The tedium day after day. It drives you crazy. What children want to do has nothing to do with what adults want to do. The world of the child and the world of the adult don't mix very often. It's frustrating. God bless work!

SELF-ESTEEM

One would think that caring for a child would create an increased sense of self-esteem and power for a parent. It is a pretty mammoth task, you know. Once again, for those with the LBP genes, this sense of self-esteem and power is evident. But for those without the LBP genes, a *loss* of self-esteem and power is evident. And this is true particularly for stay-at-home mothers. I know this from my own personal experience.

When I was a stay-at-home mom many years ago, I lost all my confidence. Other adults were out there growing, learning, being, interacting, and doing what grown-ups do. I was at home shrinking: no time or energy to learn, grow, be, interact, and do what grown-ups do. I soon felt an intense sense of inferiority. It got so bad that I was afraid to ask our best friends to dinner. One mom who had given up her career to be home with her child describes a similar experience:

> After being home with my son for a few months, I began to feel retarded. I was ashamed to go out with other adults. I had nothing to talk about except what was going on with my child. Diaper rashes, formulas, and all that interesting stuff. I envied my husband. At least he could escape to the sanity and stimulation of his job and the company of interesting people. I began to wonder why he even came home to someone as boring as me.

I interviewed a beautiful, bright, articulate woman who on the surface is a strong female with everything going for her. She gave up her very exciting and financially rewarding job to care for her two children. While she loves them very much, she finds herself paralyzed when it comes to getting herself out there again and finding a job, which she says she must do for sanity's sake. This previously confident woman now finds herself too frightened to even go for an interview. She says:

> I have moments or days when I think I don't even want to go out of the house and deal with the big world out there. It's overwhelming. I have this incredibly stressful little world in my house that I'm having a hard time handling. And I have moments and days when I don't know if I can go out there any more. You lose your confidence. You're so busy with your head down working with your kids, playing with your kids, doing whatever you have to do. You pick your head up and you see others out there learning and growing and you wonder whether you can ever catch up.

I believe that a diminished sense of self comes from the absence of adult activities and friends when trapped in a child's world. We spiral down into a very narrow space where we forget how powerful we really can be.

The conspiracy of silence also decreases our sense of self-worth. We feel as though something is wrong with us when we are not enjoying the "parent-thing," particularly when it seems everyone else is. What we don't see is that everyone else *isn't* necessarily enjoying the parent-thing! I am convinced that this is the reason for the great deal of excitement that this book generates for so many men and women I talked to. I am finally validating their feelings and restoring a sense of their sadly missed sense of self.

PERSONAL TIME

Time is of the essence for all of us in today's busy world. But when children come into our lives, personal time is typically a thing of the past—whether one is a stay-at-home parent or an off-to-work parent, male or female. Why isn't there any free time? One naively thinks that this is understandable when the baby is small, but surely not when they are older and off to school. The following are a few jobs parents feel they have to do when children are of school age: cheerleader at all events (dance and piano recitals, sports events, science fairs, plays, etc.), driver, chaperone (at social events and class trips), homework helper, committee member, resource, nurse, volunteer, club leader or assistant, chef, tour guide at museums, zoos, and parks.

You parents out there can probably think of many more. And imagine doing this for not only one child, but two or three or more! For some of us, these activities are meaningful, joyous, and fun and we wouldn't want to miss them for the world. But for those of us without the LBP genes, they can be pure and unadulterated torture.

Some books and articles suggest simplifying your life in order to have more free time. Simplifying sounds like a good idea. However, so many tips are simply rearrangements of the time you don't have, like setting the breakfast table at night instead of the morning. Some are simply objectionable, like getting up earlier. Some are seemingly impossible, like teaching your kids to clean up and enjoy the meaning of solitude. There really is only one way to have some personal time: HIRE FULL-TIME HELP! That's it. End of story. Of course, that's easier said than done, since there are few that can afford the luxury.

Full-time help or putting a child in daycare doesn't guarantee a great deal of personal time, but it certainly helps. Susan Maushart gives us a dose of reality when she points out that even if a child is in daycare or with a nanny or grandparent 50 hours a week, this still leaves 118 hours where kids need us. She says: "All the on-sight childcare in the world will not change this basic arithmetic by a single digit."[6]

One woman told me that when asked what she wanted for Mother's Day, her answer was that she wanted her husband to take the kids and just leave her alone for the entire day. And so he did. A new slant on Mother's Day! Oh, yes . . . many parents finally obtain a degree of freedom—after a divorce. Alternate weekends with kids also means alternate weekends *without* kids. Free time at last—but what a price to pay!

There was a time when children were freer to roam about than they are today, leaving us more free time. My son was taking public transportation in New York City at the age of eight, as were all his classmates. I've been told this is unthinkable today as a result of increased violence. For the same reason—increased violence—those in small towns report a hesitance to allow their kids to go out and play all day as parents used to do. As a result, more planning and attention are needed for a child's spare time, taking more spare time away from parents. So many mothers' lives are consumed with driving them here, driving them there, driving them everywhere.

In the end, we find that our prior estimation of the demands of parenthood were wildly *under*-estimated.

FUN

I recently read an article lamenting the cost of children. The author concludes his article by reassuring parents that while they may be a lot poorer than those who are childfree, they have a lot more fun. Let's use a little common sense here. How can you be having more fun if so many of your adult delights are taken away from you? Sleep, privacy, money, mobility, personal time, peace of mind, camaraderie, all come to mind. I don't question that many parents have fun with their children, especially parents born with the LBP genes. But I would venture a guess that those without children are winners in the "fun" department.

George Bernard Shaw once wrote, "*If parents would only realize how they bore their children!*"[7] Mr. Shaw, I'm sure that is true. But you forgot the other side of this equation. "*If children would only realize how they bore their parents!*" I've heard it said, "It's so interesting to watch a child grow." It's more than interesting; it's a miracle! If you see a child once a month you are astounded by the changes occurring. But on a day-to-day basis, there's not much to see in the way of visible growth—B-O-R-I-N-G.

It's like planting a seed and watching it grow. Day after day, nothing seems to be happening and then all of a sudden a little green breaks through the soil. And you think to yourself, "Wow! Isn't that amazing!" There are also the moments of "Wow!" with children, such as when they take their first step. But these "Wow!" moments are few and far between. Growth is slow. And the endless routine of feeding, diapering, bathing, going to the park, and pushing a swing can be daunting.

I have often jokingly thanked my son for my Ph.D. If it weren't for the fact that I was so totally bored staying home taking care of a child, I might never have gone back to school. My son knows this is nothing personal; he was a very bright and inquisitive little boy and continues to be so as an adult. But what a child must do to learn, grow, and develop is miles apart from what an adult must do to learn, grow, and develop. It makes sense, doesn't it?

Again, let me emphasize that there are those who thrive in the presence of children. They truly enjoy them most of the time. But very few parents enjoy interacting with a child for a lengthy period of time. After an hour or less of being with a child, even a child they madly love, a roaming thought pervades their mind: "*Please deliver me from this.*"

A pizza ad I recently saw on television captured this reality beautifully. A man and wife are alone in a room when one says to the other, "Didn't we used to have more fun?" On cue, a baby howls in the distance. They look at each other in dismay. At this point, the doorbell rings and a pizza is delivered. The next scene is mother, father and baby sitting on the couch eating pizza and watching television. The father says glumly, "Well, I guess this is fun." Cute commercial; desperate message.

Playing with a child isn't fodder for an inquiring mind. As Kathy Lette says:

> I get so bored doing creative things with Play-doh, that I can see my plants photosynthesizing.[8]

I believe that we are all meant to expand and to grow. It is very hard to expand and grow doing "kid" things. It's great for the kid, but not great for most moms and dads.

Even when children get older, their interests seldom match those of most adults. (Thank goodness for those blessed moments when they do!)

Boredom is one of the many reasons why so many mothers are today *choosing* to be out in the world of work, even though they don't necessarily need the money, and leaving the care of their children to daycare centers or child-minders, most of whom seem to enjoy the job . . . or at least enjoy getting paid for their efforts. (Of course, many mothers have no choice but to work.)

I recently read a magazine devoted to child-rearing. It covered topics such as nailbiting, yeast rashes, booster seats, bathtub risks, infant acne, the childcare crisis, picking the right preschool, and fighting fair. I know that these are important things for parents to investigate, but that's the problem! Who wants to investigate these things? Most adults are much more interested in other things like politics, career, the Internet, racy novels, playing golf, volunteer work, and so on. But for the sake of our child, we must learn an awful lot that most of us are truly not interested in learning.

When in the presence of a child, the boredom can be constant as they never seem to leave you alone. I remember sitting in the waiting room of a doctor's office. I sat there reading the latest magazines about style, gossip, and all sorts of juicy things that are a wonderful diversion in my busy life. There was peace in that. In walks a mother and a child. He appears to be adorable and well-behaved. As his mother picks up one of the magazines sitting on a table, he goes over to the toys the doctor had provided for the little ones, and says, "Mommy, play with me." I'll never forget the look of despondency that came over her face as she moaned, "*Oh, please don't make me play with you. I want to read a magazine.*" Translated, that means "*I want to do something adult; I don't want to do something that is of no interest to me.*"

Given all of the above, I hope I have made a dent in any erroneous impression that parents have more fun. While there may be many rewards in parenting, for most of us, having more fun isn't one of them!

RELATIONSHIPS

Perhaps one of the most astounding changes that occurs after children are born is the dynamic of your relationship with your partner. The loss of so many delights in life as described in this chapter invariably take their toll on romance, togetherness, pleasure, and solidarity. In fact, this is such an important area to explore, I've devoted the next chapter to the effect of children on relationships.

PEACE OF MIND

I leave the most important for last: I think that what you are least prepared for when you have children is how much you love them. And therein lies the rub. It is this very love that makes having children so miserable!

From the minute our child is born (or adopted, if that's the case), some unidentifiable source inserts a worry chip in our brain that is never removed. Forevermore, there is an umbrella of conscious or unconscious worry that permeates every inch of our being. And when you look around, it seems as though worry is a logical response to the emotional and physical dangers of today's world. What do we worry about? We worry about practically everything: their health, their future, their education, accidents, their diet, their safety, crib death, drowning, whether they like us, their looks, whether their schoolmates will like them, whether their feelings are hurt, whether their long-anticipated first date shows up, whether their caregivers are qualified, whether they are taking drugs, whether we are doing the right things for them, violence, speeding while driving, eating disorders, and I could go on and on and on and on and on and on . . .

This worry can cast a pall on all that is beautiful in our lives. For example, I remember my ex-husband and I taking our first vacation leaving our children with their grandmother and a nanny in our high-rise apartment in Manhattan. In the middle of our much-needed romantic dinner, my then-husband stiffened and, with a frightened look in his eyes, said, "I wonder if they know to keep the windows closed." At this point, we both had a frightened look in our eyes as we imagined our kids falling many floors to their death. Immediately, we ran to the phone to call my mother and the nanny to remind them to keep the windows closed . . . as if they didn't know! So much for our romantic dinner.

What we read gives us no respite from our worry. Giannetti and Sagarese point out that:

> In the 1940s the top seven school problems [in the US] were (1) talking out of turn, (2) gum chewing, (3) noise, (4) running in halls, (5) cutting in line, (6) dress code infractions, and (7) littering. They seem quaint compared with the list compiled as the 1980s wound down: (1) drug abuse, (2) alcohol abuse, (3) pregnancy, (4) suicide, (5) rape, (6) robbery, and (7) assault.[9]

Lynn Ponton, an adolescent psychiatrist in San Francisco, tells us:

> In my work two things have remained absolutely clear over the years: adolescents are going to take risks, and most parents of adolescents are terrified about this. In 1995, when the Carnegie Institute published its findings on youth and risk, its report suggested that American youths today are at greater risk because they take more risks and are exposed to even more opportunities for dangerous risks than at any other time in American history.[10]

(And I'm sure this is true of the entire Western world.) She qualifies her words by saying that risk-taking is "developmentally appropriate," that is, that risk-taking is perfectly normal for teens in their effort to grow up. But that reality doesn't make many parents breathe any easier; in fact, it might make them feel worse! So many teenagers seem to go to the dark side of the moon for too many years, and their parents live with the fear that they'll never come back. Some do and some don't. A very sad and frightening feeling for a parent who feels so much love. All things are chancy in life and I'm a great risk-taker; but few things carry the immense emotional cost that children carry.

And when we read about people losing their children, our heart skips a beat. Even the privileged among us are not exempt from such a loss. Richard Todd, who lost his child, tells us of his grief:

> To lose a child by suicide without knowing the cause is indescribably unbearable.[11]

Our heart hurts when we read of such tragedy as we know the incredible pain that parents feel with the loss of a child.

And I think of the children who commit heinous crimes. We can only imagine the pain their parents carry around in their hearts. The guilt peddlers tell you that you control what happens to your child. This is a peculiar and cruel thing to say. Don't they know that a decided lack of control is a fact of life when a child is born? And it is this very lack of control that takes away your peace of mind. If you are a "control freak" as I tend to be, this is not a good feeling.

In the book *Everyday Blessings,* the authors tell us there are times when they feel things are basically sound in their family, their children seem happy, strong, and balanced, but:

> The very next day, or moment, all hell can break loose. Our world fills with confusion, despair, anger, frustration. What we thought we understood is of no use. All the rules seemed to have changed overnight, or in an instant. We can feel like we have no idea what is going on or why. We can feel like the biggest of failures, like we don't know or understand anything.[12]

Lack of control is a fact of life in many areas of our lives, but when it comes to our children, the stakes are higher and our peace of mind suffers more than words can say.

A number of sources have described the love we have for a child as a "terrible love" because it comes with a terrible fear. Few of us are prepared for how much responsibility we feel for our children. Ultimately, one has to let go and trust in our children's own destiny, but to say that this is easy is far from the truth. It is the hardest thing we can ever do. My children and stepchildren now range in age from 25 to 40, yet, there is a part of me that is never free from a very conscious concern about their health and mental well-being. On a very deep level, these children are always with me. And they always will be.

Looking at all of the above—the loss of freedom, sleep, mobility, privacy, money, possible career opportunities, camaraderie, "sanity," adult activities, self-esteem, personal time, fun, relationships, and peace of mind—one can understand why Myla and Jon Kabat-Zinn talk of parenting as "the full catastrophe."

> It makes us vulnerable in ways we weren't before. It calls on us to be responsible in ways we weren't before. It challenges us as never before, and takes our time and attention away from other things, including ourselves, as never before.[13]

It is understandable that many parents look forward to the times when the kids are sleeping, or are at school, or at their friend's house, or at summer camp. A friend of mine told me the following story which was passed along the "parent grapevine":

> A group of teenagers were going off to camp for the two-month summer holiday. Parents and children gathered together as the camp bus pulled into the parking lot. The children's suitcases were loaded onto the bus and with tears and hugs the children said goodbye and climbed aboard. As parents waved and screamed, "Have a great time!" "We'll miss you!" "Don't forget to write!" the camp bus pulled away and a few tears were shed by all concerned. In the midst of this touching scene, one parent slowly began to clap. And then another . . . and another. It didn't take long before all the parents joined in and whoops of joy and exhilaration filled the air.

Children going off for two months: how sweet it is! I recently spoke to a British single mom living in Los Angeles who sent her seven-year-old back home to attend school and to be closer to his grandparents. She said that friends ask her if she is devastated, but, in truth, she loves having her life back again. But, doesn't the question pop up in your mind, "Why have them to begin with when your favorite times are when they are not around?"

The only logical answer is that the good old conspiracy of silence hides the truth from so many would-be parents. They simply don't understand what they are getting into. As this conspiracy of silence is broken apart, perhaps some, not all of course, will choose not to have children to begin with. Given what overpopulation is doing to this earth, this may be a blessing in disguise!

Many parents secretly live for the day their children grow up and finally leave home. It's not that the worries disappear—they never do—but so much of what we had been robbed of so many years ago is returned to us and we accept these gifts with great appreciation and joy.

You might be thinking, "What about the empty-nest syndrome? I thought that parents feel a sense of loss and depression when their kids leave home." I suggest that those who experience this syndrome, and there are those that definitely do, have made their children their whole life. Anything we make our whole life will be missed when it's gone! Such parents are far more dependent on their children than their children are dependent on them. Not a healthy situation, but in such a case, the empty-nest syndrome is understandable.

But for those of us who are able to create a life that is rich with friends, a good relationship, interests outside the home, and a sense of meaning in the community, a child leaving the nest creates anything but depression. In fact, Jane Bartlett cites a number of studies that show both men and women are happiest when the children leave home.[14] One woman I interviewed joked. . .

> My parents are having the greatest time now that we are gone. I've never seen them happier.

This isn't to say that as our child walks out the door to begin his or her new life, we may not have a day, or week, or even a month of a bittersweet sadness that signifies the end of an era, but then we go on to welcome our "new" lives and our freedom once again. It occurs to me that the empty-nest syndrome implies that our life is nothing without our children. For those of us with a rich, full life, of course, this simply is not true.

There is no getting around the fact that by having a child, you give up many aspects of yourself. Again, I must repeat:

Those with the LBP genes willingly give up much of their lives because of the wonderful benefits they experience in raising their children.

Those without the LBP genes love their children, but feel as though they have been imprisoned without any chance of parole!

And of course, there are various shades in between. Yes, some feel they enjoy their child so much that *nothing* has been sacrificed. But many of us yearn for the world as we once knew and loved it. But because we have no choice, we find a way to live with it . . . or better yet, we find a way to make it a triumph. Clearly that's the wisest course to take!

Endnotes

[1]Reynolds, Rick. From the theatrical stage production of Rick Reynolds' wonderful one-man show, *All Grown Up . . . and No Place to Go*. Written and directed by Rick Reynolds. Originally produced in San Francisco, 1995.

[2]Franze, Janet Maloney. "A Creation Story," in *Child of Mine*. Edited by Christina Baker Kline. Hyperion, New York, 1997, p. 132.

[3]Joyce Purnick is quoted by Theodore Gideonese in an article entitled "Mommy Track at the Times," in *Newsweek*, June 1, 1998, p. 61.

[4]Bombeck, Erma. *Forever Erma*. Andrews and McMeel, Kansas City, 1996, p. 23.

[5]Vivian Dai being interviewed by author Laurie Wagner in *Expectations: Thirty Women Talk About Becoming a Mother*. Chronicle Books, San Francisco, 1998, p. 29.

[6]Maushart, Susan. *The Mask of Motherhood*. Random House, Australia, NSW Australia, 1997, p. 246.

[7]Shaw, George Bernard. *Misalliance*, Episode 1, 1910.

[8]Kathy Lette quoted by author Hester Lacey in "Motherhood: The Big Lie," in the *Independent on Sunday* (British), 1998 , p. 1.

[9]Giannetti, Charlene C. and Margaret Sagarese. *The Roller-Coaster Years*. Broadway Books, New York, 1997, p. 127.

[10]Ponton, Lynn E. *The Romance of Risk: Why Teenagers Do the Things They Do*. HarperCollins, New York, 1997, p. 2.

[11]Todd, Richard. "To Lose a Child," in the *Sunday Times News Review*, Section 5, February 1, 1998, p. 1.

[12]Kabat-Zinn, Myla and Jon. *Everyday Blessings: The Inner Work of Mindful Parenting*. Hyperion, New York, 1997, p. 29.

[13]Ibid., p. 89.

[14]Bartlett, Jane. *Will You Be Mother?: Women Who Choose to Say No*. New York University Press, New York, 1994, p. 172. (Originally published by Virago, London, 1994.)

3

OIL AND WATER: SEX AND DIAPERS

It's hard to say which was the first casualty of childbirth—your waistline or your relationship with the man you married. But clearly both have suffered. Not so long ago, he was your friend, your lover, your confidant. Today he is primarily "your dad," as in "Go ask . . ."
Mary C. Hickey and Sandra Salmans[1]

"Kids" and "romance" do not belong in the same sentence, let alone the same household! The loss of so many delights in life as described in the last chapter—freedom, mobility, privacy, peace of mind, self-esteem, camaraderie, sleep, "sanity," adult activites, personal time, money, fun, flexibility, career opportunities—can't help but take their toll on a previously close-knit relationship. As Nora Ephron puts it:

A baby is a hand grenade tossed into a marriage.[2]

While seldom discussed among friends, family, or acquaintances, *all* couples, even those with the LBP genes, experience difficulties in their relationship after the birth of their child. Many ultimately pass the test with flying colors; many do not. But one thing is for sure – *nothing stays the same!* And I will go so far as to say that if anyone tells you otherwise with a straight face, they are lying. My heart goes out to expectant parents who actually think their child will have no effect on or will improve their relationship. They are in for a big shock. The relationship is first in the line of fire.

In the last chapter, I gave you many reasons why the birth of a child is "the great catastrophe" in many aspects of our lives. Perhaps the greatest catastrophe of all is what it can do to our relationship. It's amazing that beautiful, darling, cuddly, lovable, little beings can create such havoc in the lives of two loving and willing people. But they can. Here are a few eye-opening realities as to why relationships are so much at risk when a child is born:

THE "PACKAGE" CHANGES

People usually get married because they like the "package," i.e., they like the way it is. They have a fairly good way of relating to one another; they enjoy sex together; they enjoy and respect each other as human beings; and they enjoy their life together and they want it to continue "until death do us part." Otherwise, why would they have gotten married? When two people have a child, they are totally altering those things in their relationship which make it beautiful just as it is; that is to say when the little bundle enters their lives, the package changes considerably:

- The couple's way of relating to one another alters because of their offspring's unceasing need for attention
- Sex is greatly diminished as exhaustion, lack of privacy, and/or resentment take over
- Who they are as people changes as the new role of "parent" infiltrates their mode of being and new responsibilities fall upon their shoulders
- Their lifestyle changes dramatically as so many joys of adulthood disappear and the dirty diapers appear

Many new parents look back and think to themselves, "*We had such a good thing. What happened?*" What happened is that they changed the package, the unwritten contract that brought them together in the first place. Of course, there is no guarantee that the package wouldn't have changed over time *without* a child in the picture. After all, divorce occurs even with childless couples. But there is some evidence that, contrary to popular opinion, *those who choose not to have children make much happier couples.*

It also stands to reason that for many couples who survive the assault of parenthood, love blossoms once again when children go off on their own. Why? They re-discover the original package that brought them together in the first place.

Strangely, in this world of male and female equality, the package changes much more dramatically than the bad old days when mother's place was in the home. This is especially true when a woman chooses to leave her gratifying career and become a stay-at-home mom. In this case, the original package changes enormously. As Susan Maushart points out:

> One day a woman is conducting herself like an emancipated, autonomous adult, sharing equally in the challenges and triumphs of public life, and the next day she has turned into Beaver Cleaver's mother. The metamorphosis is Kafka-esque.[3]

Needless to say, this changing dynamic can be more than a hand grenade tossed into a relationship, it can be an atomic bomb! Naturally, all this assault on the original package can lead to deep-seated anger and resentment. In a thankfully honest article, psychotherapist Joseph Reiner reveals the following:

> Before having children, my wife and I had worked out a fairly harmonious way of living together. Our first baby ripped that apart. Shouting at each other at three in the morning while our infant son screamed, my wife and I saw each other's ugliness as never before.[4]

While the original package brought out the beauty in the relationship, the new package can bring out the ugliness. This doesn't mean a couple necessarily divorces; in fact, when children are in the picture, we think much longer and harder about leaving the relationship. The responsibility of a single parent is overwhelming, as any single parent will tell you. One woman admitted:

> At one stage we considered splitting up, we'd been so foul to each other, and I really think what kept us together was that neither of us wanted to be alone with the baby, poor little soul.[5]

THREE IS TROUBLE

Don't let the pictures of togetherness in the family album fool you. Underneath the surface of all the smiles and hugs, all sorts of changes in the original package are in play once a child enters our lives. In the first place, you and me and baby definitely make three.

There are few relationships where three are involved that remain a love-bath; one of the three is usually excluded while the other two embrace. That is the nature of triads. True to form, when a child comes into the picture, one of the three is usually excluded. In most cases, it is the father. This is understandable, since mothers are still more often the primary caregivers—and children definitely need a lot of care! Also understandable is the fact that many husbands feel rejected when they are left out. Some women truly love the exclusivity of the mother-child relationship and push the father away. When the father is not invited into the circle of love between mother and child, they often feel they are valued only for the financial support they offer. And in some cases they're right.

As the child gets older, sometimes the father and child become the dynamic duo. Here, the mother feels rejected. On rare occasions, when lots of help is affordable, the parents focus all their attention on each other and exclude the child. The relationship thrives, but the child feels rejected. Talk about a no-win situation. Indeed, you and me and baby does make three . . . and when it comes to romance, three is definitely a crowd. You can see the problems inherent in this simple reality.

LACK OF TOGETHERNESS

As one young man observed on the eve of his wife's scheduled cesarean delivery:

> Do you realize that this is the last time we will sit here and have supper like this for twenty years?[6]

He didn't know how right he was. This stunning reality can hurt marriages irreparably. Parents spend much too little time alone together enjoying the simple pleasures they used to share. The week is filled with work; the weekends are filled with doing things with children. Stay-at-home moms often hand the child over to dad with a snide, "It's your turn now!" Understandable, but no love here! And when there is more than one, it is often the case that one parent goes off with one child and the other goes off with the other child. No togetherness there! I was scanning the Internet one day and I came upon this tip from a parent:

> Trade time-outs with your partner. Say "Honey, I would like to take four hours off on Saturday afternoon. Why don't you take four hours on Sunday?" During your time-out, go out—leave the house.

Yes, this might be great for handling the problem of lack of some personal time, but it isn't great for romance—aside from the fact that four hours is hardly enough personal time!

As part of my research for this book, I became a people-watcher at the beach, in shopping malls, amusement parks, or anywhere children and parents would be likely to congregate. Here is predominantly what I saw:

- Mothers catering to the needs of their children—*no father in sight*
- Fathers catering to the needs of their children—*no mother in sight*
- Parents catering to the needs of their children—*no "togetherness" in sight*

These are in contrast to:

- Couples walking together arm in arm, hand in hand, kissing, talking, hugging, watching the world together—*no children in sight*

I suggest you see for yourself. Watch couples interacting with their kids. The togetherness of the parents is rarely seen—children are always in the middle, literally and figuratively.

Also pay attention to the difference between couples having dinner by themselves or with friends . . . and couples having dinner with children. It's very revealing. The former socialize, share in each other's lives, "hang out" together, and relax. People having dinner with children present a very different picture. Attention is primarily on the children—even the well-behaved ones. (You can be sure that when focus is not on them, kids will make certain it is! Children are attention-addicts, even when they are older.) When they clamor for attention, often in loud and obstreperous ways, the tension at the table is tangible. Often, one parent ends up eating alone as the other parent walks around outside calming a screaming baby. Then they reverse roles. No togetherness here.

One woman I interviewed told me that she and her husband had not been away one night in five years, ever since her child was born, and rarely went out to dinner alone. That means not one night with the privacy, romance, and intimacy that all couples need. True to form, she says sex has gone out the window. She trusts when the children (there are now two) are older all the romance will come back. I hope she's right.

This lack of togetherness is one of the big reasons love flies out the window. Couples forget how joyful a "twosome" can be. Anne Morrow Lindbergh reminds us in her wonderful book *Gift from the Sea*:

> How wonderful it was to leave the children, the house, the job, and all the obligations of daily life; to go out together, whether for a month or a weekend or even just a night in an inn by themselves. How surprising it was to find the miracle of the sunrise repeated. There was the sudden pleasure of having breakfast alone with the man one fell in love with. Here at the small table, are only two people facing each other. How the table at home has grown! And how distracting it is, with four or five children, a telephone ringing in the hall, two or three school buses to catch, not to speak of the commuter's train. How all this separates one from one's husband and clogs up the pure relationship. But sitting at a table alone opposite each other, what is there to separate one? Nothing but a coffee pot, corn muffins and marmalade. A simple enough pleasure, surely, to have breakfast alone with one's husband, but how seldom married people in the midst of life achieve it.[7]

A beautiful reminder about what is of key importance in a relationship—your mate, *not your child*, that is if you want to be together "until death do you part." And this reality is often not recognized until it is far too late.

I might add that if you don't particularly enjoy spending quality time with and romancing your mate, this lack of togetherness is not particularly upsetting; it may be a Godsend! But for many of the unsuspecting, this is one of the biggest and most difficult life changes for a couple to accept. And it is worth our while (with or without children) to make sure that we make time for each other in a meaningful and loving way.

RESENTMENT

Resentment is also a big separator in relationships. It starts insidiously with the lack of sleep that parents experience from day one. I know this one well. Let me share something I wrote in my Journal so many years ago:

> My life took on the feeling of a monotonous routine, made even more difficult with the baby's bouts with colic. They seemed to occur every night between eleven and three in the morning. One long night, as I paced the floor of the nursery trying to calm my screaming baby, uncontrollable tears started to flow down my face. I was slowly hit with the realization that the fun and games were ended and we weren't playing house any more. The reality hit me with a stunning blow.
>
> The tears kept streaming down my face as I continued to walk in circles with my little one. As I tried to ease his pain, I realized that there was no longer anyone to ease mine. My husband had his responsibilities and I had mine. I deeply resented him as he slept in the other room. I so wanted him to take over, yet, I couldn't expect him to be up all night and go to work the next day. And for the first time, I started to see myself as a "victim". I was the one stuck at home—taken out of the mainstream of life. Strangely, I held little resentment for my son. I saw him as my "soulmate". We were both helpless and pathetic. It was "poor us," alone in this world. My husband became the enemy.

Resentment is an ultra-destructive feeling. It puts cracks in the solidness of formerly beautiful relationships. And as the cracks continue to appear, the relationship by definition falls away. Unless the resentment is dealt with satisfactorily, it just grows and grows and grows.

So many women at home resent their husband's "freedom"; sadly, their pain does not allow them to see the loss of freedom the increased financial responsibility creates for the men. Both feel unfulfilled. And instead of consoling one another, they often blame one another. They would feel too guilty to blame the arrival of an innocent child, so they blame each other instead.

I once counseled a couple whose seriously handicapped child was creating extreme difficulties in their marriage. The husband was able to take much of the responsibility off his wife's shoulders as his job allowed him great flexibility. Yet she raged at him constantly—which brought them in to see me. The husband was a very loving man who truly adored their child and was able to cope beautifully with his deformities. He also adored his wife and couldn't understand her rage toward him. After each of them presented their side of the story, it was so clear to me what the problem was. I looked at the wife and said with great compassion, "Why don't you just admit that the problem here is not your husband; it has to do with the fact that there is a part of you that is sorry you ever had this child to begin with?"

For a moment she looked stunned. She then softened and started to sob. Her husband's arms immediately went out to comfort her. "Yes," she finally said. "You are right. I couldn't understand my anger toward my husband. Now it makes sense. It's hard to admit you are sorry you had your child, especially when he is so helpless, but it is true." I told her that her feelings were very human and nothing to feel guilty about. As the years of pent-up feelings came tumbling out, she was overcome with an intense sense of relief. And by being able to place her upset in the right place, she was able to deal with her pain, see her husband for the wonderful man he truly was, and the last time I spoke with them, she and her husband—and the child—were all doing fine.

We need to place "blame" where it truly exists—on the changes in our life that the presence of our children demand. It's nobody's fault; it just is a reality of life. We need to admit that parenting is really tough. Then we need to work with our mates to heal whatever anger, pain, or resentment may exist, so that love can continue to flow.

THE LOSS OF SEXUAL ACTIVITY

This one *really* hurts. When a child enters the picture, satisfying sex for many couples becomes a distant memory. Geoff Deane in his inimitable voice puts it this way:

> On the odd occasion that you can both muster up the energy you will discover that nature has installed a modem connecting the man's erection to his son's lungs. You get a hard-on and he starts to cry. Soon the moment has passed and so has your boner. What have you done to deserve this?[8]

No more lying in bed on the weekends reading the newspaper or making long, passionate love. Attention to the baby is the order of the day. Again, if you don't particularly enjoy sex with your mate, this is not so upsetting, but for the rest of us, this is a difficult part of the package to give up.

And who has the energy for sex? The demands of parenthood create fatigue and often depression. By definition, fatigue and depression kill our desire for sex, let alone enjoyment of everyday life. Yes, Mom and Dad want to go to bed, but for sleep, not for sex. Oh, my! And for those moms who are enjoying the exclusivity of the mother-child relationship, sex is the furthermost thing from their minds. Some have reported that it has taken a very long time, sometimes over a year or more, to even think about such closeness with their husbands. This doesn't make an already left-out father feel great. When we are not paying attention to lost intimacy in a relationship, we are asking for trouble.

Another reason for decreased interest in sex is that "sexy wife" is often replaced by "maternal wife" which isn't much of a turn-on either for the woman or the man. I love what one woman had to say:

> I felt like I'd been a prisoner for five months . . . a stinky one at that. Who had the time or energy to take a shower

> or wash my hair? I was pathetic. And this child of mine spent its life pooping and peeing and spitting up all over my shirt. My breasts were so sore and scabby that I wanted to scream. Sex? Are you crazy?

Not a sexy picture! (And the breast-feeding mystique is a disaster for some, as you will see in a later chapter.)

Believe it or not, I feel much sexier and more attractive now (mastectomy and all) than I did when I was in my twenties raising children! Today, there's just my wonderful husband and me . . . and no babies making three, four, and more. And with that goes a delicious sense of "us-ness" that is very sexy, indeed.

One couple I interviewed reported:

> Yesterday was such a nice day. Usually we're so consumed with the kids' activities. One of us goes with one kid; the other goes with the other kid. Yesterday, they were both off on a school activity. It was so wonderful; we just hung out in the house and made love. Usually we're so tired from all the hassles that we don't make love. We forgot what we were missing.

It is lucky for them that the urge was still there. Others just lose the desire. Hickey and Salmans have this view on the situation:

> Who can think about sex with a man you haven't had a one-on-one conversation with in months? Come to think of it, you barely even see the guy any more.[9]

One woman told me:

> I don't need to go to the gym. I am lugging, schlepping, and running all day. Then I'm exhausted. Sex has gone out the window. Anyone who says they are having sex with little kids is lying. Totally lying. Who has the energy? It's hard to think about sex when you are changing a diaper or the baby is spitting up on your shirt. My husband is exhausted also. What a team!

One woman felt all was not lost. She said:

> I look forward to great sex when the kids are gone. My husband and I work on keeping enough passion and playfulness and rapport. Nobody's angry at the other. I feel parents are pressured to believe that if they are not having sex like they did before, something is wrong. Not necessarily. It's just how it is. It goes with the territory. I think it's something to think about before you have kids. Nobody tells you your sex life will wane. But even if they were told, people don't believe it will happen to them. I wonder why they think that?

So do I. It seems to be a fact of life, that the only people whose sex life doesn't change after a child enters the picture are those who rarely had sex before!

INCREASED RESPONSIBILITY AND DELEGATION OF TASKS

This one is a biggie! While women have come very far in attaining equality in the workplace, they forgot to demand equality in the home. It is a rare couple that gets the balance right. Even if a mother is working and doesn't feel the resentment of being stuck in the house when he goes off to the "freedom" of work, her resentment comes when she gets home and takes on the bulk of responsibility in caring for the children. While there may be an honest intention to co-parent before a child is born, true co-parenting is a rare occurrence. Men "baby-sit" or play with the child, while the actual drudgery often reverts to the woman. In fact, many a working woman comes home to what is now being called "the second shift." Joan Peters tells us:

> Most childless couples share in the financial and domestic maintenance of their homes. But when these same men and

> women become parents, instead of modernizing motherhood and fatherhood to preserve their equality, they unthinkingly submit to the traditional roles their mothers and fathers have struggled to expand these last thirty years.[10]

Women sometimes inadvertently create this inequality. They often covet control in the home as men often covet control in the workplace. Talk about cutting off your nose to spite your face! As a result, women sometimes push willing men away . . . and then complain about the heavy load. I am always amused when women complain about all the things men can't do right when it comes to laundry, shopping, and childcare . . . as if there is a "right way." Soon the men give up and the women get angry.

What doesn't help the situation is the destructive myth that men don't know how to nurture and only women do. Again, many women love feeling that sense of importance. But in reality, most men are wonderful at caring for children if given the chance. Most men, however, are not given that chance. And they rarely fight for it. I wonder why! Could it be that a round of golf on the weekend is a much more gratifying alternative than lunching with a bunch of rowdy kids?

The complexities of the division of labor are huge. And it is a daily struggle to keep it all in balance. Some succeed beautifully; others never get it right.

DIFFERING PARENTING STYLES

How do we raise our children? Many arguments occur as this question is acted out. Are we strict or lenient? Do we give, give, give or do we make them earn? Do they need to keep their rooms tidy or do we allow them to be slobs? Do they date when they are 15? When do they drive? Many parents don't agree to the answers to these questions and the countless others that come up. And often it's a fight to the finish. As one woman told me:

> We thought our house would be filled with love; it is now filled with fighting. It is amazing that something we looked forward to with such joy can end up so miserably.

The fighting is actually fruitless because there are few situations in life where two people actually know so little yet *think* they know so much! Even the childcare experts are deceiving you when they tell you they know how to raise a healthy, well-adjusted child. It's a mystery that no one has yet solved. But the fighting goes on anyway. Each wants what is best for the child, but what is "best" too often differs from person to person.

EXHAUSTION

Aside from a lack of sleep, exhaustion also occurs from the extra work, responsibility, and attention that children require. Exhausted people have short tempers and booming anger. Needless to say, this combination is not great for relationships. Again, Reiner tells us:

> Our family has known much sweetness: bringing our new babies home, watching them crawl, then toddle, then run. Our house has echoed with much laughter. Yet in the moments when their needs exhaust me, I become bitter, angry, wishing only to be left alone. Being a parent has often made me very unhappy. It's no fun seeing how selfish, or angry, or limited I am. The happiness I experience in being with my children gives me the resolve to go through these hard times. But it's a piece of work, being a parent.[11]

I ask you: what if these hard times go on for years at a time . . . sometimes 18 years . . . sometimes longer? Can the love survive? Nina Barrett tells us:

> I had always felt about my marriage that we were so in love that if one of us were ever asked, "Would you give up

> your life to save your spouse?", we would both unhesitatingly answer "Yes." But, to mix my metaphors, we were like two drowning people, each of us expecting the other to save him without being aware that the other one was drowning, too. I was too exhausted to care about his needs and he was too exhausted to care about mine.[12]

How poignant and how common a situation. Some of the people I interviewed had full-time childcare to help with all the drudgery. Even here, the burden can be overwhelming. One woman told me:

> I don't know how people do it without help. I am overwhelmed, even with full-time help. I am exhausted and I yearn for private time with my husband. It rarely happens.

THE MANIPULATION BY CHILDREN

Very early on, children master the art of divide and conquer when it comes to their parents. As infants, they need to be the center of attention or they could literally die. As they get older, they have a very hard time relinquishing center stage and will cause all manner of trouble to make sure that the center of attention remains theirs. They don't like you relating to each other; they like you relating to them. They are not interested in your needs; they are interested in their own. This is just the nature of children. "*Over here. Pay attention to ME.*" And we oblige, just to keep the screaming down. Ultimately, parents have to ask themselves, "Do we allow our child to divide us or do we stand together?" The couples who choose the latter obviously have a better chance of surviving the melee.

I've presented just a few reasons why oil and water are as compatible as sex and diapers. And certainly many marriages do not survive the raising of children. Some survive legally, but not emotionally. For example, I know a number of cases where women have stayed in unhappy marriages because of their fear that they couldn't make it financially or otherwise on their own. In reality, these marriages are over, despite the fact that these couples are living together. What a waste of a life.

Interestingly and understandably, when a divorce occurs, parents reassure their children that the break-up has nothing to do with them. Of course, it is humane and caring to spare the child's feelings at such a difficult time. I strongly advise it. But, just between you and me . . .

Of course, it has something to do with them!

When we have lost so many wonderful aspects of our lives in order to raise our children, how can it not create problems in our relationships? It must be clearly understood that *children cannot be blamed for the break-up of a relationship and no children of a divorced couple should feel guilty.* It isn't their "fault." It simply is a fact of life—a reality of nature—that all of us come into this life helpless and need constant care for many, many years. But the enormous chasm created when a couple brings a child into the relationship cannot be denied.

For those who are contemplating having children, it is unfortunate that the conspiracy of silence has hidden such an important reality . . . the reality that a precious being that is supposed to be the glue of a relationship and that is supposed to enhance the love a man and woman feel toward each other, a being that is made from the two of them, can actually tear them apart. But that is the way it is, for many, many couples.

Given all this, there are obviously many marriages with children that survive the hand grenade. Which marriages are they and what is their secret?

- Perhaps those marriages where both parties have a realistic expectation of what having children entails and are willing for a number of years to accept less intimacy, romance, and togetherness in the relationship, trusting that it will all be restored when the children are grown.

- Perhaps those marriages where both parties have the Loving-Being-A-Parent (LBP) genes and truly enjoy sharing all that parenting involves.
- Perhaps those couples who are so close that they become the dominant twosome and simply don't allow children to interfere with their intimacy and great times together. Most of these have outside help allowing them time alone. They see themselves as a team and rarely will allow a child to pit one against the other.
- Perhaps those who weren't that close to begin with—those who didn't thrive on intimate moments, time together, passionate sex, those who had separate lives and separate interests. These couples may find it easier to be child-oriented and may welcome the glue that a joint endeavor provides. In such cases, the problems in their relationships may occur when the children are gone.

While they survived the melee, many couples would admit to very difficult times along the way. Many would also admit that although they enjoyed the process while it was happening, they couldn't imagine starting all over and doing it again. This doesn't mean that there aren't couples who miss having kids around and adopt or start a new family once their "first" children leave the nest. But they are certainly not the norm.

It stands to reason that would-be parents are well-served by having intense reality training before they make up their minds to have a child. But because of the conspiracy of silence that exists in Western society today, such reality-training is hard to find. One woman says she borrows children to remind herself why she didn't have any. I've joked that perhaps some entrepreneur out there could start a new business called "rent-a-baby," where a couple has the opportunity to get a taste of what parenting is *really* like before they jump into the fray.

I remember a wonderful segment of the television show *Frasier* where his brother, Niles, decides to carry around a sack of flour as a "pretend-baby" to get a sense of how it would feel to be constantly responsible for a little being. At the end of the day, after a hilarious series of events where the sack of flour ends up tattered and torn, he tells Frasier, "Yes, I want a child, but not badly enough."

It's time we put more thought into what we are doing when we are thinking about having a child. "Do we really want it badly enough?" And as I will discuss in a later chapter, "Do we really want it badly enough, for the right reasons?" Essential questions for one of the most important decisions in your life.

Endnotes

[1]Hickey, Mary C., and Sandra Salmans. *The Working Mother's Guilt Guide: Whatever You're Doing, It Isn't Enough*. Penguin Books, New York, 1992, p. 37.

[2]Nora Ephron quoted by author Susan Maushart in *The Mask of Motherhood*. Random House, Australia, NSW Australia, 1997, p. 101.

[3]Maushart, Susan. *The Mask of Motherhood*. Random House, Australia, NSW Australia, 1997, p. 243.

[4]Reiner, Joseph F. "Those Mixed-Up, Painful Feelings of Being a Parent," in the *Washington Post*, January 10, 1982. As cited in *How Men Feel: Their Response to Women's Demands for Equality and Power*, by Anthony Astrachan. Doubleday, New York, 1988, p. 242.

[5]Ruth Parker as quoted by author Hester Lacey in "Motherhood: The Big Lie," in the *Independent on Sunday* (British), 1998, p. 2.

[6]Green, Maureen. *Marriage*. Fontana Paperbacks, Great Britain, 1984, p. 125.

[7]Lindbergh, Anne Morrow. *Gift from the Sea*. Pantheon Books, New York, 1955, p. 64.

[8]Deane, Geoff. "Life After Birth: When One and One Makes Three," in *Arena Magazine*, Spring, 1994, p. 56.

[9]Hickey. Ibid., p. 38.

[10]Peters, Joan K. *When Mothers Work: Loving Our Children Without Sacrificing Our Selves*. Hodder Headline Australia, 1998, p. 10.

[11]Reiner. Ibid.

[12]Barrett, Nina. *I Wish Someone Had Told Me: A Realistic Guide to Early Motherhood*. Academy Chicago Publishers, Chicago, Illinois, 1997, p. 137.

4

THE UNSPEAKABLE TRUTH ABOUT KIDS

Stephen: What have you got against having children?
Simon: Well Steve, in the first place there isn't enough room. In the second place they seem to start by mucking up their parents' lives, and then go on in the third place to muck up their own. In the fourth place it doesn't seem right to bring them into a world like this in the fifth place and in the sixth place I don't like them very much in the first place. OK.

Simon Gray
from *Otherwise Engaged*[1]

I once heard a well-known author and therapist addressing a group of mothers. He began by telling them that they should learn from their children, that children come into this world as loving and caring beings, messengers of peace. He didn't get very far when one of the mothers couldn't take it any more. She raised her hand and asked incredulously, "Which planet are you from? I have children of my own and I used to be a teacher of young children. Obviously I love children, but I don't see "loving and caring." I see "needy, selfish and cruel." I nodded my head in agreement as did the other parents in the room. I don't think the speaker ever recovered from that one!

Perhaps there exists in this world a few wise souls who begin their lives as loving and caring beings, messengers of peace, but frankly, I haven't heard of any. Most children, *by definition*, belong in the "needy, selfish and cruel" category and, as you will see, for a very logical reason.

It's hard to imagine where the myth got started that children come into this world as loving little beings. All one has to do is look around and see the colossal absurdity of such a belief. Yes, when things are going their way, it can appear that children are caring, loving and wise, *but*—and this is a very important *but*—when things are not going their way, children are demanding, manipulative, and sometimes incredibly hurtful. I think the story of Dr. Jekyll and Mr. Hyde must have been conceived while the author watched the behavior of his own children. One minute they are angels and the next minute they can transform into punishing monsters: loud, cruel, demanding, whiny, needy, self-centered, greedy, unreasonable, hurtful, spoiled, uncooperative, untruthful, manipulative, uncaring, sneaky, sloppy, and selfish.

And that's when they're three! It can get worse as they get older, reaching a crescendo of horror in their teens. No getting around it. No rationalizing their behavior. No making excuses for them. Kids can, indeed, be horrible.

Society today tends to focus primarily on the angel-side of children and omits the horrible side—the omission of which is a dirty trick on those deciding whether to have children or not. These poor souls never hear the whole truth and nothing but the truth. There's the old conspiracy of silence again.

You may be interested in knowing that the idea that children come into this world as little angels is a relatively new concept. Earlier in history, people were far more observant—and far more honest. It was believed that children came into this world evil and needed a great deal of discipline to rid them of the deep darkness within. I don't believe either the "angel theory" or the "evil theory" so I created my own theory. It's called the "needy theory."

Have you ever observed a newborn infant? It is astonishing how helpless they truly are. They can't turn over, feed themselves, change their diapers, make themselves understood. They can't even hold up their little heads. They are totally dependent on us for their survival. That's needy, indeed! Now, what does a needy child do? TAKE, TAKE TAKE! CHILDREN HAVE TO TAKE OR THEY WILL DIE! Of course, a child's taking is not bad; it is simply "needy-nature" in action. Their survival is dependent on their ability to take. Their survival is also dependent on what they are given. And who is the giver? Usually a parent. And thus we have the give and take of parenting:

Parents give and children take!

You may be saying, "Oh, children give you so much back with their smiles and hugs and kisses." In *Feel the Fear and Do It Anyway*, I point out that: "Yes, parents often get a feeling of joy from the smile or the touch of their child and, in that sense, the child is a giver—but I doubt if the child spent the night pondering: 'My life is abundant. I have so much to give away that I think I'll reward my parents with a great big smile tomorrow morning.' No, their 'gift' is on a rather primitive or reflexive level. In fact, a hungry belly in the morning will produce only loud shrieks of impatience."[2]

A friend of mine moaned when going through a sleepless patch with his infant son:

Children have no mercy!

It's true. They really don't care if you have the flu and need your sleep; they really don't care if they embarrass you with all their demands at the supermarket; they really don't care that they hurt you when they scream, "I hate you." It's true that a needy child has no mercy and *all children are needy!* In any other relationship, we would never put up with such blatant disregard for our feelings; hopefully, we'd get out of the relationship as quickly as we could.

But with our children, we have no choice but to put up with their needy nature and handle it as best we can. One woman says of her relationship with her two-year-old child:

> It's like being madly in love with a man but the hardest relationship you ever had. Never more in love, but never in more misery. It's like the unhealthiest relationship with a man you ever had. Every day is hard, hard, hard.

The naïve among us think, "Surely things have to improve once the baby stage is over." *Wrong!* For a long, long time, they continue to need us for all the necessities of life, such as food, clothing, shelter, and love. And for a long, long time, they continue to take, take, take without giving much in return . . . except with the threat that their television set will be turned off. Or something just as dire.

One woman told me that every time her teenage daughter didn't get what she wanted, she would go into her room and slam the door—loudly. Despite multiple attempts to stop her daughter's noisy and disrespectful behavior, the door continued to slam . . . and slam . . . and slam. What did this ingenious mother finally do? She removed the door! And it stayed in the basement for a week. In the interim, her daughter discovered what living in a glass bowl felt like. A nightmare for a teenager! When the door was replaced a week later, you can be sure, it was never slammed again.

One of my favorite tools in making life beautiful is to say Yes to life.[3] Children don't say Yes to life; they say No . . . a lot! When they are young, the No is stated in the form of a temper tantrum. As they get into their teens, it is stated in many forms, such as silence, disdain, anger, promiscuity, drugs . . . and sometimes a temper tantrum. Many children moving from infancy through their teens and beyond give their parents many periods of intense difficulty. That process can be a torment for both . . . and it can be a very long process for all concerned!

Contrary to what we have been told, *this is not necessarily a failure of parenting.* In fact, the process of moving from childhood to adulthood *requires* that the child pull away from parental control and stand on his or her own two feet, literally and figuratively. Still, knowing that the upsetting traits of your children are all a natural part of the process doesn't make them any more pleasant. "Oh, darling, you threw your food on the floor. Isn't that developmentally wonderful!" On the other hand, knowing it's not your fault certainly brings a measure of relief.

The descriptions of some of the stages of childhood are very revealing:

terrible twos
tantrum threes
roller coaster middle years
turbulent, terrible teens

I've never heard of anyone writing about the terrific twos, satisfying sixes, or great eights. Have you? Just as we get over one terrible, turbulent, or tantrum stage, we seem to come face to face with the next. Many of us wish each child came into this world with a survival guide—not for the child, but for the parent! Raising kids is akin to a warring state, not a state of continuous joy and fulfillment as some would have us believe. Again, this doesn't mean that there aren't glorious moments of closeness, cuddling, caring, and all good things. There has to be or surely you would see a lot fewer kids on the planet! Yes, kids are a lot of great things. They are at times funny, clever, a miracle, joyful, cuddly, loving, attentive, adorable, winsome, lovable, bright, delicious, co-operative.

I'm sure you can think of many more wonderful adjectives to describe children at their best. But we can't just skirt over the needy side of children's behavior which makes them behave in very ugly ways. Katherine Anne Porter describes children as follows:

> They are human nature in essence, without conscience, without pity, without love, without a trace of consideration for others—just one seething cauldron of primitive appetites.[4]

Not a pretty picture of human nature! While children can have adorable exteriors, the spill-over of their internal "cauldron of primitive appetites" can be very disturbing to watch.

I think what is most disturbing about children's behavior is their cruelty. I passed a school yard recently and watched children teasing one of their classmates so cruelly that it made me cry for the little boy being teased . . . and for the boys doing the teasing. I recently heard a man explaining that he had contracted polio as a young boy which left an obvious deformity in one of his legs. The dress code at his school was short pants, which, of course, exposed his deformed leg. He reported that his classmates never stopped their merciless teasing.

Jenny Alexander wrote a book about bullying with a title of the same name, *Bullying*. She talked about the shock she felt as she did her research. Kids are perpetrators of many hurtful acts including physical bullying (kicking, hitting, pushing, spitting, damage to property, theft, and extortion) and non-physical bullying (teasing, name-calling, threatening, excluding, and whispering campaigns).[5]

Over the years, I have watched the cruelty of children toward their siblings. They take special delight in physically hurting their brothers and sisters or getting them in trouble. And we can't forget the cruelty they show toward their parents as well—from the three-year-old screaming, "I hate you," to the disdain, disregard, and lack of respect and caring that are a signature of the teenage years.

Children think the world revolves around them. Their narcissism is unbelievable at times. A friend told me a story that would make any parent's hair stand on end:

> I lived alone with my mother. My father was dead. When I was 15, I decided that it was time to leave home and go off to see the world. I left a note saying simply, "I'm leaving home. Thank you for everything." And I disappeared for two weeks, at which point I realized that there's no place like home. When I returned, my mother became hysterical. She ran into her room, composed herself and never brought the subject of my disappearance up again.

A parent's nightmare . . . the disappearance of a child. I asked him if he ever, for one moment, thought about his mother's feelings in the matter. He shook his head in disbelief at his own insensitivity and said, "Never. I never for one moment thought of her feelings." I'd like to think that my friend's lack of regard for his mother is unusual. But it isn't. Again, this is simply needy-nature in action, but this reality doesn't make it any easier for parents. Just watching children's cruelty and insensitivity to each other, to their siblings, and to their parents can't help but dispel any myth that children are angels.

I could go on showing you unarguable proof that at times children are all manner of hateful things, but I think I've made my point! Given their distasteful behavior, one can understand why many people, if they were truthful, would admit to not liking children very much. Gore Vidal gives us a logical reason for this dislike of children when he talks of "*the nakedness of their bad character.*" That phrase hits the nail on the head. "The nakedness of their bad character." Screaming, yelling, shrieking, slamming, and hitting is as naked as you can get. Just as we can't avoid their cuteness, we can't avoid the nakedness of their bad character no matter how hard we try.

Gore Vidal doesn't let us forget one very important reality: *we adults have the same bad character, we have just learned to hide it a little better!* Of course, that's true. Some adults never grow up and continue to be needy until the day they die. Their neediness can be seen in many forms: men who can't tolerate their wives' independence; employees lying about a co-worker to get the boss's approval; owners of companies who lie and cheat to put more money in their pockets; sports figures desperate to win—at any cost. And so it goes. Needy people can't give; they can only take.

Needy-nature is unattractive both in children and adults, but neediness in adults isn't so obvious. It's rare that you find an adult kicking and screaming at the next table in a restaurant putting a damper on your romantic dinner!

Also many adults learn over the years how to side-step or transcend their neediness and become "givers" instead. When this happens, the "nakedness of their *good* character" shines through! But children don't have the ability to side-step or transcend their neediness. A sense of power and love and all good things comes only with adulthood, if it comes at all.

A word about teenage behavior: while the behavior of young children is often difficult, teenage behavior can send us over the top. I have known many parents who have enjoyed parenting until their children reached their teens. And then all hell broke loose, leaving them emotionally bloodied and battered. When you are in a bloodied and battered state, it is not surprising that all the enjoyment ceases! Many children who may have been sweet and easy in the early years often become disdainful, angry, and contemptuous as they hit the teens. And even if they are not so easy as kids, bouts of horrible behavior are at least interspersed by lovable behavior which makes the *horrible* more tolerable. It goes like this:

horrible > **lovable** > horrible > **lovable** > horrible > **lovable** > horrible > **lovable** > horrible > **lovable** > horrible > **lovable** > horrible > **lovable** > horrible > **lovable** > horrible > **lovable** > horrible > **lovable** >

There is an ebb and flow and a surety that "this too shall pass"—that bad always follows good, and good always follows bad. That's reassuring. In their teens, the pattern changes. It looks something like this:

horrible > horrible > horrible > horrible > **lovable** > horrible > horrible > horrible > **lovable** > horrible > horrible > **lovable** > horrible > horrible > horrible > horrible > horrible > horrible > horrible > horrible >

No more balance. The *horrible* greatly outweighs the *lovable*. For some, the *lovable* disappears altogether. There is no ebb and flow, but a long bout with *horrible* that could go on for years and years and years. Certainly, not all teens create so much havoc; just as certainly, many of them do.

Teens push away for a very rational reason, but it doesn't make it hurt any less. What is this rational reason? They have to grow up and away from the influence of the family and become independent individuals. It is during this time that we realize everything we did right when they were young may be totally inappropriate when they enter their teens. Where we once protected, we now have to let go. Where we once did everything for them, we must make sure they do things for themselves. Where we once may have really enjoyed them, we now find them awful to be around. And where they once were affectionate, they now turn their backs.

We stand by helplessly and watch their talk becoming disrespectful and sarcastic . . . if they talk to you at all. Sometimes their silence is even more devastating. I nod my head in disbelief when articles and books tell parents to "create a healthy dialogue with your children—a give and take of feelings where each can have their say." How do you create a dialogue with someone who won't talk . . . no matter how you plead? Or if they do have an easy dialogue with you, who says they are going to tell you the truth? They have a way of omitting the important things, such as drugs, sex, and the like.

I had a good relationship and a lot of dialogue, relatively speaking, with my parents as a teenager. I was the "good girl"—good marks, a cheerleader, Queen of the Ball, lead in the high school play and all the rest. My parents never suspected that my extracurricular activities included great sex, or drinking in bars with friends long before I was old enough to legally drink. Luckily there were no drugs around. My behavior in front of my parents was one thing; my secret behavior with my friends was another.

And then there are the extremes. One woman, who went through hell because of her daughter's behavior, reported that her daughter finally graduated college and moved into her own apartment. Her comment said it all: "*My nightmare is finally over.*" I asked her if she loved her child. Her answer was a sad one: "*In truth, no. But I still feel responsibility, guilt, sadness and a desperate wish she were happier than she is.*" A mysterious bond, an intense responsibility, perhaps, but when you cringe at the sound of your child's key turning in the door, it can't be called love.

I know that there are those who profess that a parent-child relationship is the supreme example of unconditional love. But is it? Harriet Lerner suggests that if we want to practice unconditional love, we should get a cat. "But even here," she warns, "one may discover one's limits."[6] Love is not an automatic feeling, not even in a child-parent relationship. It has to be earned. And some children don't earn it. (Of course, neither do some parents. But that's another book!) I loved the honesty of a parent whose response to her child's screaming, "I hate you," was "Right now, I hate you, too!" instead of the questionable platitude we often hear: "I love you, it's your behavior I can't stand."

Of course, on a spiritual level, all beings are lovable; one only needs to look to the light inside. I believe that and, in fact, have written about it in a few of my books. But when the devil incarnate seems to be living in our home, it feels as though the light has definitely gone out. Most human beings are not that spiritually enlightened. It's hard to see the light inside another person when that person is driving you crazy. Who blew the light out? You didn't. No matter how many articles will blame you for your child's bad behavior, you can rest assured that it probably wasn't you who caused it, as you will see in a later chapter.

I was told the story of one woman who had a double mastectomy. At a time when she most needed support from people who cared about her, her daughter treated her with extreme cruelty, as she had done for many years. But this particular act of cruelty opened the mother's eyes. Soon afterward, she took her child out of her will without telling her. She was chastised by a friend for not giving her child another chance to heal the relationship. Her answer was, "*Nothing she has ever done lets her deserve that chance.*" Unconditional love? I don't think so. Justified? Perhaps, as there was no evidence that her child would ever change. Sad? Indeed.

At the extreme, children can be violent against parents. Again, the media distorts. While they report the numbers of parents who physically abuse their children (which, of course, is totally unacceptable), they forget to mention the large number of children who physically abuse their parents (which is also totally unacceptable).

And there's the emotional abuse. One mother says of her young child:

> I just feel tortured. Parenthood has to be the closest thing to boot camp. Why is he torturing me? Boot camp has to be better. Actually war has to be better!

One woman said to her husband as they looked at their perpetually screaming infant, "Do you think we will ever love this child?" He nodded his head and answered, "I don't know." They told me that their first child had been so easy and that, certainly, had their second child been born first, there never would have been a second child! One thing is for sure:

Some people make hateful parents; but it is also true that some people make hateful children.

There are so many books today that focus on the pain that parents cause their children. To be sure, parents, wittingly or unwittingly, make many mistakes that cause their children pain. It goes with the territory. What we don't notice on the bookshelves, are books that focus on the pain that children cause their parents just in the process of their growing up. I believe that . . .

If children knew the intense hurt they cause their parents in the process of growing up, it would be they who would be infused with guilt . . . not their parents!

The pain inflicted on parents by their children starts when they are very young. I recently read a letter in an Agony Aunt column written by a young parent whose three-year-old keeps telling her "I hate you." She expresses her hurt and concern. "What am I doing wrong?" What makes matters worse for her is that the child adores his father. She feels left out in the cold. On a rational level, we can assure her that children are children and not to worry about it. He'll outgrow it. It's just a phase. But will she outgrow her pain of being rejected? Of course, that one incident doesn't amount to much. But compound that one little incident into years and years of almost daily assaults of one kind or another and the pain eventually becomes imprinted on your heart.

Here's an experiment: With your knuckle, lightly tap your arm. It doesn't hurt. But keep tapping your arm over and over again on the same spot. Slowly but surely it starts to hurt. The longer you continue to do it, the worse it hurts. Ultimately the pain becomes agonizing. Children are like your tapping knuckle. They have a way of tapping away at your heart until the pain becomes agonizing.

By virtue of the fact that children are children, it is a guarantee there will be times that they will lash out at their parents when things don't go their way—and one has to be made of steel for it not to hurt.

Parents are supposed to be understanding, have compassion, rise above the subtle or not so subtle attack most children wage on their parents in their process of becoming independent human beings. But most parents are not so spiritually evolved that they can always rise above the storm in such a supremely noble way. They can "act" in a loving and forgiving way, but in their heart of hearts, the pain is there. Not only the pain of their children's behavior, but the pain of all their disappointments, all their frustration, all their guilt, and all the other hurtful feelings they experience in the process of raising their children. Even when we are blessed with relatively good kids, there are always the hard, hard times. There was not one parent I interviewed, even among those who adore children and loved raising them, that said it was easy. "Difficult" was the most commonly used adjective.

Susan Forward wrote an excellent book called *Emotional Blackmail*. There is no question that kids are emotional blackmailers, par excellence. Forward talks of "FOG," which is an acronym for fear, obligation, and guilt, the three feeling states that all blackmailers, no matter their style, work to intensify in us. Who is more capable of creating fear, obligation, and guilt than our children? She says: "FOG is penetrating, disorienting and it obscures everything but the pounding discomfort it produces. In the midst of FOG we're desperate to know: How did I get into this? How do I get out? How do I make these difficult feelings stop?"[7]

Children go through ages where they are embarrassed by you . . . where anything you do will be thrown back in your face— if not today, at some time in the future.[8] The father of a thirteen year-old sadly reports that:

> My son always depended upon me for help and advice. Now he credits me with as much intelligence as a sow bug.[9]

Hurtful, indeed. Naturally, we shouldn't take their behavior personally, but it's very hard not to take it personally when you are the target of the day—seemingly every day. It's so hard to understand their outbursts when you are trying the best you know how to be a loving parent. When my daughter was in her mid-teens, she wrote me a letter which was amazingly insightful and loving and may give you some understanding of a teenager's hateful behavior. With her gracious permission, I offer you her letter:

> Dearest Mom,
> I wrote this note in my journal after our very special evening at the ballet.
>
> "There is something so brilliantly frightening about mom sometimes. It's as though I have absolutely no guard around her. She knows the truth about me all the time whether or not I do. I think it's why sometimes I get so ugly with her because very often I'd just as soon not look at or see the truth and looking at her, or hearing her voice, I see/hear nothing but what it is I'm trying to avoid. It is much clearer than a mirror. It's like a window with a magnifying glass. Thank God it's a glass that doesn't succumb to my lashing out. It is shatterproof, strengthened by her love."
>
> I wanted to share this with you because I love you so deeply and intensely that sometimes it confuses me. I guess it's the intensity behind all my feelings about you that gets

crazy, the love is so strong and so is the fear and anger. I'm learning so much about myself and about love itself through my relationship with you. How lucky I am to have your undying love and support and your strength to never ever give up on me and the courage to let me go while all the time nurturing me. You are extraordinary. I thank you by doing my best to take the risks and chances to become the most I can be. You showed me I too have this strength and ability.

Forever yours,
Leslie

I was one of the lucky ones. Leslie had the insight to know that her lashing out had something to do with *her* growing pains, not my actions. And she mercifully shared her insight with me. Few parents are ever given such a gift. They just feel the pain of their children's lashing out without any understanding whatsoever. I hope Leslie's letter provides some measure of understanding for those of you who are looking for reasons why children lash out.

It's almost as though we need a mourning period after a child reaches a certain age. Because, at least temporarily, we seem to lose them. Their bodies are there, but their hearts and minds seem to have been abducted. Giannetti and Sagarese agree:

> Soon it seems like all your close encounters—with an alien being who bears just a passing resemblance to your son or daughter—are of the angry kind. Two-way communication stops. You feel your offspring spinning out of control, out of your orbit.[10]

During their difficult teen years, I used to look at pictures of my kids when they were very young and think to myself with great sadness in my heart, "Where did you go? I miss you." It took many painful years, but ultimately they did come back again. I recently asked my son, now 40, "Where did you go all those years?" He said, "I never really left." We both cried. Some aren't so lucky. One woman says she lost her child to drugs and he has never returned:

> I rarely talk about it because it is so painful. A horrible blow. When he was small, there was a lot of pleasure and joy. It's a horror to watch a child transform. I didn't think I would survive his adolescence. He's grown now. But he's still very disturbed as a result of drugs. I rarely see him. It's too painful.

I was so moved by the following quote by Katherine Gordy Levine:

> Being a parent is tough. Bad follows good. Good follows bad. And you never know when one will replace the other. The bad is rarely in your power to predict, and often not in your power to change. One thing is predictable, though: by the time a child makes it through the early years and into the teens, most parents identify at one time or another with this African proverb: "A cow gave birth to a fire. She wanted to lick it, but it burned her. She wanted to leave it, but it was her child."[11]

Obviously, parents are "burned" by their children all over the world. Africa. Britain. America. Wherever. And, while they probably wouldn't admit it, there are many who, at times, "want to leave it, but it is their child."

It is the very blessed parent who breezes through the parenting process without too many knuckle taps to the heart. If you are one of them, I suggest you kneel and kiss the ground and have compassion. Many aren't that lucky.

As always, humor helps. One man told me his grandfather refers to his grandkids as "RK1, RK2, and RK3." I asked what that meant. He said, "Rotten Kid Number 1, Rotten Kid Number 2, and Rotten Kid Number 3." I believe it is the Irish comedian Noel V. Ginnity who is credited with the following:

> My father had ten kids. He said he had no favorites. He hated everyone of us.

Humor helps, indeed. So does honesty. Knowing we are all in this together . . . that we are not alone in our experiences, is the biggest help of all.

Endnotes

[1]Gray, Simon. *Otherwise Engaged.* 1975, Act II. Found in *Bartlett's Familiar Quotations*, by John Bartlett (Justin Kaplan, general editor). Little, Brown and Company, Boston, 1992, p. 768.

[2]Jeffers, Susan. *Feel the Fear and Do It Anyway.* Fawcett Columbine, New York, 1987, p. 171.

[3]See the addendum of this book for suggestions on to how to say YES to Life!

[4]Porter, Katherine Anne. Found in *Child.* Edited by Helen Handley and Andra Samelson, Penguin Books, New York, 1990, p. 44. (First published by Pushcart Press, 1988.)

[5]Alexander, Jenny. *Bullying.* Element Books Limited, Shaftesbury, Dorset or Boston, 1998, p. 2.

[6]In Harriet Lerner's Good Advice column. *New Woman,* September, 1997, p. 60.

[7]Forward, Susan, with Donna Frazier. *Emotional Blackmail: When the People in Your Life Use Fear, Obligation and Guilt to Manipulate You.* HarperCollins, New York, 1997, p. 39.

[8]Unfortunately, it is not uncommon for adult children in their twenties, thirties, and beyond, to admonish their parents for something they said or did when they were ten!

[9]Giannetti, Charlene C., and Margaret Sagarese. *The Roller-Coaster Years.* Broadway Books, New York, 1997, p. xii.

[10]Ibid.

[11]Levine, Katherine Gordy. *Parents Are People Too: An Emotional Fitness Program for Parents.* Penguin Books, New York, 1997, p. 2.

PART II

SEND THE "EXPERTS" BACK TO SCHOOL

5

WHAT YOU PUT IN DOESN'T NECESSARILY COME OUT

We have the mistaken idea that where we lead, they will follow. They may or they may not. If they do, it probably is a coincidence.

Susan Jeffers

When my son was about two years old, we used to make daily trips to the sandbox in the park, weather permitting. I remember the day when a little boy came over and picked up my son's pail. Without a moment's hesitation, my son picked up his shovel and hit the "intruder" on the head.

Now, trust me when I tell you *I did not teach my son to hit other kids on the head when they touched his pail!* Honest! What did I teach him? SHARE! SHARE! SHARE! That was what I taught him. Did he listen? No! My son definitely had a mind of his own! Naturally, the other mother was furious at *me*! What did *I* do? *I* didn't hit her kid on the head with a shovel! But that's the way it goes: parents being blamed for the way their children behave.

I shudder when I hear of city ordinances which hold parents responsible for their children's damage to other people's property or for their acts of violence. If this doesn't put people off having children, nothing will! In truth:

Parents have very little control over their children whether they are infants or teenagers.

While Western society loves to blame parents, usually mothers, there are many influences that determine our children's behavior. *This should be an incredible relief to parents out there who have been to hell and back with their children thinking it was all their fault.*

What I am about to tell in this chapter will be received first with upset and then with relief:

***Upset,* when you realize how little control you have over your children, then**

***Relief,* when you realize how little control you have over your children.**

Let me explain. When we feel the deep love most of us feel for our children, of course we want them to grow up as caring, loving, healthy, happy human beings. The thought that we have very little control over how they grow up can be very upsetting. We worry, worry, worry. *On the other hand*, the thought that we have very little control over how they grow up takes a HUGE responsibility off our shoulders and allows us to breathe a sigh of relief. This means that while we can't take the credit when things go right, we can't take the blame when things go wrong. Of course, this doesn't take us completely off the hook. It is our responsibility to do our very best to love and care for the being we have brought into this world; at the same time, we must let go of the outcome. *The outcome is out of our control.*

Parental blame has reached the level of the absurd in today's child-centered world. It is clear that this blame is sadly misplaced. James Hillman, a Jungian psychologist, agrees as he tells us:

> If any fantasy holds our contemporary civilization in an unyielding grip, it is that we are our parents' children and that the primary instrument of our fate is the behavior of our mother and father.[1]

A long hard look at reality shows us that there are many influences on a child's development; parenting is only one of them. *And I believe that, while very important, it is an influence that is greatly exaggerated!* (Again, I know there are many parents who don't really want to hear this. Rather, they need to feel that they are or have been the sole sculptor of their child's life . . . especially if the child turns out wonderfully. I also know that there are parents who really *do* want to hear this. They need to feel that they are not the sole sculptors of their child's life.)

"Well," you may ask, "if it isn't the parents who are the instrument of a child's fate, who (or what) is?" It is my theory that:

What determines a child's fate is the child's Circle of Being.

"And what, Susan, is that?" The child's Circle of Being consists of the seemingly infinite number of forces that affect a child before conception until the end of his or her life. Here are only a *very few* of the huge number of components inherent in a child's Circle of Being:

- which man and woman happen to get together
- which egg and sperm happen to get together
- the child's genetic makeup
- what happens in the woman's body during the time she is carrying a child
- who their grandparents are
- what doctor delivers the child
- if they had an easy birth
- who takes care of the child
- if there are siblings

- birth order
- how siblings interact
- how much money the family has
- what the parents do for a living
- what music the child listens to
- what movies, video, and television they watch
- what friends they make
- what they do at their friends' houses
- what kind of parents their friends have
- what schools they go to
- how they react to a competitive world
- how they are treated by their friends
- how healthy they are
- how intelligent they are
- what personality they came in with
- if they are accident-free
- what teachers they have
- what books they read
- what food they eat
- what town they live in
- what policemen are on the beat
- what culture they live in
- what their physical attributes are

- the "fit" between parents, child, and siblings
- the child's "calling" (which I will explain)
- the parent's "calling"
- what their religious leaders tell them
- societal customs at the time

And this only scratches the surface. Not only does each factor have an important influence in its own right, so does the *interaction* of all of these forces. And the reality is that *very little about the effect on the child of the above or the interactions of the above is predictable or controllable by the parent.*

It is all chancy!

As I said, these are only *some* factors influencing a child's life; but the list goes on and includes the not so obvious. I always loved the story of a child with a history of bad behavior being admitted to a Catholic school. He became a model student. His teacher, of course, felt very proud of herself for the obvious influence she had on him. But when the headmaster asked the little boy what created the enormous change in his behavior, the child pointed to a figure of Christ on the cross and exclaimed with wide eyes, "Look what they did to him!" Sorry, teacher, in this case, it had nothing to do with you.

What is the lesson? How can we ever know what sights, what images, what experiences in the child's Circle of Being impinge on the senses of our children when they are growing up? The answer is, "We can't!" Nor can anyone else, including the childcare experts who blame it all on the parents. In fact, if you consider the huge array of factors that affect the development of a child, you see that:

The parents' interaction with a child is only one piece in a massive array of factors that determine how a child will turn out.

One might rightfully take the position that some factors are more important than others. I'm sure that's true. The problem is that *we really don't know what those factors are.* Is it genes, peers, siblings, parents, teachers, social environment, or whatever? And how do all these factors combine? And which factors more deeply affect which child? And at what age do they have an effect? Oh, chanciness, indeed![2] What does this mean? It means that *when we consistently blame the behavior of the parent, we are seeing only a teeny, tiny part of the big picture.*

When I was young, I remember hearing a fable which taught me an interesting lesson: five blindfolded men who had never seen an elephant are asked to describe an elephant through the sense of touch. One man feels the trunk. One feels the ears. One feels the legs. One feels the sides. One feels the tail. Naturally, they disagree hugely about what an elephant looks like. And, of course, they are all wrong in relation to the big picture that is known as "elephant." I maintain that:

Anyone who says that one factor, such as the mother or anything else, is of ultimate importance in determining the fate of a child is, like the blindfolded men in the fable, unable to see the big picture.

Unfortunately, there are many blindfolded men and women trying to convince mothers today that it is only they who determine the outcome of their child, with a resulting level of guilt that is sky high.

I'm here to tell you that you can relax!

While we all have our hopes and dreams for our children, *we are not that powerful!* Nor would most of us want to be. When we are told we are that powerful, we can't help but carry a mammoth weight of responsibility on our shoulders and enough guilt to break the elephant's back!

Let's look at it. If a child turns out to be violent:

- I could make the argument that it's the violence in our society. (Blindfolded Man #1)

- You could make the argument that it's the parents who must not have paid enough attention to him. (Blindfolded Man #2)
- Someone else could argue that it's the poverty in which he grew up. (Blindfolded Man #3)
- Someone else could argue that he's a bad seed. (Blindfolded Man #4)
- Someone else could argue that it's because of the teasing of his peers. (Blindfolded Man #5)
- Someone else could argue that it's probably the drug culture. (Blindfolded Man #6)
- Someone else could argue that it's the moral decay in our society. (Blindfolded Man #7)
- Someone else could argue that it's his teachers. (Blindfolded Man #8)
- Someone else could argue that it's our competitive society. (Blindfolded Man #9)

We have a lot of blindfolded men and women in our society! If only everyone would take their blindfolds off, they then would be able to see how the combination of factors in a child's Circle of Being is the hero or the villain in a child's life; but to blame the parents is an erroneous and hurtful conclusion. Recently, a few authors have reported that parents are not that important an influence on how a child turns out. One points to the importance of birth order, another points to genetics, another points to the peer group. While I applaud them for taking away the onus of parental guilt, they, too, are focusing on only a limited part of a much larger picture—the child's Circle of Being.

You may say, "Oh, other things may have *some* influence, but not as much as the mother. And maybe, if the mother did her job right, her children wouldn't be involved in drugs, or teasing their classmates, or dishonesty, or violence, or whatever other evil confronts our children." Maybe; maybe not. *But no one really knows*. Let me give you a few examples:

- My mother had a lot of prejudices, as did many others in the little town in which I grew up. Some of us abhorred the prejudices we saw in our parents and went the other way, fighting prejudice wherever we found it. Others followed in their parents' footsteps and became prejudiced as well. Same prejudice in the parents; different results for different children. Could you say my mother's prejudice was a great model because she taught me what not to be? Confusing, isn't it?

- A particular mother is abusive, absent, and uncaring towards her child. The child grows up to be a wonderful human being who contributes much to society and is very happy in his personal and professional life. If only good mothers produce good kids, by logical extension, she must have been a good mother! Why not? She raised a good kid. And there is no question that many wonderful, successful human beings have had horrible upbringings. This gives us further proof that it wasn't the mother who created the child's successful outcome—it was the child's Circle of Being!

- One woman I interviewed recently told me that her birth mother tried on many occasions to smother her with a pillow. Finally, she was adopted by a loving couple and grew up to be a wonderfully happy, healthy human being. If those early times with the mother are so critical, as we are led to believe by some experts, was her birth mother the perfect mother? Of course not. We must look to the child's Circle of Being.

- I know a full-time mother who gave mountains of love, care, attention, and all those things we are constantly told will produce successful children. Her child is in jail today. He was convicted of dealing drugs. What is our conclusion then? Was she a bad mother? Of course not! Tricky, isn't it? It was her child's Circle of Being that determined his behavior.

- I used to be the Executive Director of the Floating Hospital in New York City.[3] Over the years, I watched the growth of the children who came regularly and was often amazed at what I saw. I remember a wonderful little boy who had been horribly abused as a child. I knew this from his records, but the proof of the pudding was that he had cigarette burns all over his body. Over the ten years I was at my job, I watched him grow and couldn't help but notice the beauty in this child's behavior. He was caring, kind, inquisitive, joyful, and funny. What were the factors in his Circle of Being that created such a beautiful human being from such a dismal beginning? Since I was Director of The Floating Hospital at the time, I would like to believe it was his lengthy association with The Floating Hospital that made the difference. But I have to keep remembering reality: it was his Circle of Being that ultimately made the difference.

- Two young college students were recently sentenced to two and a half years in prison for killing their newborn child. These kids came from a privileged neighborhood and had seemingly loving and close relationships with their parents. Both excelled at school and had brilliant futures. All was well . . . until it wasn't. Two Circles of Being converged and caused them to act in such a reckless and heartless way.

- A 15-year-old boy killed two classmates and wounded 22 others. According to a family friend, his parents were living in a nightmare for the previous two years because of his uncontrollable temper and his obsession with explosives and guns. These were not horrible and heartless parents. In fact, they were both teachers, widely respected for their devotion to kids. His older sister turned out beautifully—a university graduate and a loving and successful human being. From an objective standpoint, there is no obvious explanation for what went wrong with this teenager. Somewhere locked in his Circle of Being lies the answer; but one thing is sure: we cannot solely blame the parents—or any one thing or anyone else.

- On television, I watched the trial of three youths who had been accused of removing a number of stop signs as a prank. This thoughtless and stupid act ultimately cost the lives of three young men whose car didn't stop when it was supposed to, because the stop sign was no longer there. Ultimately, the three accused were sentenced to 15 years in prison. I watched the anguish on the faces of the parents whose children were killed. But one couldn't help but notice the anguish on the faces of the parents of the accused. These were just parents who did the very best they could do in raising their children. I'm sure they worked hard, tried to instill values and common sense into their children's hearts and minds . . . and in the end, their children behaved in such a careless and stupid fashion that it caused the death of three other youngsters. Why did it happen? You now know the answer to that—the interplay of all the factors in their Circles of Being. And it's all chancy . . . chancy . . . chancy.
- I know of a couple who moved out of New York City into the quiet suburbs of Connecticut to put their kids in what they thought was a safer environment. Even though they regretted leaving the city which they loved, they did it for the good of their children. They felt the city offered too many dangers relative to drugs and violence. Within a very short time, the behavior of their son changed dramatically. Ironically, the drugs of the city had never reached him; but the drugs of the beautiful suburbs found their way into his body. The parents did what they thought was best for their child. But in the end, the child's Circle of Being ruled the roost.

These examples show us that a child with an uncaring, abusive, absent mother can turn out to be a wonderful, productive, caring human being. And a mother can be wonderful, devoted, and caring, and her child can turn out like a demon. I've seen it happen over and over and over again. Imprint this on your mind:

There are really no tools available at the present time to determine the factors in a child's Circle of Being and how these factors interact to determine his or her behavior. And be suspicious of anyone who says that there are.

And how about this? If the parent is the prime determinant of a child's behavior, how do you explain two children in the same family turning out differently—one turning out like an angel, the other turning out like the devil? Same parents, different outcome. There is only one answer: each child's Circle of Being was different. Genes, birth order, calling, physical health, classmates, teachers, and the infinite number of other factors that enter a child's Circle of Being. My sister, Marcia, always jokes that our mother used to say when we were young, "When Susan speaks, jewels come out of her mouth. When Marcia speaks, snakes come out of her mouth!" In my mother's mind, she had created both jewels and snakes! I'm glad my mother lived long enough to see my sister turn into a jewel!

Judith Viorst wrote an article entitled *Bones Break, But Boys Endure.* While she credits herself and her husband for doing a good job of parenting, she said:

> We're painfully aware that there are forces inside our children and out in the world over which we possess very little control. And so, in taking credit, we also nervously knock on wood and thank the uncertain benevolence of fate.[4]

To be painfully repetitive with the hope that you will fully absorb this important message that will bring you peace of mind: it is clear to me that if we climbed out of the fog of our conditioning, we would notice that "bad" parents sometimes raise great kids and "good" parents sometimes raise bad kids. It is the child's Circle of Being that determines all, and as you've already learned, it comprises an infinite number of factors. So how can the "experts" say that it all hinges on the mother? And, even more astonishing:

Why do we believe them?

We believe them because of the brainwashing to which we have been exposed, as I will discuss in the next chapter. My hope is that this book will help all of us to think for ourselves.

One woman wrote a letter to the editor after reading a story about a teenager convicted of murder. She said that her biggest fear about having a child was that he or she would turn out evil. Her friends reassured her that this couldn't happen. She and her husband were loving, responsible, and caring adults, and couldn't help but raise a loving, responsible, and caring child. They reassured her that killer-kids are the products of horrible parents and grim childhoods. She said she wanted to believe them, but her fear was that her child was more likely to be influenced by outside forces than by her husband and herself. Here was a woman who thought for herself and she thought correctly.

Now what could her friends have told her that reflected the truth? They could have told her, "*Look, you do your best, enjoy your children as much as you can, and then you work on letting go of any expectations. There are no guarantees. If that doesn't sit well with you, you would be wise not to have a child.*" That's the truth. By the way, let's follow the logic of her friends through to a different conclusion: if her child turned out to be violent, immoral, or badly behaved, can we assume that she too was violent, immoral, or badly behaved? I don't think so.

There are so many factors entering into the child's Circle of Being that you can't assign blame (or credit!) to anyone or anything.

There is one item in the child's Circle of Being that needs some explanation. Conventional psychology and most of our childcare experts insist on explaining human behavior as a *reaction* to external people in their lives, mostly their parents. As a result, we have lost sight of what James Hillman calls "the Soul's code" in his book of the same name.[5] In it, he talks of the acorn theory, which suggests our lives are guided by an inborn image, just as the oak's destiny is contained in the tiny acorn.

Hillman wrote his book to try to shift our perception that who we are is dependent only on our pasts, our parents, our culture, and other externals. He says there is something more . . . and it is the "Soul's code" or "calling." Hillman presents the idea that we come into this world with a predetermined *daimon*, a Greek word meaning the map of our soul, which ultimately directs the course of our lives. A similar belief in the Soul's code can be found in the Kabbala. Native Americans have it. West Africans have it. Hindus and Buddhists have it. Basically, they all believe that we come into this world with a particular destiny. It is only in Western conventional psychology that this phenomenon is absent.

Maybe Western psychology has omitted an important part of the child's Circle of Being, and would serve itself and its patients well by paying attention to alternative theories of child behavior.[6]

Hillman believes his idea is a gift for parents and I agree. He states that because children enter this world with their own calling, it isn't "This is my child," it is "Who is this child?" One woman I interviewed instinctively understood this concept. She told me:

> I remember when my daughter was born, I looked at her and said "Show me who you are. Because I don't know. Show me who you are and we will muddle through together." I know we have to get rid of expectations. We all want to mold them to our image. We're in trouble right there.

A belief in a child's own calling allows him (or her) to be his own person, not ours. It relieves us of our expectations that create so much disappointment when children do not grow up as we would like them to. Children who rebel may be on the right track relative to their calling, a better track perhaps than those who become what we consider models of behavior. Hillman points out that when children seem to go their own way, we don't consider their calling, we only think of errors we must have made. We continually try to make them follow our lead. In fact, their diversion may be leading them to exactly where they are supposed to be going in the grand scheme of things. Hillman states very poetically:

> Mothers and children may worship at very different altars and serve very different gods, even if they are placed all day long in the same family. No matter how close physically, they may have immensely different fates.[7]

We, as parents, all start out wanting to do our best, but in truth we don't know what the best is for our child. Although there are those who try to tell us, *they really don't know*. They don't know if a particular child is best served by a working mother or a stay-at-home mother; or a mother who is strict versus a mother who is lenient; or a mother who plays with her child versus one who doesn't. And so on. And if they say they know, they see with blindfolded eyes. As Jerome Kagan told us as far back as 1984, scientists haven't been able to discover many profound principles that relate the action of parents or siblings to psychological characteristics in a child.[8] The evidence simply does not support a direct cause and effect situation.

Logic betrays us. Logic tells us that if you are loving, caring, and giving to your child you will raise a loving, caring, and giving person. And logic tells us that if you treat a child badly, the child will turn out badly. But, in the case of child-rearing, *logic doesn't work*. Some children give us great joy, some give us heartache, no matter what we do. A woman once came to me in tears lamenting her daughter's mental state:

> I don't think she's had a happy day in her nineteen years. I don't know what I did wrong. I did everything to make her

happy. I applauded her in every way. Why does she have such low self-esteem?

I explained the concept of the Circle of Being and she was greatly relieved and better able to cope with her daughter without guilt. Trust me when I tell you that guilt makes us treat ourselves and our children in very unhealthy ways.

Some people are so proud of their children; others are more disappointed than they care to admit. One reason it is hard to admit our disappointment is that our society teaches us we are responsible for their behavior. One acquaintance told me how proud she was of her 30-year-old son and how he was the greatest achievement in her life. A mutual acquaintance later revealed the truth: her son, who she claimed was the greatest achievement in her life, is the ultimate taker who can't hold a job, and who is very demanding of and unkind to his mother, despite the fact that she supports him financially. I suspect if his mother understood that she wasn't to blame, she probably would be reacting in a stronger and more appropriate way to his child-like behavior. I don't know if it would help her son, but it certainly would help her in terms of her self-respect!

If the child's Circle of Being provides that the child doesn't turn out in the most desirable way, that does not mean we failed. It means that chance stepped in and created the conditions for the child to turn out the way that he did. It also means that if a child turns out well, it doesn't mean we succeeded; it means that chance stepped in and created the conditions for the child to turn out the way that he did. We are only guardians; we cannot control so much of what makes a child succeed or fail. And, again, that should come as a relief.

Am I absolving parents from doing the best they can? Of course not. We need to feed, clothe, care for, educate, love, and guide our children as best we can. For our own self-respect, we all want to put something good into our child's Circle of Being and into the world in which we live. But we can't listen to the advice of others as to what comprises that "something good." It is our child and it is our life. And it is certainly preferable that we care for our children with all our hearts, without any expectations about how they turn out. We take a deep breath and cut the proverbial cord. I know this isn't easy, so I have provided a few "let go" exercises in the Addendum to help you along the way.

What does all of the above mean in terms of how you live your life? That's simple:

> Live your life as is appropriate for who you are as a human being and stop feeling guilty if your children don't turn out the way you want them to. *It is not your fault!* Look to the child's Circle of Being and take heart in the wonderful fact that you are important, but not that important, to the outcome of your child. Hallelujah!

Endnotes

[1]Hillman, James. "The Parental Fallacy," in *The Sun: A Magazine of Ideas* (Issue 267). The Sun Publishing Company, Inc., [107 North Roberson Street, Chapel Hill, NC 27516, (919) 942-5282], March 1998, p. 13.

[2]In her book *Burst Out Laughing*, Barry Stevens introduces us to the word "chanciness." What a wonderful word to describe the infinite number of forces that impinge upon a child before conception and until the end of his or her life. (Celestial Arts, Berkeley, California, 1984)

[3]The Floating Hospital in New York City is a wonderful health and recreational facility for the poor. It exists aboard a ship that sails around Manhattan Island during the summer months and has dockside programs for the community during the winter months.

[4]Viorst, Judith. "Bones Break, But Boys Endure," in *Newsweek*, May 11, 1998, p. 61.

[5]Hillman, James. *The Soul's Code: In Search of Character and Calling*. Warner Books, 1997.

[6]Certainly, non traditional psychology, sometimes called Transpersonal Psychology or Height Psychology, which has a more spiritual base, has recently come into being. While denounced by many traditionalists, its wholesome focus on love is very reassuring.

[7]Hillman. Ibid., p. 16.

[8]Kagan, Jerome. *The Nature of the Child*, 1984. Quoted in *Wrestling with Parenthood*, by Irwin Matus. Gylantic Publishing Company, Littleton, Colorado, 1995, p. 31.

6

DOWN WITH THE GUILT-PEDDLERS!

Mother guilt. It comes with the birth, is brought forth from us with the placenta, grows like the piles of laundry, and stays with us forever like we believe the child will.

Abigail Stone[1]

*(**Note:** Before I formally begin this chapter, let me remind men not to skip a chapter that seems to be written about women's issues. Men have guilt too. Also, it is important for men to understand the problems women face as primary caregivers to the children and then become part of the solution.)*

Never was there a time of such pervasive guilt in women when it comes to the raising of their children. Men experience a touch of guilt themselves, but nothing compared to the guilt women take on with the birth of a child. One might think mother-guilt just comes with the territory; in fact, mother-guilt, in the extreme form it is today, is a relatively new phenomenon. It has been created by a society that has gone slightly mad when it comes to the raising of its children.

Mother-guilt in its present form suggests many things to me. It suggests we live with a deep lack of trust in ourselves, in our children, and in what I love to call "The Grand Design"– that is, the bigger plan for our lives and the lives of those we love that our limited mortal minds cannot see. It also suggests a sad lack of entitlement on the part of women. Hopefully what I offer in this book restores some of that trust and entitlement.

As you learned in the last chapter, what you put in doesn't necessarily come out."Chancy" is the name of the game.The huge number of variables in a child's Circle of Being rule the roost. What these variables are and how they interact with each other are all meaningful in determining how a child turns out—body, mind, and soul.

Why, then, are women given—and, more importantly, *why* do women take—all the rap, when it is virtually *impossible* to pinpoint any one factor in a child's life that determines what that child becomes?

One of the reasons is that mother-guilt has become part of the collective unconscious of our culture. And the collective unconscious is very hard to escape, even if it is based on error. Barry Stevens gives us a wonderful example of this as she talks about her daughter:

> There were all the other influences in her life, which I was only faintly aware of in spasms. There was herself and her own choosings. There was herself and the radio, which said things I did not agree with. When I tried to discuss this with her, I lost to the radio. She was nine years old. Tenaciously she clung to what the radio had said. Whether she was right or wrong is not what I am considering. She and the radio got together and I had no power over her at all. Yet I still felt responsible for what she did! *The culture in which I was embedded insisted on it and this got between me and my own observations.*[2] (My italics)

Stevens's last sentence hits the nail on the head. Our culture insists mothers take all the rap and, since we are all so embedded in the culture, we allow its beliefs to get between us and our own observations. A tidal wave of brainwashing has programmed us not to think for ourselves, but to believe others, *even if what they say makes little common sense.* We have been led to believe that it's *all* up to us and that if we don't do it "right" from the minute a child is born—and even before—we will ruin our children forever. It's hard to believe we fell for that one, but we did. There is an old Yiddish saying that I love:

To a worm in horseradish,
the whole world is horseradish!

Yes, we are like worms in horseradish. We can't see beyond the horseradish of our conditioning. By definition, guilt signifies that we haven't poked our heads out of the muck, and as a result, we can't see things as they really are. It's now time for us to climb out of the horseradish and gain the clarity that will allow us to get rid of the guilt forever.

In order for us to climb out of the horseradish, it is necessary to identify those who peddle the guilt mentality and learn how to say, "Thanks, but no thanks." Guilt-peddlers come in all sizes and shapes and they are everywhere we turn. Ours is a culture immersed in mother-blame—and guilt-peddlers are, after all, part of the culture.

MEET THE GUILT-PEDDLERS

Society-in-general is a guilt-peddler.
Society loves to blame mothers. Why? Diane Eyer has an interesting explanation backed up with much evidence. She says:

> Behind all the mother blaming, there is a rather nasty reality. No-one wants to pay for the care of our young children. Rather than putting forth the effort and providing the funds for a first-rate daycare system for these young

> children, for whom all the blamers profess such concern, mother castigation provides the useful smokescreen.[3]

If society is not willing to support a childcare system, what's left but to glamorize, romanticize, and invent the theory that the child's welfare depends on the mother being home with the child? Since mothers aren't paid for staying at home and taking care of the children, full-time mothering is a cheap solution to an expensive problem.

It isn't only effective childcare that society avoids paying attention to when it blames mothers. It also avoids paying attention to increasing violence, inferior education, availability of illegal drugs, the demoralizing emphasis on competition and external gain instead of partnership and internal fulfillment, as well as many other societal influences on a child's life. Yes, mother-guilt allows society-at-large (and that includes all of us) to turn our backs on the many difficult, expensive, and controversial issues in society that need to be addressed.

I am reminded of the silly, yet telling, story of a man looking under a streetlight for a coin he had dropped. A passerby stops to help him and asks, "Can you remember where you dropped the coin?" The man answers, "Oh, I dropped it further up the street, but it's so much lighter over here." Our society is much like the man who dropped his coin. A lot of work needs to be done "over there," but it's much easier to cast blame "over here," right in the laps of mothers who are trying their very best to raise happy and healthy children.

As you can see, mother-blame is very dangerous. It gives society permission to turn its eyes away from the many issues that need to be addressed, all of which affect the bodies, minds, and souls of our children—and ourselves.

The media is a guilt-peddler.

The magazines and newspapers we read and the television shows we watch are part of society's effort to blame mothers. Let me give you a telling example: it was recently reported that a television program had been aired which purported to show that the children of working mothers achieve poor exam results. According to the report, it was subsequently revealed that the program had had access to other research showing that having an employed mother actually increases a child's educational attainment, but had opted not to feature this.

If this is correct, you see an example of a television show reporting only one side of the story, thus throwing pain and guilt in the face of working mothers. The question we must ask is, "Can we trust the media?" The answer is "No." Some members of the media, of course, aim for the truth; but others go astray in order to prove a position.

I recently heard a radio talk-show host ask, "Where are the mothers when kids are doing drugs?" (Guilt! Guilt! Guilt!) What kind of a question is that? The mothers are probably at home or at their job doing what adults do. The children are probably at school, in an alleyway, in their car, or wherever teenagers hang out doing what children do. Does anyone really believe a mother can stop a kid from doing drugs? No way. "Well," the argument goes, "if parents trained them right, the child wouldn't do drugs." When we climb out of the horseradish, we see that this argument just doesn't hold up. So many adults set a good example and impress upon the minds of their children that drugs are bad, but that doesn't stop kids from trying them. Peer pressure is strong. Many kids will try it. Some will get hooked, others won't. *The child's Circle of Being rules, not Mother!* It's certainly much easier to blame Mother than to handle the burgeoning drug culture that affects all of us in a very negative way. Another example of "It's lighter over here."

A panel on a recent television talk-show discussed violence in the media and children's games and its deadly effect on children. The very last line of the show was "It's clear that when children get into trouble, it's all the mother's fault." All the speakers on the panel nodded their heads in agreement and the show ended. The program was all about violence! The word "mother" had never entered the content of the show! Yet, the uncontested conclusion, based on no evidence whatsoever, was that "It's the mother's fault." Does this make any sense? Of course not. But when you are swimming in the horseradish, you just go along with the program. And the program of the day is called, "Just Blame Mom."

Our children's teachers are guilt-peddlers.
When my children were little, we were told by their teachers not to help them with their homework. "If you help your kids, we won't know whether your child is learning or whether you are!" I thought that was wise advice. Today, the tables have turned. Mothers are supposed to be "partners in education." How's that for a con job! That's all you need . . . to spend the time you don't have helping your child with his or her homework, an activity that, in times past, was frowned upon. One woman I know does practically all her child's homework for her. I recently asked her what grade she got on her child's last term paper!

Not only are you supposed to help your children with their homework, you are supposed to volunteer . . . in the library, on class trips, for special projects and whatever else the school can invent for you to do. And if you miss a school function, you will certainly hear, at some future time, "Gee, we missed you at the last meeting." You, of course, translate that into, "We noticed you are not taking enough of an interest in your child's education." (Guilt! Guilt! Guilt!)

All of the demands the school places on parents' time, together with the long periods of time in which the children are on vacation, put mothers at a distinct disadvantage when it comes to their careers. Fathers have not as yet been affected. You say, "But what's the point of having children if you don't want to be involved in their lives?"

Involved is one thing; *over-involved* is another!

The expectation of mother-involvement with a child's life has reached a point of absurdity. And I don't believe it is good for either parent or child.

Schools have a responsibility to educate our children. It is time we held them accountable. This is not to entirely blame teachers or the school system entirely. The "blame" goes back to society-at-large which doesn't feel education is important enough to receive appropriate funding for a sufficient supply of qualified teachers. Yet another, "It's lighter over here" kind of situation. Certainly, teachers are underpaid and adequate supplies are not available. But we cannot allow teachers to hurl guilt at mothers; they are simply hurling in the wrong direction.

Strangers are guilt-peddlers.

One day, when my son was a toddler, he was drawn to a toy in the window of a store very near our apartment building in New York City. Since his room was overflowing with toys, I told him he couldn't have the object of his desire. As is common for a child in the middle of the infamous tantrum stage, he immediately began screaming, ranting, and raving. I thought to myself, "What do I do now?" There I was on a busy street in Manhattan with an inconsolable child beating my leg like a punching bag. Knowing that talking logically to a child in the middle of a tantrum is about as effective as trying to stop the sun from setting, I made what I thought was a brilliant plan of action. I decided to simply walk slowly toward our apartment building knowing my son would follow. Thankfully, I was right. Of course, as he followed behind, his screaming and hitting continued without abatement. Not a pretty sight!

A woman who was walking toward us surveyed the scene, stopped, glared at me with great contempt in her eyes, and began shrieking, "What a horrible way for a mother to treat her child!" I turned to her and with my head held as high as I could get it, retorted, "Madam, what a horrible way for a child to treat his mother!" That stopped her in her tracks and I maintained a modicum of my self-respect. But there she was—a bona fide guilt-peddler—intent on making me feel guilty for the normal, albeit miserable, behavior of my child. We must all learn how to hold our heads up high when strangers (or anyone else) treat us with such disdain!

Family and friends are guilt-peddlers.
Even our family and friends join the enemy camp when it comes to mother-guilt. When I went back to school many years ago, they all joined the choir of, "How can you leave your children?" The fact that I had wonderful childcare in place and a husband who was actively part of the team seemed irrelevant. "How can you . . . ?" is the telling phrase. Run when you hear it! My friend, Donna, was recently asked in an accusing tone, "How can you send your child to sleep-away camp for two whole weeks?" She felt very strongly she was making a wonderful choice for her young daughter. When I told her it was common practice when my children were young to send them for two months, she was astonished. It was her turn to ask me, "How could you send your child to sleep-away camp for two whole months?" We laughed when we saw the irony and realized how much of what is considered proper childcare is based purely on the fashion of the times. And fashions change frequently.

"How can you?"s follow mothers everywhere they go. "How can you do this?" "How can you do that?" I suggest that every time a mother is asked, "How can you . . . ?" she responds with "Because I think it's the right thing to do." End of story. That won't stop all the accusers from uttering all the "Yeah, but's," but she should just keep repeating "I hear you, but I think it's the right thing to do." It goes like this:

Guilt-peddler: How can you send your child to camp?
Mother: I believe it's the right thing to do.
Guilt-peddler: Yeah, but, he might feel lonely and abandoned.
Mother: I hear you, but I believe it's the right thing to do.
Guilt-peddler: Yeah, but, something could happen to him.
Mother: I hear you, but I believe it's the right thing to do.
Guilt-peddler: Yeah, but he might have horrible camp mates.
Mother: I hear you, but I believe it's the right thing to do.

The scenario may vary somewhat, but you get the point. You don't need to defend yourself. You don't need to argue. You just need to keep repeating your statement, "I believe it's the right thing to do." Eventually your "friend" will get tired and you will still have your peace of mind intact. This self-defense mechanism keeps you from engaging in a meaningless discussion that could end up making you feel guilty!

I guess most annoying are our friends or family who have no children of their own. They know *exactly* how to raise a child, don't they? "Oh he's so good with me. You must be doing something wrong." "If he were my child, I'd . . . " We can only feel delicious revenge when they become parents . . . and perhaps a little, very little, compassion in our hearts!

Our children are great guilt-peddlers.
My daughter introduced me to the line:

If it's not one thing, it's your mother.

One blatant characteristic of children is that they love to blame others, particularly their parents, for anything that goes wrong in their lives. This is perhaps one of the most painful parts of parenting. Instead of acknowledging all you have given them, their focus is on everything you do or have done wrong. Some eventually grow up and take responsibility for their lives, and some never do.

I always joke with parents that you do your best . . . take your children to the museums, take them on vacation, read to them before they go to bed, find the right schools, worry about their safety, make them beautiful birthday parties, shop for them, feed them and their friends, play with them, help them with their homework . . . and on and on and on. In the end, it will never be enough. Until they truly grow up, they will blame you for everything anyway! Sometimes they will alight on one insignificant event that sticks in their mind that they are convinced messed up their lives. "When I was ten, you cut my hair too short." "When I was twelve, you and Daddy went on vacation and didn't take me." Usually, they are in their twenties or thirties when casting these "horrible" accusations. And you sit there in shock, wondering why they never noticed all the sacrifices and wonderful things you did for and with them.

What is vital is that parents give themselves a pat on the back and acknowledge the many, many things they give to their children in the process of their growing up. We all make mistakes, but on balance, most of us tip the scales on the side of love, caring, and all good things, and we deserve to be congratulated—if not by our children, then certainly by the voice inside our heads.

I have come up with an appropriate answer for all parents when children dump blame upon them: simply look your children squarely in the eyes and with great conviction simply say:

I'm okay; you're a brat.

Again, I think you should repeat this statement over and over again until it registers into your psyche. Let me hear you . . .

I'm okay; you're a brat.
I'm okay; you're a brat.
I'm okay; you're a brat.
I'm okay; you're a brat.

Oh, if only I had thought of this simple phrase so many years ago. Well, I didn't, but I offer it to you now. So put it to good use.

Conventional parent/child therapists are guilt-peddlers.
Therapists are very much into parent-blame as I found out in my interviews with a number of therapists. I should not have been surprised . . . even therapists are steeped in the horseradish of their conditioning. And, as Paula Caplan, an enlightened psychologist, points out:

> "Mother blaming" is the bread and butter of traditional psychotherapy.[4]

That's a scary thought. My advice is that if a therapist makes you feel guilty, get out of that office just as fast as you can and find a more compassionate therapist. A sign of a great therapist is that he or she makes you feel powerful and loving so that you can effectively change what doesn't work in your life.

What about child therapists? If mothers are being told that everything is their fault, what do you think children are being told? "It's your mother's fault." Sometimes they throw in father for good measure, but the bulk of the blame lies firmly at the feet of mother. The modus-operandi is to "suggest" to children—young and old—that the behavior of their parents in some way made them feel unloved, unworthy, unhappy, abandoned, or whatever else is the negative adjective of the day. And in so doing, therapists let us all down—parent and child.

I believe it is the purpose of child therapists to teach their young clients that blame is a powerless act and that we all need to take responsibility for how we live our lives . . . despite what happened in the past. Taking responsibility for our own lives is key. Therapists should know that *blaming parents, no matter how they treated us, is not a prescription for good health.*

As I point out in all of my books, the victim mentality can only sap us of dignity and strength and ultimately bring us down. We all need to pick up the mirror instead of the magnifying glass, not to blame ourselves, but to empower ourselves, so that we can change what doesn't work in our lives.

I find it ironic that parents pay a lot of money for a child to hear from his (or her) therapist that his parents let him down. He wasn't loved enough, or he was abandoned when his mother went off to work, or his mother didn't breast-feed him, or his mother didn't bond enough, or whatever is the fashion of the week for good parenting. I believe that therapists need to help children focus on appreciation . . . appreciation for all that their parents have given to them throughout their life. They need to help children understand that parents are human beings . . . and human beings aren't perfect. And they need to help children learn how to say to their parents, "Thank you for all you have done." "Thanks" is not on the lips of most children today often enough and this omission hurts their parents very deeply. As William Shakespeare once said:

> How sharper than a serpent's tooth it is to have a thankless child![5]

I guess they had ungrateful children even in Shakespeare's time!

Here's a radical thought: could it be that our children themselves are experiencing tremendous guilt because the world is not holding them accountable for their horrible behavior? In the process of growing up, they do so many things that all of us would feel terribly ashamed of. They defy, they scream, they ignore, they utter cutting remarks, they lie, they steal. They get away with many things that were impossible to get away with in times gone by when punishment would have been swift. And, if they go to therapy, instead of dealing with their own soul-destroying behavior and the guilt that inevitably goes with it, the focus is often on what their parents have done wrong. In the end, nothing is healed. The anger and the righteousness on the part of the child continues. "It's your fault" remains the silent and not so silent way in which many of our children live their lives. How sad for both parent and child.

It's time for child-therapists to take responsibility for helping their young clients to take more responsibility. I ask you:

How can any child build a sense of self-respect by not acknowledging the gifts their parents have given them and, instead, hurl hurtful blame upon them? I don't believe they can.

Our "Chatterbox" is a guilt-peddler.

If there is any legitimate blame to be placed in the laps of mothers (or fathers), it is that they allow themselves to be blamed. Too many mothers can't climb out of the horseradish long enough to say, "Hey, wait a minute! I'm not going to take the rap for all of this. I did the very best I could."

In *Feel the Fear and Do It Anyway,* I introduced you to the little voice inside our heads that tries to drive us crazy—the Chatterbox, the voice of the Lower Self. It's the same voice that tells us we are bad if we work after our children are born, if we leave them with a sitter, if we think The Bad Thoughts, if we want to read a book instead of playing with them, if we let them cry themselves to sleep, and so on. The Chatterbox is immersed in the horseradish. We need to learn how to silence the Chatterbox and listen to the voice of the Higher Self, that part of us that honors and trusts who we are, the part of ourselves that is never affected by horseradish, but sees with clear and loving eyes.

Guilt for parents also masks a great deal of anger. How many of us, for example, would like to scream from the top of our lungs to our troubled adolescents, "TAKE RESPONSIBILITY FOR YOUR OWN LIFE, FOR GOD'S SAKE!" Very often, when the anger is acknowledged and dealt with in a healthy way, a lot of the guilt goes away.

There are many tools to help us silence the Chatterbox and find our way to the wisdom of the Higher Self. *Feel the Fear and Do It Anyway, Feel the Fear . . . and Beyond,* and *End the Struggle and Dance with Life* are filled with such tools. These books were designed to teach you—step-by-step—how to walk out of the horseradish and into a wonderful way of being in this world.

Our childcare experts are the biggest guilt-peddlers of all.
It seems to me that many of our childcare experts need to hide their heads in shame for what they are telling men and women today. I believe that . . .

Many of our present-day collective beliefs about parenting are purely myths and half-truths perpetrated by a bunch of "guilt-gurus" who are seriously lacking in information, good judgment, and common sense.

That's strong language, but I have even stronger feelings about the matter. What is most disturbing is that these guilt-gurus are putting forth edicts that are based on flawed research or no research at all. Unfortunately, because they tell us that their principles are based on research, we tend to believe them. That is our first mistake.

My academic background included a great deal of study of the scientific method. Part of my doctoral program included the studying of an amusing and informative book, which is still available today, entitled, *How to Lie with Statistics*.[6] What an eye-opener! I learned that certainly in the area of human growth and behavior, let the buyer beware. And, in this case, *that means you*. The author of this enlightening book, Darrell Huff, quotes Disraeli who said, "There are three kinds of lies: lies, damned lies, and statistics." It is important to understand that psychological research in the area of human development has accurately been called a pseudo-science, a scientific fiction and, as such, it is certainly not to be trusted.

To dig into the various studies is to uncover a mass of errors of scientific design and interpretation. So beware of comments such as "studies show"—*even of the ones I present in this book that support my views*. (For the interested, I list in the endnotes a few reasons why this is so.[7])

As I stated earlier, no one really knows the one big secret to raising a healthy child if there is one—not even the experts. This is evidenced by the fact that child-rearing fashions change with the times. And they change quite dramatically. Let me give you a stunning example: My mother was a student of the childcare guilt-guru, John B. Watson, who wrote a best-selling book in 1928 entitled *Psychological Care of the Infant and Child*.[8] His theories were in vogue until the late Fifties and early Sixties when my children were born. Let me give you a sample of the kind of things Watson and others of his day instructed women of that era to do. You may be very surprised.

> No hugging, kissing, snuggling. Strict, strict, strict. Don't create dependency in the children. Children have to learn how to live in this world and adapt to the schedules of their

> parents. Let them cry when it is bedtime. If you must kiss them, do it once, and only once. And do it on the forehead at night and shake hands in the morning. No breast-feeding. You can cripple and torment children by giving them too much love and affection since they would be miserable when you were away from them. Children have to be trained. Crying is good for them . . . it clears their lungs. Children must have multiple caregivers, as too much emotional closeness between mother and child is crippling to a child. Institutions like boarding school are a good thing. Conclusion: *If you don't do the above, they will grow up psychologically damaged.*

My mother trusted Watson's instructions and raised me accordingly, and frankly, I can see no ill effects in my development. I felt very close to both my parents. Watson was at the end of his reign when my son, Gerry, was born. I loved to pick him up and cuddle him, and I remember my mother shaking her head in disgust as she pleaded, "Susan, put him down. You're going to spoil him!"

What a difference a few decades make! The guilt-gurus of today are telling us just the opposite of Watson.

> Bond, attach, pick them up when they cry, feed them when they are hungry, carry them around close to your bodies, be their only caregivers, hug them, kiss them, cuddle them, breast-feed, don't toilet train, sleep with them, no spanking, give them all your attention, quit your job, make them the center of your life, make their needs more important than your needs. Conclusion: *If you don't do the above, they will grow up psychologically damaged.*

It is important to note that, although the childcare experts of yesterday and today have varied their instructions from one end of the behavior spectrum to the other, *what has never varied is the message that Mom is totally responsible for what happens to the child.* One must notice that it is a sad state of affairs that those to whom trusting parents look for help and advice can be their worst enemies by creating a guilt mentality and taking away all peace of mind.

Understand that guilt-gurus don't do it out of malice (I hope); they do it because they, too, are stuck in the horseradish of their conditioning. Most of them truly believe the guilt-producing thoughts they are peddling. So we can't place blame; we can only look at what is the truth for each of us without regard to the guilt-gurus, and slowly but surely, recondition ourselves to see the state of mothering and fathering in a much healthier light. And one day maybe the "experts" will learn from those who *really* know. I recently bought a bumper sticker that said, "If the people will lead, the leaders will follow."[9] Great message. Maybe we also need a poster that says . . .

If parents will lead,
the childcare experts will follow!

I have spent a lot of time in this chapter talking about the guilt-gurus because I believe it is their words that have an inordinate impact on parenting today. They are the umbrella under which many of us go for shelter, but too many of us only find pain. I wonder if our guilt-gurus feel any guilt for what they are doing to parents today! Nina Barrett conjectures:

> Perhaps the children of the expert you're consulting grew up and joined a religious cult and never called home again.[10]

It would be an interesting touch of irony, wouldn't it?

All of the above can't help but make us ask, "Why do we have such a strong need to believe the words of the guilt-gurus today?" Sylvia Bigelsen and Virginia McCullough give us one answer:

> Sometimes being a parent—especially a first-time parent—can turn an intelligent, independent, confident person into an insecure mouse. We are so afraid of making a "mistake" that we turn to the printed word for a voice of authority rather than using our own good sense to solve the problem—if there even is a real problem.[11]

We also turn to the printed word because moms are isolated in their role of parents as never before. For most of us, gone is the village or extended family where we can turn for help as we could in the past. And we become desperate. Unfortunately, we are not aware of the huge amount of wisdom we hold within our being to handle all that needs to be handled. Like children, we have given away all the power to our surrogate mothers and fathers that come under the heading of "guilt-gurus." It is time for us to grow up and take back our power.

The experts tell us that if we don't listen to them, disaster will follow. Well, we've listened to them for quite a while now, and I only see parent-child interactions getting worse and worse. I also see a tremendous decline in the satisfaction parents get from the parenting role. I have found that when we deflate our respect for the experts, and increase our respect for ourselves, we derive much greater satisfaction and happiness in the parenting process. So the advice from this "expert" is:

Don't believe everything the childcare experts say. Think for yourself. Consider your personality, your child's personality, and do what *feels* right and what makes you feel good.

It might take some experimentation to determine what feels right for you, but trust that kids are strong and resilient and so are you. Trust your common sense. Parenting is such a uniquely individual state of being. Someone else's way seldom "fits" with who you are as a human being. If you decide you want to read some childcare books to see if you can derive any good tips, go for it. Here's a formula:

If a childcare book makes you feel good, relaxed, and competent as a parent, keep reading. If a childcare book makes you feel guilty, throw the book in the garbage where it belongs.

It's really quite simple when you learn to trust your gut. One woman told me she was very comfortable with what she was doing with her child and when she read a childcare book, it told her she was doing it all wrong. She tried all the new techniques suggested and it felt awful. Finally she went back to her old ways, realizing that she knew better. We all know better!

HOW TO GET AROUND THE GUILT-PEDDLERS

A few mothers I interviewed have been able to hold their own against the overwhelming guilt I see in so many other mothers and guess what? *They report being happy in the parenting process.* They don't listen to the guilt-peddlers. They do what makes *them* comfortable and satisfied and they trust that what they do is best for all concerned. They parent from a place of great confidence and trust. Their attitude about their children seems to be, "I shall love and care for you and I shall love and care for myself as well." They are strong about who they are and what they need in life. Here is some insight into the character of three happy mothers. Their stories are refreshingly revealing.

Janet decided her two-and-a-half-year-old was ready to be toilet trained not only during the day, but during the night as well. She didn't listen to the childcare books and she didn't listen to all her friends and acquaintances who thought they had all the answers. She listened to herself. One night, she simply put a pair of panties on her daughter who was going off to sleep and told her she was now toilet trained during the night. And so she was.

The next day she told the director of her child's nursery school what had transpired. A few of the other mothers overheard the conversation and were shocked. Guilt-peddlers in action. They assailed her with, "How could you do that? Your daughter wasn't ready. She's too young. Why are you pushing her?" Janet's response said it all. "In the first place, I was ready. In the second place, obviously *she* was ready, or she would have wet the bed!" Perfect. End of story. Short and sweet and confident. Janet said she rarely feels guilt. She knows everything she does isn't perfect, but she feels she's a great mother. If her kids grow up with problems, so be it. She recognizes there are so many other forces in her child's life.

She has always had help in caring for her children. She is trained as a lawyer and helps her husband, part-time, in his law practice. She also pursues her interest in sculpting and art. Her life is rich, and as a result, she truly enjoys her children.

She talks of first-time mothers she has met who read childcare books *ad nauseam*. And the more they read, the more unhappy they become. She tells of one acquaintance who read a book telling her she must sleep with her child and so she does. She doesn't understand how this woman continues this practice when she complains that she hasn't had a good night's sleep since the child was born two years ago. *Two years ago!* Janet said, "After a week's time, she should have known it doesn't suit her. She also complains her sex life is gone and her child now refuses to sleep elsewhere." Janet shakes her head in disbelief! She has a strong sense of knowing what works for her and her children and she acts accordingly. She truly lives the philosophy that your children will grow up (and complain) no matter what you do and there is no such thing as perfection in child-rearing. This philosophy makes all the difference in the world.

Gina is also enjoying the raising of her children. She works so she can afford childcare for the kids, so someone else can handle tasks that she isn't interested in doing. For example, she doesn't like to play children's games; so she doesn't. She lets others play with them or they play with their friends. Nor will she be drawn into her children's extra-curricular activities. For example, her son belonged to the Boy Scouts. As a treat for the boys, she was asked to provide snacks and sodas on an alternating basis with the other mothers when the boy scouts met. She informed the scout leader "I don't do that." He said, "All the mothers *love* to do that." (Another guilt-peddler in action.) Holding her own, she said, "Well, *I* don't." The scout leader wouldn't take no for an answer.

Her appointed day to deliver the goodies came along and it was recorded in the annals of boy scout history that this was the only time the boy scouts did not get their snacks and sodas! Needless to say, the scout leader never asked her again. Nor did she feel guilty. And the kids survived. In fact, they probably were healthier that day without the soda and cookies! Gina has her job and she feels the scout leaders have their jobs and should be providing for the children themselves. She says, "I take to the woods when asked to volunteer for anything. I question the motives of the parents who are constantly taking part in their children's activities. It's as if they don't have a life of their own."

She tells her kids, "A lot of the time, I am a pain in the butt; and a lot of times you are a pain in the butt. Sometimes I have to get you out of my hair and have my own space. But when we talk to each other with respect, it all works out." She said that children must know that you are a person, too. And all people deserve respect.

Her other son plays soccer. She refuses to watch all the games as the other mothers feel compelled to do and, of course, they castigate her for not being at soccer practice. Some love soccer and that's great. But she doesn't enjoy soccer and believes that everyone, *including her son*, should do what one enjoys. She also says, "I want my kids to do things for themselves because they enjoy doing them, not because I'm sitting there applauding." Other mothers criticize her because they say it is good for the child's self-esteem if she comes. (Guilt! Guilt! Guilt!) She said, "I feel children have to get a sense of self-esteem for themselves. Mother and father won't always be around to applaud." She is very clear that children like to do what children like to do; adults like to do what adults like to do, and seldom the twain shall meet.

When her first child was born, her pediatrician told her, "You should breast-feed." She replied with a definitive "No! This is simply not me." She said, "My son threw his bottle away at ten months and never drank milk again. Yet the pediatricians were saying give him milk. Now they are saying milk isn't that great. Who knows?" She said neither she nor her kids ever followed the rules and the kids are turning out great.

So what does she do for her children? She is a very warm and accessible woman who has an easy way with them. It is obvious they have a wonderful relationship with her. She educates, she guides, she is very affectionate, but she doesn't put up with any nonsense. She is a source of great love in many ways. She has never read a childcare book and feels totally comfortable doing what she does. She obviously was born with the LBP genes. From the moment they were born, she loved holding them and caring for them. She says, "I loved parenting so much because I never did it alone. I always made sure I had help, and importantly, an involved husband. It blows me away when people assume mothers should do it all alone. It isn't and it was never meant to be that way. We can't take possession of our children."

The point is that despite the guilt-peddlers, Gina is doing what she wants to do and, as a result, *she is enjoying the raising of her children*, contrary to those who are doing what they *don't* want to do and are hating the raising of their children. She feels little guilt, she honors who she is. *She has the courage to honor her boundaries*, which shows a lot of confidence in herself and enormous self-respect. So few parents have this kind of confidence and self-respect. She says, "There is a French saying that it is important to feel good in one's skin. I feel good in my skin." She is a wonderful example of how important it is to set boundaries over which others will not cross. *Not* setting boundaries destroys the ability to love the parenting process.

Martha also is loving the raising of her children. She is very strong about her belief that parents have to do what they enjoy doing, not what others tell them to do. She also has never read a childcare book. She told me that she had a friend who had so many problems parenting and all she did was read childcare books trying to get it right. She said, "I decided to learn through experience." She also realized from the very beginning that children were narcissistic. She said, "They will walk all over you. You have to tell them, 'No, I won't be walked all over.' I tell them, 'I am not an object. I have feelings. If you are sick, I take care of you. When I am sick, just back off with your demands.'"

She told me she didn't go to parent-teacher meetings unless there was a perceived problem. She didn't take her kids to the park if she didn't want to. She refused to torture herself by taking them to places like DisneyWorld until they were old enough to run around while she sat and had a cup of coffee. In essence, she didn't put pressure on herself to do the things about parenting she didn't want to do. She had a job she truly loved and, thus, was able to pay someone to do the things with the children she didn't enjoy doing. She was not trying to be Superwoman. Her advice to other parents was, "Stop doing the things that are torture to you. Do the things that make you happiest."

One thing she refuses to do is sign the kids up for the ten or more after-school lessons a week as so many other parents in her area seem to be doing. The kids are stressed, the parents are stressed. One or two is fine, but no more. It gives her more time to actually be with the children in a more meaningful way. Her happiest moments are quiet times in the evening with her children. She builds a fire in the fireplace, puts on soothing music, and the children do their homework as she reads. They all enjoy their time together. She is very familiar with the 12-step program[12] and uses one of their tools, which is to remind herself over and over again, "I am powerless over my kids' irritability (or whatever it is) and I refuse to make my life unmanageable." She says her children have always been as different as night and day. "I would have had to be different people to cater to the needs of each child. Instead I choose to be myself; who else should I be?" A perfect message to all of us.

The above women are happy as parents. From them we can derive some important generalizations:

- Happy parents know how to "let go."[13] They do their best and understand that they have little control in terms of how it all turns out. Taking a very Zen approach, they are not attached to outcome. They realize they can't make their children's life right, perfect, or happy.

- Happy parents set boundaries over which their children or the guilt-peddlers cannot cross. They demand to be treated with respect and this demand is usually met. Too many parents let their children walk all over them.
- They all have help of some kind— other arms to hold their children—when they are too tired or want to pursue other interests. They never feel that it is their job to be there for their children 24 hours a day. By the way, don't think it is only the providence of the rich to have childcare. By definition, those who must work for financial reasons also must find other arms to hold their children in the form of babysitters, family members, or childcare facilities.
- They know they are entitled to pursue other interests and have a full and balanced life. By enjoying many things in their own life, they are enjoying their children as well.
- All of these women aim for a balanced life. Even though they all enjoy their work, they are not driven to work, work, work . . . any more than they are driven to focus totally on their children. Again, balance is a key to their feeling fulfilled.
- They do not live their lives following the advice of childcare books. They trust they will do what is right for themselves and their children. They are willing to make mistakes, trusting that their children are strong enough to handle their mistakes. They have thrown out the book of rules and in each situation have asked, "What am I most comfortable doing?" And they do what feels right without a sense of guilt.

There you have some of the components that I believe make a *happy* parent. You might be thinking, "Yes, Susan, but what makes a *good* parent?" As I said in the last chapter, I can't give you an answer to that. I don't believe there *is* an answer. Good for which child? Which parents? Which society? Under what circumstances? And for which results? I have seen children who have been dealt the worst life has to offer and they have turned out to be wonderful human beings who appear to be very happy. I have seen children given much love and tenderness who have turned out to be immature takers living in a perpetual state of discontent. Perhaps Gertrude Stein had the right answer when she said:

There ain't no answer.
There ain't going to be any answer.
There never has been an answer.
That's the answer.[14]

The realization that there are no absolute answers to the question "What is a good parent?" should give us a great sense of relief. It should also give us the freedom to do what we feel is right for ourselves and our children given who we are as human beings. And it should give us the freedom to let go of the outcome knowing there is so much out of our control. *Ah, peace at last.*

Endnotes

[1]Stone, Abigail. "Bye Bye Baby: On Mother Guilt and Poverty," in *Child of Mine: Writers Talk About the First Year of Motherhood.* Edited by Christina Baker Kline. Hyperion Books, New York, 1997, p. 243.

[2]Stevens, Barry. *Burst Out Laughing.* Celestial Arts, Berkeley, California, 1984, p. 74.

[3]Eyer, Diane. *Motherguilt: How Our Culture Blames Mothers for What's Wrong with Society.* Random House, New York, 1996, p. 175.

[4]As found in Maushart, Susan. *The Mask of Motherhood.* Random House, Australia, NSW Australia, 1997, p. 41.

[5]Shakespeare, William. *King Lear.* I, iv, 312.

[6]Huff, Darrell. Illustrated by Irving Geis. *How to Lie with Statistics.* W. W. Norton & Company, New York, London, 1954. (Norton paperback reissue, 1993.)

[7]Here are a few reasons to mistrust stated results of scientific data:

1. Too many variables cannot be controlled. For example, how do we control all the factors that impinge upon a child's life (the Circle of Being) in order to separate out the role of the mother? It's virtually impossible. To say that any one thing determines a child's behavior is a dangerous and misleading conclusion.
2. Researchers are often comparing the proverbial apples and oranges. To research child behavior, studies often use and rely upon artificial experimental set-ups. To compare how a child behaves in these set-ups does not really measure how a child behaves under normal circumstances. Yet, conclusions are drawn from the former that have little to do with the latter.
3. The number of people in the study is often too small and therefore filled with possible error. Obviously, a study of only ten people will not be as reliable as a study that got the same results with 1,000 people. And many of the important studies in the field of child-development have very few people in them.
4. The scientific method can easily be abused, misused, and misinterpreted by those who conduct and/or interpret it. In fact, the book, "Lying with Statistics" shows how one can manipulate the findings to prove any theory you want to prove. Often, the conclusions a researcher makes in a

given study have nothing to do with the actual findings. Or the scientists consciously or unconsciously rig the study to prove what they want to prove. The "myths of motherhood" which I will explore in the next chapter will give you some excellent examples of such abuse of evidence.
5. Exactly what the studies are measuring is often questionable. One study interpreted the fact that a woman has no guilt leaving her child with a baby sitter to mean that she is not "properly bonded" with her child. Others, including myself, would interpret this to mean that she is healthy and knows how to "let go." Same fact, different interpretation.

This is just a small sample of problems that can create false conclusions in research projects. You can see one has to be wary when anyone, including me, cites studies to prove a point.

[8] Watson, John B. *Psychological Care of Infant and Child.* W.W. Norton & Co., New York, 1928.

[9] This bumper sticker was produced by: Peace Resource Project, PO Box 1122, Arcata, CA 95521 (707) 822-4229 (#S63).

[10] Barrett, Nina. *I Wish Someone Had Told Me: A Realistic Guide to Early Motherhood.* Academy Chicago Publisher, Chicago, Illinois, 1997, p.82.

[11] Bigelsen, Sylvia, and Virginia McCullough. *When the Wrong Thing Is Right: How to Overcome Conventional Wisdom, Popular Opinion, and All the Lies Your Parents Told You!* MasterMedia Limited, New York, 1994, p. 129.

[12] The Twelve-Step Program is a spiritually-based philosophy that helps us take responsibility for our reactions to all that happens in our lives. There are many Twelve Step Programs available today, all stemming from the original program Alcoholics Anonymous (AA). Some of these are Codependents Anonymous, Workaholics Anonymous, and Adult Children of Alcoholics.

[13] There are many techniques for letting go in *End the Struggle and Dance with Life* and *Feel the Fear . . . and Beyond.*

[14] Stein, Gertrude. *Zen to Go*, compiled and edited by Jon Winokur. New American Library, Penguin Books, New York and Canada, 1989, p. 11.

7

THE TOP TEN MAD, MAD MYTHS

As we acquire more knowledge, things do not become more comprehensible, but more mysterious.

Will Durant[1]

As I wrote this book, the many mad, mad myths of parenthood kept swirling around my head. I realized that some were more insidious than others. Many people would have made healthier choices in their lives were it not for the pervasiveness and strength of these myths. As you recall, I define a myth as an *unproven* collective belief that is accepted by society at-large as true. Along with the other myths presented in this book, I thought I would share with you my pick of the top ten "favorites" in the crazy-making department. You may be pleased or displeased with what I have to say, depending on your own personal experiences. As I said earlier, this is the nature of a subject that is as personal and as controversial as this one. In any case, read with an open mind. Take what works for you and let the rest go. So here they are . . . my pick of the top ten mad, mad myths:

1. *Unproven:* There is an instinctual urge for all men and women to have children.

2. *Unproven:* Having children is the ultimate fulfillment in a woman's life.
3. *Unproven:* All women instinctively know how to care for their newborn child.
4. *Unproven:* All women have an instinctual *desire* to take care of their children.
5. *Unproven:* Breast is best for everyone.
6. *Unproven:* "Bonding" and "attachment" are essential to the well-being of the child.
7. *Unproven:* Mothers should stay home from work during the early years of a child's life.
8. *Unproven:* All that goes wrong with a child is the mother's fault.
9. *Unproven:* Women are more capable than men when it comes to the care of their children.
10. *Unproven:* Getting custody of the children is a "win" for all women.

Let's explore these mad, mad myths one by one and question whether they make any sense.

1. Is there really an instinctual urge for all men and women to have children? If such an instinct does exist, then why are more and more men and women in Western society (estimates of 20 to 25 percent) deciding not to have children?[2] There are many reasons: lack of a marriage partner, lack of community support, financial considerations, a preference for pursuing other interests in life, a dislike of all things children . . . just to name a few. No, children aren't as practical or affordable in today's world as they once were and as a result more and more people are saying no to having them. The point is . . .

If there is an instinctual urge to have children, wouldn't everyone just "do it" and put practical and financial considerations aside?

And then there is the issue of abortion. Would someone with an instinctual urge to have children choose to terminate a pregnancy without a medical reason to do so? I don't think so. I have never heard of a pigeon going for an abortion, have you? Human beings are different from pigeons and other animals in that we have the ability to think and to make choices. And the fact is that, after much thought, more and more of us are choosing not to have kids.

There is other evidence that the desire for children is not instinctual. We can look to the late 1800s when an article appeared in the Journal of the American Medical Association bemoaning the fact that upper-class mothers didn't want to become mothers at all. The explanation was that motherhood got in the way of their partying.[3] Many of us can understand that!

"But, Susan, so many people are desperate to have children. Isn't instinct the reason?" Desperation to have a child comes from *neediness*, not instinct. It comes from the expectation that a child will fill an existing hole in our heart. Children, or anything else out there, can't fill that empty space. A feeling of wholeness comes from within. Therefore it is predictable that those who feel desperate to have a child will, in most cases, feel the same desperation *after* the child is born. When we are secure and know we are meaningful adults who have much to give to this world, we are never desperate for a child . . . or anything else. Here's a thought: if anything about the experience of producing a child is instinctual, it must be the sexual urge. *That's* irresistible for most of us. And what a wonderful way to guarantee the perpetuation of the human race!

2. *Is having children really the ultimate fulfillment in a woman's life?* The following line by Kathy Lette sets the appropriate tone for what I have to say about this question:

> The myth that motherhood is the ultimate fulfillment for a female is the last great sacred cow, and it's time to whack it on the barbecue.[4]

If having a child is the ultimate fulfillment in life, why are so many women miserable after the birth of their children? For some, this misery continues for a long, long time—some report that it continues until their children leave home! This doesn't sound like fulfillment to me. I know that for some, having and raising children *is* the ultimate fulfillment. They absolutely adore the parenting experience. But certainly this is not true for all of us, arguably, not even most of us. Researcher Mary Boulton believes that most middle-class women find motherhood meaningful but cease to experience it as intrinsically rewarding. She said:

> We harbor no doubts that mothering our children is infinitely worth doing. It's only that we'd really rather be doing something else.[5]

If mothering our children is so fulfilling, why do many mothers want to be doing something else?

Also, there are studies that conclude that both men and women can be just as happy without children, in many cases, more so.[6] One woman told me that the best decision in her life was not to have children. She finds great fulfillment in her chosen profession and knows a child would have held her back from following her dream. She said:

> My life is so rich, and I am free to move around at will and do all the things I love to do. I love people and am surrounded by the company of wonderful friends and my wonderful husband. The way we are all there for each other is beautiful. A child certainly would have gotten in the way of all this.

In my professional and personal experience, and among all the interviews I've conducted for this book, I have never met a man or woman who *chose* not to have children and has regretted that decision. I'm certain that some may exist, but I have never met them. Yet, I have met those who chose to have children and have regretted that decision. So don't believe those who claim that children bring ALL mothers (and fathers) the purest happiness there is. For some, this simply is not true.

3. *Do all women really instinctively know how to take care of a newborn child?* I love Harriet Lerner's line . . .

> Being a mother comes about as naturally to me as being an astronaut.[7]

Join the crowd. Certainly many of the mothers I interviewed didn't have a clue as to what to do with their newborn. I remember visiting my sister six weeks after my niece was born. I wasn't prepared for the bedraggled figure that greeted me. She was so frazzled trying to figure what to do with this stranger in her midst that she hadn't gotten dressed since she came home from the hospital. Other than feeding her daughter and changing her diaper, which the nurses in the hospital had taught her to do, she hadn't a clue. She had no sense of what it meant to "nurture" a baby—to coo and cuddle and talk and sing and stimulate with color, music, and so on. I spent the week teaching her and consoling her with the fact that I was just as inept when my first child was born.

Hillary Rodham Clinton had the right idea when she brought her daughter, Chelsea, home from the hospital and couldn't stop her crying: She said, "Chelsea, this is new for both of us. I've never been a mother before, and you've never been a baby. We're just going to have to help each other do the best we can."[8]

As I have mentioned in a previous chapter, it hasn't always been this way. In the days of the proverbial village and extended family, infants were part of the everyday world. One *learned* how to take care of infants by consciously or unconsciously observing adults caring for the children all around them. Therefore, when it was their turn to parent, they knew what to do. This is key: *what looked like instinct was more often than not learned behavior.*

Today the nuclear family has replaced the village. No longer do most of us observe adults caring for their young; some of us have never even held a baby in our arms until we have our own. No wonder we are at a total loss as to what to do. *There goes the whole instinct theory down the drain!*

Unfortunately, society offers little in the outside world where mothers can find help. No wonder the books of the childcare experts are so popular! Having nowhere else to turn, many mothers read book after book after book seeking reassurance; but instead of feeling reassured, they report feeling inadequate.

The obsession of mothers today to do the right thing is painful to watch. And this obsession comes from the fact that they are told by the guilt-peddlers that if they don't do it right, they will damage their children forever. What an onerous and unwarranted responsibility they place on the shoulders of mothers. It's clear that parents today need a heck of a lot more support than they now are given. And it's up to society as a whole to provide it.

4. *Do all women really have an instinctual desire to take care of their children?* I don't see any evidence that all women love or want to be full-time caretakers of their children. Of course, some women (and men) definitely do—those with the LBP genes. If the truth be known, many mothers—those without the LBP genes—would prefer to take care of their children *in very small doses.* They love having someone take over when their children are taxing their sensibilities or when they want to pursue other interests.

One wonders where this idea that women have an instinctual desire to nurture their children came from. *Could our guilt-gurus have had a hand in this deception?* You may be surprised to learn that there were many times throughout history when children were not at all well-cared for by their mothers. We only have to look at what was happening in Paris in 1780. It is reported that of the 21,000 babies born that year, 19,000 were handed over to wet-nurses, many as far as 125 miles away from Paris. Were they sent away for a night, a week, a month? No. It was *common practice* for the child to remain with the wet-nurse from three to five *years*. This practice existed among the rich and poor. Because of the paltry conditions in which the wet-nurses lived, many babies died or came home in very bad physical condition. Would it shock you to learn that parents seldom went to the funerals of children less than five years old?[9]

Why did the women hand their babies over to wet-nurses in the first place? The answer is that breast-feeding was thought to harm a woman's beauty, and interfere with her desire to satisfy her husband's sexual needs. Women of that day were encouraged to organize their lives around their husbands, not their children.[10] *I don't see any instinctual desire to nurture here, do you?*

It has not been uncommon throughout history for the upper classes to turn over their children to wet-nurses and nannies and then send them off to boarding school. And many of these children grew up to be healthy adults. Compare this with the obsessive child-centered world in which we live today.

What I have just told you holds within it an important piece of information:

How women treat children seems to be *culturally,* not *instinctually,* dictated!

"Susan, are you telling us that how we treat our children today is *a fad*?" It sure looks that way. Elisabeth Badinter, who has studied various periods in history, states that the notion of innate maternal instinct is absurd. She says:

> Mothers behave as the culture dictates.[11]

And Harriet Lerner tells us:

> How the "good mother" thinks, feels, and conducts herself may have less to do with "nature" than with the economic, political, and social climate of the day.[12]

I don't see how we can refute these conclusions. If a motherly instinct to care for the child was, in fact, a reality, *methods of childcare wouldn't vary so drastically from generation to generation and from culture to culture and from mother to mother.* So if your "instincts" about mothering fail you, not to worry. You are not alone!

5. *Is breast really best for everyone?*
I was lucky. When my kids were born I felt no pressure to breast-feed. In fact, my mother felt it was a disgusting practice . . . unclean, animalistic, and all sorts of no-no things. No pressure there! Recently I was told by an acquaintance who grew up in Tennessee that when she was young, it was considered immoral to breast-feed beyond six weeks as it was sexually stimulating to the child—a dirty practice. No pressure there! My, how the dictates of society have changed!

Today mothers are pressured without mercy to breast-feed . . . breast-feed . . . and breast-feed some more. Some "experts" tell parents they should breast-feed for years! I am here to tell you that breast-feeding is not appropriate for everyone . . . yet women are constantly being prodded to do it. I just read an article that rambled lyrically about the joys of breast-feeding—how easy and natural it is, how economical it is, how healthy it is for the baby. The article even suggested that breast-feeding was great for weight loss (a low blow!).[13] Unfortunately, it omitted the possible down side . . . clogged ducts, bloody and scabby nipples, engorgement of the breast, infections, vaginal dryness, breast pumps . . . need I go on?[14] Susan Maushart reports:

> My nipples were so cracked that one of them nearly detached (leaving a fat wormlike scar still menacingly visible today).[15]

Yet she was encouraged to try, try, try. I wonder how healthy it is for an infant to suckle on a bloody, scabby, cracked breast. Yuck!

The article also forgot to mention that some people don't believe that mother's milk is always the perfect food for babies. It may have an immune benefit for the newborn child, but it may also have an immune deficit. It is believed by some, for example, that HIV can be transmitted to babies through breastfeeding.[16] This is surely something to investigate. And certainly the mother's diet, level of alcohol consumption, and the medications she takes are all believed to have an effect on the quality of her milk.

Or the mother may unknowingly not be producing enough milk. Shirley Radl tells us she was trying do the "right thing" according to La Leche, an organization that strongly promotes the idea that "breast is best."[17] It was clear that, after a while, her child was not doing so well. Finally she took him to the doctor where she was informed that her child was starving to death and should be put on formula immediately. A few days on formula and a happy, healthy child at last! One woman still has nightmares thinking about the times when she was breast-feeding:

> I was so exhausted, I would dream I had a litter of puppies pulling at my breasts instead of waking up to face the reality that my baby was pulling at my breast. There were four of us in bed: the baby pulling at my breast, my older child who was jealous of the attention the little one was getting and my husband. Horrible. So much of that time was so horrible, that I don't remember it. It's amazing what one tolerates. There were so many arms and mouths touching me when I wanted to sleep that, to this day, so many years later, I can't even stand for my husband to touch me once I'm going off to sleep.

This doesn't sound like "breast is *always* best" to me. Of course, it is for some, but not for everyone.

And what about Dad? One eminent guilt-guru proclaimed that mothers bond with their children hormonally through breast-feeding and, since dads don't have breasts or hormones, they should just stay out of the way and support their wives. I find this advice abhorrent. Mothers need all the help they can get and dads need every opportunity they can get to establish their own closeness with their children. Bottle-feeding is one way of bringing men into the picture and offering relief to women. Of course, a woman can use a breast pump to pump milk in a bottle for a father to use, but it makes me tired (and sore) just thinking about it.

There are many grounds on which to argue that bottle-feeding is far more desirable. But, *that truly is not my goal.* It is obvious to me that breast-feeding and bottle-feeding each have advantages and disadvantages. But the guilt-gurus don't tell us that. They insist that "breast is best" and infuse women with guilt if they take the bottle route. This is unfair to everyone concerned. The truth is that there are generations of people who have fared beautifully having been breast-fed. There are generations of people who have fared beautifully having been bottle-fed. It all boils down to this:

Breast-feeding is right . . . and bottle-feeding is right. It all depends on the mother, on the child, and on the situation!

Yet, in today's crazy world, women are considered bad mothers when they don't want to breast-feed. Don't you think this nonsense has to stop? It seems so obvious to me that a mother who, for whatever reason, wants to breast-feed should breast-feed. It also seems so obvious to me that a mother who, for whatever reason, doesn't want to breast-feed shouldn't breast-feed. Everyone is best served doing what is right for them. Doesn't it make you want to scream . . .

It's so simple! Why does everyone make it so difficult?

6. Are "bonding" and "attachment" really *essential to the well-being of the child?*
Of all the mad, mad myths of motherhood, those involving the ideas of "bonding" and its counterpart, "attachment," have to be the most cruel, given the amount of disappointment, pain, and insecurity they create in the hearts of so many mothers today.

Before I go any further, let me give you the definitions of bonding and attachment as I am using them here:

Bonding refers to a maternal instinct that kicks in with close physical contact with her child immediately after birth and beyond.

Attachment has to do with an instinct in the child, activated by early physical closeness to the mother over a period of many months—some say years! I have seen these terms used interchangeably.

It has been claimed by certain childcare experts in recent years that unless bonding and attachment are part of the mother-child interaction, the mother will fail in her parenting role and the child will grow up damaged as a human being . . . or worse. For example, a boy burned down the hotel in which his family was staying. The conclusion was that his behavior could be a failure of postpartum bonding because his mother went back to work too soon.[18] Unbelievable! What is so irresponsible about such a guilt-making speculation is that there seems to be no reliable evidence that bonding and attachment are essential factors in the healthy development of a child. Research on both has been discredited over and over again. Hear it from Diane Eyer who has done much investigation on the subject:

> Mothers told me they were being advised to stay home from work for the entire first year of the child's life in order for proper bonding to be attained. I was astounded. There was absolutely no research that I knew of to prove the existence of a special "bonding" period during this time or to show that women's employment interfered with mother-child relationships.[19]

In addition to the fact that there are many problems in research design and interpretation regarding the issues of bonding and attachment, Eyers suggests there is much evidence actually *contradicting* these ideas. What does this tell us about all the childcare experts who are "pushing" bonding and attachment theories? Maybe they need to be sent back to school!

Certainly, the childcare experts are being insensitive, as they are using the concept of bonding as an instrument of guilt. Yes, some mothers (and fathers) report feeling an intense and wonderful sense of closeness and connection the minute their child is born. Unfortunately, many do not. According to Jane Bartlett:

> Recent surveys have shown that only about half of all women feel an immediate sense of love for their babies. Four out of ten first-time mothers recall that their predominant emotion on holding their baby for the first time was indifference![20]

For some, a feeling of intense closeness and connection with their child can take a year or more, if ever! This isn't bad or good, it just is. But because of the myths of bonding, so many women today experience an extreme sense of failure when this idyllic sense of connection just doesn't happen. They feel they have let themselves and their child down. One woman I interviewed has been trying to "bond" for two years. She quit her job (with great sadness) in order to bond with her child and it simply hasn't happened. She says with a great deal of confusion and sadness in her voice:

> I'm afraid to leave him with anyone for fear of missing an opportunity to bond. Like I'm missing this perfect feeling of togetherness we're supposed to be having. I just never have this feeling.

I reassured her that, while she probably would never have this sublime feeling with her son, she really didn't need to, since the so-called bonding phenomenon is not at all the determinant of her child's future behavior or happiness. While she was disappointed that she would not have the exquisite feeling she was so looking forward to, she was also relieved that there was nothing wrong with her.

If you think about it logically, the concepts of bonding and attachment conjure up something particularly neurotic. Stickiness. Glue. These terms smack of co-dependency. To me, cutting the umbilical cord, literally and figuratively, signals the very moment in which a baby begins its journey away from, not toward, dependency on a parent. Of course a child has to be loved, fed, cared for, clothed, educated, and protected from harm, but it seems to me that the more people involved in the process, the merrier. There was never a time in history where children were expected to be so close to their mothers exclusively. And, as I will discuss in the next chapter, this creates a very unhealthy environment in so many ways. It seems to me that a mother, who is *not* so "attached" to her child and allows others to share in the child-rearing process can handle the parenting role in a much healthier, happier, and more objective way.

7. *Is it really that important for mothers to stay home during the early years of a child's life?*
Given what I have just told you, it is shocking that the theories of bonding and attachment are still being used by the guilt-gurus to keep mothers in the home. "If you don't stay home, your child will be 'maternally deprived.'" Don't you love that term—"maternally deprived"?

You will be amazed to learn where much of the theory of maternal deprivation was derived . . . from orphanages in Romania and Russia where babies were left in their cribs for 16 to 20 hours a day "curled against feeding bottles, their heads flattened, and their faces peaked."[21] Needless to say, they were in bad, bad shape, physically and emotionally. The diagnosis? "Attachment disorder as a result of maternal deprivation." If you believe that one, I will, as they say, sell you some swampland in Florida! *No, they didn't suffer from maternal deprivation, they suffered from woeful physical and emotional neglect—a lack of any stimulation or meaningful personal contact whatsoever.*

What is unbelievable to me is that a number of guilt-gurus decided that this extreme situation could be equated, if not in degree then in kind, to a mother going off to work and leaving her child in the hands of responsible caregivers. A classic case of comparing apples and gorillas. They claimed that the orphanages gave them "scientific evidence" that continuous care by the mother was needed. This is one of the most outrageous examples of faulty interpretation of research I have ever seen . . . using the example of squalid orphanages in Romania and Russia to determine that mothers shouldn't work. Unbelievable![22] Personally, I feel offended by such nonsense obviously designed to manipulate women.

Although the number of women in the workplace keeps growing, women feel an enormous amount of guilt as they are told over and over again that they should be home with their kids. Well, women, you can breathe a sigh of relief. According to Diane Eyer:

> There is no research to suggest that constant time with a child is necessary for the healthy development of that child; in fact, there is evidence that children do as well, *if not better,* with multiple care-givers.[23]

There is something else you should know. Upon looking over some old research, I noticed that it was common practice to use the phrase "mother *or mother substitute.*" Somehow the "mother substitute" part has in recent years been dropped and only "mother" remains. A huge omission, indeed . . . one that has caused grief in the lives of too many mothers.

Even with all of the above information, women are still being pressured left and right by magazines, books, pediatricians, and guilt-gurus to stay home with their children. I think it's time we tell them to sell their wares somewhere else.

Bottom line: It doesn't matter what mode of care a child has, just so long as it's good care. And maybe even that doesn't matter . . . considering the fact that so many children grow up healthy despite an unhealthy upbringing. As I have already discussed, the child's

Circle of Being rules the roost, not *just* mother and father. You do the best you can . . . and then, it's time to let go.

8. Is all that goes wrong with a child really the mother's fault?
The entire last chapter dispelled this hurtful myth. Indeed, what you put in doesn't necessarily come out. The child's Circle of Being holds the upper hand and not Mommie, dearest—or for that matter, Daddy, dearest. If you are still not convinced, reread the last chapter—over and over again!

9. Are women really *more capable than men when it comes to the care of their children?*
You may be surprised to learn that there have been many times in history when men played a far more important role in child-rearing than women. In Colonial times, for example, it was the fathers who had a much more important role in their children's lives. In an agricultural society, mother and father worked together and shared the responsibilities of child-rearing.

Certainly men are just as capable as women in the raising of their children. And don't let anyone tell you otherwise. In fact, some studies show that when raised by men, children do better in a number of areas. Of course, it *looks like* men are not as good at caring for their children. Why? Because in our society, they don't have an opportunity to practice as much as women. And, as you just learned, *we all need practice!* But when men do practice, they are great caregivers. While the term "nurturing" is associated with women, it is clear that some women aren't nurturing at all and many men are. One woman told me:

> After my child was born, I kept waiting and waiting for the maternal instinct to kick in. It didn't. My husband was the one with the maternal instinct. It was so frustrating to watch him do everything with such ease. It was a vision watching him feed the baby. He was so relaxed and content; I was a nervous wreck.

So why aren't men more involved in childcare? One reason is that many women, consciously or unconsciously, push men out of the picture. Why? Perhaps women see it as the one area where women have been designated in our society to reign supreme. Perhaps they see it as their territory and don't want to give it up. Perhaps mothering gives them a sense of importance. Perhaps they feel jealous and/or excluded when a closeness between father and child develops. Perhaps they feel guilty when they don't shoulder all the responsibility. Who knows why, but many women will admit they do push the men out of the picture. My advice is, "Women, think about what you are doing. Enjoy, in fact, *demand* the help of your men!"

Some men really don't want to get involved in the parenting process . . . and, luckily for them, society has given them a way out: "It's the mother's role." *No guilt here!* It's not that they wouldn't be great caregivers if they had to; it's just that they would rather be doing something else . . . as many women would! Other men *want to be* more responsible for the raising of their children. They feel very badly when they are excluded. They feel their only value in the family is as a money machine. They yearn to establish a deeper feeling of closeness with their children.

Predictably, those with working wives don't suffer such exclusion. In the first place, they don't have sole responsibility for the family income, and as a result, may have more time available to spend with the children. In the second place, because their wives work, they are "expected" to share the burden at home. And this is good. Too many children grow up never having known their fathers. Some of my most wonderful memories of childhood came from the easy access to my father who owned a pharmacy two blocks from our home. A short walk and I was guaranteed a big hug and kiss from a man I deeply loved. I was fortunate indeed.

We live in a transition period and I am hopeful that as time goes by, men will demand a more active role in the raising of their children. At this point in time, too many are intimidated by the fact that society believes that parenting is a woman-thing. And too many women don't want to have responsibility for the family finances . . . they feel it's a man-thing.

We must call on women to be "new mothers" who refuse to have full responsibility for the well-being of their children as mandated by their husbands or by society-at-large. We must call on men to be "new fathers" who refuse to be excluded from the raising of their children by their wives or by society-at-large. Happily, more and more fathers are opting to get more involved. In fact, the number of men as primary caregivers is on the rise. The truth is that men and women are both equipped—body, mind, and soul—to raise their children. And it's time that both were more *equally* involved.

10. Is custody of the children really *a "win" for all women?*
Of all the myths of motherhood, this is probably the hardest for all concerned to look at clearly and dispassionately. I will probably be branded a heretic for some of what I have to say. I'm willing to take this risk since the shattering of this myth could give a number of women a whole new lease on life. I know whereof I speak.

Way back in the Seventies when my children were 11 and 15, I made the unheard-of, *shocking* decision to give physical custody of the children to my husband when we divorced. While we had joint custody, the children lived with him. For many reasons I felt this was clearly the right decision for all concerned. Needless to say, I was severely castigated for my decision. In fact, over 20 years later, you may be reading this and castigating me as well. Societal change is slow. The criticism I got came mostly from women—but a few men got into the act. I remember having a date with a divorced man who lived in my apartment building. His ex-wife and four children lived in the suburbs while he was having a fine time living in the city. When I told him I had given physical custody of my children to my ex-husband, he looked at me in disbelief and said, "I don't understand how you could walk out on your children." I looked at him with amused astonishment and answered, "I guess the same way you 'walked out' on yours!" Needless to say, that was the last time I went out with him! Here in action was the familiar assumption that it is okay for a father to "give" his children to the mother, but a woman "abandons" her children when she gives them to the father. How unfair to both sexes!

When my daughter was in her late teens, I invited her to one of my women's workshops to answer questions about a child's feelings when Dad has physical custody. Predictably, the first question asked was, "Didn't you feel your mother abandoned you?" My daughter responded: "Why do you think a child feels less 'abandoned' when a father leaves? If you love both your parents, it's sad to see either one of them leave . . . but no more for the mother than the father." My daughter delivered a powerful message to my class that day—one I hope she is delivering to you today.

Even though I was criticized for my decision, waiving physical custody was a choice that, for many reasons, I have never regretted. A few of these reasons are as follows: My ex-husband was born with those wonderful LBP genes, and as such, totally enjoyed the process of parenting. He was also earning a great deal more money than I was at the time and was able to give the children a much more desirable lifestyle. And, strangely, it was a decision that brought me closer to my children. While I had frequent physical contact with them, the shift in the dynamics of our relationship definitely made the heart grow fonder . . . for both my children and myself. Mommy was no longer the "bad guy" making all the house rules; now it was Daddy's turn! And my career flourished as it probably would not have, had the children lived with me. (As you will learn in a later chapter, a flourishing career and primary care of the children are often incompatible.) Hence, I held no resentment and I more fully enjoyed the time my children and I spent together. My decision gave me an awareness of the advantages—and freedom—most men, as typically the non-custodial parents, had over the years. For these reasons, and others, it is my belief that, in my case, it was to the advantage of all concerned that Daddy, not Mommy, had physical custody of the children, and I'm sure this would be the case for many other families as well.[24]

History tells us that there was a time when fathers always got custody of the children; women had no legal rights. That was the "fashion" of the time. Then women fought hard and won many rights, including the right to retain custody of their children. *That* became the "fashion" of the time. Presently, various forms of joint custody and shared physical custody are becoming the new "fashion." While there are difficulties to overcome, I see joint custody and shared physical custody as steps in the direction of equality between men and women—if handled correctly.[25] Another step toward equality between men and women is to give fathers physical custody of the children where appropriate, as it was in my case.

I often joke that women shot themselves in the collective foot when they insisted the children live with them. To further the interests of equality, perhaps there will come a day when women will *demand* that men take physical custody of the children . . . and for the first time in history, true women's lib will have been accomplished! As Jessie Bernard puts it:

> Rocking the cradle has been precisely what has prevented [women] from ruling the world.[26]

While some undoubtedly consider my "joke" a shocking concept and are already throwing tomatoes at me, others realize it holds a great deal of insight. Women constantly complain, and rightfully so, that in most cases women carry much too much of the burden after a divorce. They end up with less time for themselves, less money, less of an opportunity to advance their careers, and less of a social life. What they have is more responsibility, anger from their children, and blame for everything that goes wrong. Yes, they have more contact with their children, but, as in my case, sometimes "less is more" in terms of a richer relationship with our children.

Would women be shortchanging their children by insisting that men shared or took sole physical custody? (Again, *why are we not asking the same question of men when they give sole physical custody to women?)* It is clear to me and verified by research in the field, that most men and most women *both* have wonderful things to offer their children. It's a sign of misinformation to say one gender is inherently better at being a parent or one is worse. With the same kind of practice that women usually have, men are just as adept at child-rearing as women—if not better in some areas. Yet the myth that it is to the advantage of all concerned that mother has custody of the children persists without abatement. The words of Richard Warshak may shock you, but will certainly give you something to think about:

> Mother custody, far from being a historical imperative, was virtually unknown to our ancestors. The belief in a mother's singular importance to her children arose in response to economic pressures and was buttressed by sentiment, unproven theories, and faulty interpretation of earlier research. Recent research has underscored the father's immense contribution to his children's development and documented the psychologically harmful effects of his absence. Research with father-custody families has proved that fathers are able to manage competently the responsibilities of single parenting and that their children are no worse off than their peers in mother-custody families. In the light of this evidence, reason beseeches us to revise the cultural and judicial standards that have guided custody decisions during the past seventy years. It is time we release judges, attorneys, and divorced families from the grip of the motherhood mystique.[27]

It would be wonderful if our culture embraced the possibilities inherent in Warshak's statement and realized that, in some families, custody for the father would be an appropriate decision. But, as yet, mothers are still criticized and made to feel guilty, often by other women, when they make the choice of giving physical custody to the father. It is clear to me that much more flexibility is needed on a case-by-case basis for fairness to occur. And this certainly will require a release of the motherhood mystique that has held us in its grip in recent years.

Let me tell you an interesting story. Although he is British, my husband's early years were spent in Singapore where his father was a member of the colonial police. At the age of seven, he was sent back to England to attend boarding school as was the custom of the day, and he did not see his parents again, except for one summer vacation, until the age of 13—*six years later.* Again, nobody gave this practice much thought as it was the "fashion" of the day for members of the colonial service to send their male children back to England for an education.

Given this as background, understand my amazement when, on my first meeting with my present mother-in-law, she expressed shock that my children lived with their father. I found this to be astounding. She didn't see her son for six years; I saw my children most weekends and often during the week . . . but she was the one that was shocked. One can see how blinding the collective beliefs of a culture really are. Thankfully, our different cultural beliefs didn't destroy our relationship before it even started. I might add that Mark grew up to be the most wonderful human being I have ever known.

I tell you this story so that you can understand the power of the myths of motherhood to create an inability for people to think rationally. And I find it ironic that no matter how cultures vary, the people in each culture think that only they are *right.* I guess that explains why wars are started!

It is interesting that in spite of how far women have come in so many areas, non-custodial mothers are still considered failures. As a result, even if the heart and soul of a woman knows, consciously or unconsciously, that she does not want physical custody, she will demand it anyway because of her intense sense of guilt and fear of what others will say. Perhaps this is why there are so many burnt out, frustrated, and angry women trying to do it all.

Anger is often the driving force in the battle for custody; each wants to hurt the other partner. While many men and women truly want custody, others truly do not. But because they want to hurt their partner, they go for custody anyway. For these misguided souls, those who want to hurt their partner, *the biggest hurt may come when they actually get what they demand—sole custody of the children.*

More and more men are actually stepping up to the plate and more and more women are understanding that fathers can raise children beautifully. Dana Milbank wrote an article in the *Wall Street Journal* describing a new type of father that is emerging in the United States—the single dad with physical custody of the children.[28] Milbank points out that in 1970, the number of such fathers was 393,000 while today it is 1,860,000 . . . and this number is growing exponentially. Her explanation of this increase is that career track mothers have given men more options at home. If you think about it logically . . .

One way of assuring mothers true equality in the workplace is to give fathers more equality in the home.

As women make more money, it is logical that men who don't make as much money choose to be the stay-at-home parent—if the parents believe one parent should be home with a child. When divorce happens, it is perfectly logical that the children stay with the stay-at-home father and receive child-support from the mother . . . just as the reverse has been true for so many years. Yes, while equality may be wonderful for many women, it may be difficult for many other women to accept at times! The increasing numbers of custodial fathers may herald a new "fashion" in parenting. Milbank points out that five American sitcoms in a recent television season were based on custodial fathers. Custodial fathers are also creating support groups on the Internet. I see this as a very liberating trend.

Again, I know this section of the book may be the most controversial, but I felt it truly needed to be written. We all need to open our minds enough to think of the inherent possibilities for every man, woman, and child if a shift in consciousness about custody issues takes place. In truth, both sexes are equally capable of caring for their children . . . and we need more flexibility when the decision of custody is made. And if you are still resisting the possibilities presented here, ponder the following quote by Vicki Lansky:

> Who is the better parent? There is no answer to such a question. If you think there is, be assured it is probably not you.[29]

While there are, of course, exceptions, most parents—men and women alike—are equipped to do a fine job in raising their children. Hard to take, perhaps, depending on your situation . . . but certainly something to think about.

Now that you've had a chance to explore my top ten, I think most of you will agree that it's time for these myths, and the many others that exist, to go the way of the dinosaur. Remember that, as I define it here, a myth is an unproven collective belief; yet when it is drummed into our heads long enough, it can be made to look real. Don't trust societal beliefs; trust your own common sense instead and be flexible. When you do, the whole picture of parenting will change in a way that will make parenting easier, more equitable, more humane, and certainly more enjoyable.

Endnotes

[1]Durant, Will. *Zen to Go*, compiled and edited by Jon Winokur. New American Library, Penguin Books, New York and Canada, 1989, p. 105.

[2]For example, Cherry Norton reports in the *Sunday Times* (October 25, 1998, p. 11) that Britain's birth rate has fallen to its lowest level since records began 150 years ago, with increasing numbers choosing not to have children.

[3]Herst, Charney, with Lynette Padwa. *For Mothers of Difficult Daughters: How to Enrich and Repair the Bond of Adulthood.* Villard Books, New York, 1998, p. 9.

[4]Lette, Kathy. Quoted by Hester Lacey in "Motherhood: The Big Lie" in the *Independent on Sunday* (British), 1998, p.1.

[5]As found in Maushart, Susan. *The Mask of Motherhood.* Random House, Australia, NSW Australia, 1997, p. 177.

[6]For example, in her book *Will You Be Mother?: Women Who Choose to Say No* Jane Bartlett cites a survey carried out in the Netherlands that concluded that men and women can be just as happy without children as with them. Bartlett, Jane. *Will You Be Mother?: Women Who Choose to Say No.* New York University Press, New York, 1994, p. 55. (Originally published by Virago Press, London, 1994.)

[7]Lerner, Harriet. *The Mother Dance: How Children Change Your Life.* HarperCollins, New York, 1998, p. xiii.

[8]Clinton, Hillary Rodham. *It Takes a Village: And Other Lessons Children Teach Us.* Simon and Schuster, New York, 1996, p. 70.

[9]Badinter, Elisabeth. *The Myth of Motherhood.* Souvenir Press, London, 1980, as reported by Jane Bartlett in her book *Will You Be Mother?: Women Who Choose to Say No.* New York University Press, New York, 1994, pp. 53-54. (Originally published by Virago Press, London, 1994.)

[10]Elisabeth Badinter's work is cited by Braverman, Lois. "Beyond the Myth of Motherhood," in *Women in Families: A Framework for Family Therapy.* Edited by Monica McGoldrick, Carol M. Anderson, and Froma Walsh. W. W. Norton and Company, Inc., New York, 1991, p. 229.

[11]Ibid.

[12]Lerner, Harriet. *The Mother Dance: How Children Change Your Life.* HarperCollins, New York, 1998, p. 253.

[13]Springen, Karen. "The Bountiful Breast," *Newsweek* magazine, June 1, 1998, p. 71.

[14]Barrett, Nina. *I Wish Someone Had Told Me: A Realistic Guide to Early Motherhood.* Academy Chicago Publishers, Chicago, Illinois, 1997, p. 86.

[15]Maushart, Susan. *The Mask of Motherhood.* Random House, Australia, NSW Australia, 1997, p. 189.

[16]Lerner, Sharon. "Striking a Balance As AIDS Enters the Formula Fray," *Ms.* magazine, March/April, 1998, p.15. In this article it is reported that in developing countries at least 300 infants per day are being infected through breast-feeding, accounting for one third of all HIV-infected babies.

[17]Radl, Shirley L. *Mother's Day Is Over.* Charterhouse, New York, 1973, p. 51.

[18]Eyer, Diane. *Motherguilt: How Our Culture Blames Mothers for What's Wrong with Society.* Random House, New York, 1996, p. 71.

[19]Eyer, Diane. Ibid., p. x. To learn more about the faulty research and the ultimate damage it has caused, I suggest you read this book, as well as her other telling title *Mother-Infant Bonding: A Scientific Fiction.* Yale University Press, New Haven and London, 1992. Telling titles and even more telling books.

[20]Bartlett, Jane. *Will You Be Mother?: Women Who Choose to Say No.* New York University Press, New York, 1994, p. 55. (Originally published by Virago Press, London, 1994.)

[21]Talbot, Margaret. "Attachment Theory: The Ultimate Experiment," in the *New York Times Magazine,* May 24, 1998, p. 24.

[22]What is even more maddening is that if the orphanage children were adopted before six months of age, the data suggests that they do comparably well to birth children. If they were adopted a year later, although some children fall behind in certain areas, the evidence suggests that they recover. Contrast this with the fact that mothers are told that if bonding didn't occur very quickly, children were damaged forever.

[23]Again, you could read more about fathers and childcare in Diane Eyer's *Motherguilt* and *Mother-Infant Bonding: A Scientific Fiction.*

[24]Of course, if a father or mother is unfit, that parent should not have custody; but if both are good parents, there are many variables to consider as to which parent gets custody of the children.

[25]The argument of feminists is that with joint custody, many men do not take more responsibility for the children, yet they have a greater say in raising

them. On the other hand, we see that more and more parents are splitting physical custody giving each parent more time with the children and more time for themselves. For an informed discussion of joint custody, read chapter 9 entitled "Joint Custody: Panacea or Pandemonium?" in *The Custody Revolution: The Father Factor and the Motherhood Mystique,* by Richard A. Warshak, Poseidon Press, New York, 1992.

[26]As found in Peters, Joan K. *When Mothers Work: Loving Our Children Without Sacrificing Ourselves.* Hodder Headline Australia, 1998, p. 44.

[27]Warshak, Richard A. *The Custody Revolution: The Father Factor and the Motherhood Mystique.* Poseidon Press, New York, 1992, p. 135.

[28]Milbank, Dana. "Demographics: More Dads Raise Families Without Mom," in the *Wall Street Journal,* October 3, 1997, page B1.

[29]Lansky, Vicki. *Vicki Lansky's Divorce Book for Parents.* The Book Peddlers, Deephaven, MN, 1989, 1996, p. 135.

8

THE DANGERS OF FULL-TIME PARENTING

For those of you who are traveling with small children, be sure to put on your oxygen mask first before assisting your child.

Instruction to Airline Passengers

Every time I board an airplane, I am struck by the above instruction given to passengers relative to the use of oxygen masks. The underlying message is, "For the safety of the children, *adults come first.*" This is contrary to today's rule in Western society where we are always admonished that "*children come first.*" Maybe the airlines are onto something important. Common sense tells us that . . .

> We can take proper care of our child only when we ourselves are physically and emotionally healthy.

It is my contention that for most women, *even those with the LBP genes*, being a full-time mother is not necessarily a physically or emotionally healthy thing. And as I am using it here, a full-time mother is one who has no help in caring for her child other than for the short spans during the evening when a supportive mate (unless she is on her own) or other family member takes over. Despite what the guilt-gurus tell us, I strongly believe that such long stretches alone with a child is punishing to even the most devoted among us. *Everyone*, even those who absolutely adore parenting, needs regular breaks from the unrelenting demands of their children. My question is:

While the guilt-gurus are working very hard to get mothers back in the home as full-time caregivers, especially in the early years, could they be putting mother and child in jeopardy?

Let's look at it.

In her well-known book, *It Takes a Village,* Hillary Rodham Clinton tells us that there was a time that "village" meant a "geographic area where individuals and families lived and worked together."[1] *In such a village*, the children were safe as everyone kept a watchful eye. *In such a village*, there were arms to hold a baby when mother got weary. *In such a village*, mother was surrounded by familiar faces and knew that she was never alone. This kind of village no longer exists for most of us in a world that has become incredibly mobile. Far away are the grandparents, siblings, aunts, uncles, and "villagers" who would have been there in days gone by to ease our burden. Some close-knit little towns exist, I am sure, but they are not the norm in today's big, wide world of opportunity. They are, in fact, a rapidly vanishing element of Western society.

Historically, when we were an agrarian society, male and female were in it together. Their responsibilities overlapped—both worked and both took care of the kids. Mother was never alone, day in and day out; relief was always there. Then came the industrial revolution and family problems began with a vengeance. Women became over-involved in the home and began feeling quite alone; men weren't involved enough. And so it has remained—a lopsided world, a very unnatural way of raising children. A similar scenario has been playing itself out in other countries of the Western world.

It is worrisome to me that if many of today's guilt-gurus had their way, all the mothers would wave goodbye to all the Daddies every morning, close the door, turn around . . . and find themselves alone with their little ones all day, every day. Some of these guilt-gurus say we should wave goodbye for at least one and a half years. Some say at least three years. Others say we should be permanently ensconced in the home until the day we wave goodbye to our little ones as they go off to make their own way in the world. I don't agree. What seems self-evident to me is that:

The idea of a mother alone with her baby, day in and day out, is a totally unnatural state of being—a potential for psychological and physical danger.

To begin with, the unrelenting demands of babies can't help but cause extreme emotional distress for many. Some statistics compiled both in the United States and United Kingdom speak for themselves.

Jane Bartlett tells us that: "research presented at the autumn meeting of the Royal College of Psychiatrists in 1986 demonstrated that up to 50 per cent of UK mothers with small children under the age of five have symptoms of intensive emotional distress on a regular or continual basis. Women are five times more likely to be diagnosed as mentally ill in the year after their first child's birth than at any other time in their lives. At least one in ten women suffers from post-natal depression, and more than half of those who are not treated are still depressed a year later."[2]

Susan Maushart points us to research that tells us that "women in the first year of motherhood are five times more likely to suffer mental illness than at any other stage in their life cycle, and a horrifying 16 times more likely to develop a serious, psychotic illness." Also, "estimates of the incidence of mild depression among mothers with preschool children range from 30 to 80 percent . . . four out of five new mothers go through a reactive depression (often patronizingly dismissed as 'the blues')." Maushart also cites Annie Oakley's research in Britain, where it was found that 75 percent of the women studied reported times they were "overwhelmed by anxiety," and two-thirds admitted feeling "ambivalent" about their babies.[3]

Can you understand why it is not a good idea to leave a helpless, screaming, and demanding baby with someone who is not in a great mood? Maushart asks the critical question:

> Can it be "right" or "normal" that, as a society, we have constructed the mothering role in a way that quite literally makes women sick?[4]

It is obvious that, while this unnatural situation can be disastrous for parents, it can be even more disastrous for a helpless child. What is hidden in the closet of the world of the nuclear family is the large number of stay-at-home moms who are frightened that they will cause bodily harm to their children . . . or themselves. As one mother told me:

> It's like after a while, with all the shrieking and screaming until all hours of the morning, I'd have such thoughts as, "You could end this." "You could kill him." "You could jump off the terrace." "You could kill yourself." "This torture could be over." I had a little postpartum depression which didn't help. And, thank goodness, a friend told me I might have thoughts like I wanted to hurt my baby—that it's normal to have these thoughts. And her consolation gave me so much help because without it, I would have thought I was losing my mind. And there's the hormonal imbalance after a baby. My baby is two years old and I don't think my hormones are normal yet. To this day I still have these feelings.

I don't think anyone could disagree that this mother should not be the sole caregiver for her child . . . but she is. Unfortunately, she believed the guilt-gurus who told her she should be home to "bond." So she quit her job, became the sole caregiver for her child and is wondering what it's all about. Because she quit her job, she has no money for help in the form of other arms to hold her child. Nor do she and her husband have available cash to even enjoy a romantic dinner out together or a movie once in a while. This does not sound healthy to me.

Another woman tells me:

> If you would have told me that I would have basically been going out of my mind with boredom and loneliness, I wouldn't have had a child. The truth is, I am so afraid to be alone with my baby. He doesn't want to be in the house and he lets me know by raging and raving and spitting and hitting and crying. I can't keep him amused. You can't be out when it's raining or night-time, so I've been afraid to be alone with him. Because I don't know if I can handle his tantrums. Some people have more patience than I have. "Oh let him rave," they tell me. But when he is so upset, it really upsets me. Would I have had a child, had I known all this? No, I wouldn't.

And another:

> When my first was born, I was young, inexperienced and she had colic. And I thought I literally could kill her. I would put her in the crib for fear I would throw her against the wall. I would leave her there screaming and run around the block and keep running and running until I was exhausted. I would come back and she was still there screaming. Screaming and screaming. But the running took out the tension and I was then able to deal with it.

And yet another:

> I have screamed until I have seen red and lost my voice. I ask myself, "Where does this anger come from? Where does this rage come from?" I am beside myself asking, "Who is this person deep inside me?" One day I called my husband. I screamed, "You have to come home. I am afraid I will kill this kid. I am out of my mind."

It is important to know that these thoughts are not unusual for full-time moms, the sole caregivers for their children. You might be thinking, "Oh, Susan, come on! I never heard mothers talk like this before." No, you probably haven't. There aren't many in today's society (where guilt is born with the baby) who have an easy time announcing they want to kill their kid! The conspiracy of silence zips most mouths shut. In fact, three of the above mothers told me they have *never* expressed such feelings to another soul. On the surface, these women present a picture to the world of composure and happiness at being parents . . . but underneath a cauldron of dissatisfaction brews. Maushart reports:

> Research suggests that such destructive impulses are probably as universal among new mothers as sleepless nights and shapeless days. Yet to admit as much publicly remains a deeply subversive social activity. Indeed, even admitting to such feelings privately is more than many of us can manage.[5]

The conspiracy of silence keeps many parents in the closet about their true feelings. The unsuspecting buy into the mad, mad myths of motherhood, quit their jobs, and become full-time caregivers. In so doing, they discover the dark side of parenting that was not properly explained to them before, not from the guilt-gurus, their parents, their friends, nor from society. It is only the bright side of parenting that has a public face.

I remember the day an au pair was accused of shaking a baby to death. The cry that went out was, "Mothers, go home!" (Notice society didn't say: "Mothers *or fathers*, go home." It lay the guilt upon the shoulders of the mothers.) The message was "don't leave your child in the hands of caregivers." It would have been helpful if someone had pointed out that a very small percentage of abuse is perpetrated by caregivers. In a number of studies, abuse in daycare, foster-care, or other childcare arrangements has been reported to be in the area of only two or three percent.[6] You may be surprised (even shocked) to learn that the majority of physical abuse of children under the age of eight is perpetrated by mothers.[7] And the reasons for maternal abuse are many. They include the frustrations of poverty, the irresponsibility of youth, substance abuse, raising a child alone . . . and, for the purposes of this book, *losing control when a child is excessively demanding and no support system is available to relieve the unrelenting tension.*

I will wager that all mothers, even those who adore parenthood, have at some time had emotionally or physically violent thoughts or behavior aimed at their children. (It isn't that fathers are less capable of violence toward their little ones; it's that they normally spend less time with them and, as a result, their rate of "eruption" is lower.) Radl tells us:

> It is quite possible for the tenderest and most loving mother to feel absolute hatred for a child who has been making that terrible noise for hours on end.[8]

Emotional and physical violence of varying levels happen often when our sanity is compromised with the unrelenting responsibilities of parenthood. One mother admitted that her son was frightened of vacuum cleaners and when he was in his walker, she used to deliberately "go after him" with a vacuum cleaner while he screamed with terror. One mother remembers slapping her child uncontrollably. Another remembers slamming a wall and wishing it could be her child. Are you beginning to get a sense of how damaging, even deadly, parenting without respite can be? And how damaging the conspiracy of silence is to all concerned?

The despair that full-time mothers somethimes feel should be shouted from the rooftops![9]

There is no question in my mind that mothers need help in the course of their everyday living with their children.

Let it be understood that mothers are, for the most part, very loving beings who adore their children and would do everything they could to help them grow up to be healthy and happy adults.

Mothers are also human; they can explode when they have reached the limits of their patience. To always have helping hands available when they have reached this limit can be a life-saver—literally and figuratively.[10]

One parent I interviewed asked me what to do when she is enraged to the point of wanting to beat her child into silence. I said that the most important thing she could do was to leave the scene and take care of herself (put on her oxygen mask!). That meant putting her child in the playpen or another area where he is safe and then leaving the room. Read a book. Sing. Polish her nails. Put make-up on. Talk to a friend who can help her calm down. Call a help-line. Anything to get herself in a good space. The key is for her not to feel guilty as he screams and screams and screams, as long as he is safe. I told her to console herself that screaming is thought to be great for their lungs! And when she feels ready, she should return, but not before. There are times we can't stop a child's screaming, but we can change our reaction to it. If we do this long enough, the screaming may even stop. Hallelujah!

In telling this mother what to do, I was speaking from experience. I once lost control when my son was having one of his tantrums. It was at the moment when I began to hit him that I discovered what a volcano must feel like when it erupts. Thank goodness, I quickly stopped myself before I hurt him, but I was very much aware that if I had not been able to stop myself, I could have seriously hurt him. Some are not able to stop themselves. The minute I stopped hitting him, my entire body started to shake uncontrollably and I vowed I would never allow myself to be put in such a position again.

The next time I felt one of his tantrums coming on, I ran into the bathroom, locked myself in, and began to sing—loudly—until his tantrum petered out. I kept repeating this scenario each time a tantrum was coming on and, blessed relief, his tantrums soon stopped. Why did they stop? Because he knew that if he had a tantrum, he would lose me to the bathroom, that is to say, his tantrums weren't working for him any longer—unless his original purpose was to train me to run into the bathroom, lock the door and sing!

It is important to note that because I had caregivers and outside interests four years later when my daughter was born, I don't remember ever having that kind of rage when she went into her tantrum stage. It wasn't that she was better behaved than my son. It was that I had taken care of myself (put on my oxygen mask) and therefore was much better able to take care of both my kids.

What I am saying here needs to be taken very seriously. Most first-time moms in today's world of the nuclear family are novices. And to hand all the responsibility and unrelenting demands a child brings into this world to a novice is asking for trouble. I don't care if this first-time mom is 20, as I was, or 40, as many new mothers are today, the responsibilities and demands can be overwhelming if there is no one there to help. Parents need relief. And the fact that today's guilt-gurus are telling Mom to be the only caregiver for the first year or more of a child's life could spell disaster. Obviously, a restructuring of the full-time parenting model is in order to protect children from physical and emotional danger. Jane Swigart concurs with my "oxygen mask" theory when she says:

> We must be reminded that there are times when the needs of the care-giver are more important than the needs of the child. We must consider the care-giver's need for refueling—for care, nurturance, support—to counteract the insidious myth that mothers are an endless source of love and emotional sustenance.[11]

I don't know where this mythology of mother-as-saint came from, but it's time to explode the myth. Mothers are human. And human beings need help when taking care of children . . . whether it's in the form of nannies, childcare facilities, relatives, mothers pooling their efforts to substitute for one another, or mothers and fathers having more equitable responsibility in the raising of the children. But something must be done to relieve mothers of the awesome responsibility of being primary caregivers to their little ones.

There is something else to consider as well: a restructuring of the full-time parenting model is in order to protect children from psychological danger as well. For example, stay-at-home moms are more prone to be "enablers." What is an enabler? As Angelyn Miller tells us, an enabler is one who prevents growth and promotes weakness in others by assuming their responsibilities and protecting them from the consequences of their behavior.[12] Not good!

One can understand why stay-at-home moms would become enablers. To justify their "job," they pride themselves on "being there" for their child in every way they can. But the reality is that children have to learn how to be there for themselves. Miller, who learned the error of her ways, had this to say:

> I lived through Stan's and John's traumas—I made them my own. There were many times during the years of juggling the whole mess that I thanked God that I had been there for them and had been strong enough to handle the burden. I didn't know that God would have been likely to reply: "Would you get the hell out of the way, so I can help these people learn to help themselves?"[13]

Think about it:

Full-time parents get their sense of self from being needed. And to be needed they must have children who are forever needy.

Way back in 1946, Dr. Edward Strecker was on to something when he identified a syndrome called "momism," where a mother harmed children by making home such a haven that he or she didn't ever want to leave it or manage on their own.[14] Certainly in 1998, momism remains an ever-present danger when women leave their job in the workplace and replace it with the full-time job of "mom." I've witnessed full-time moms who are so eager to get it right that they are prone to over-do everything. They are over-parenters, over-protectors, over-doers, over-carers . . . in summary, over-bearing mothers. It was Margaret Mead's daughter, Catherine Bateson, who said that her mother's exposure to different cultures in her career as an anthropologist strengthened her belief that it is "preferable that children feel a part of several households and have several caretakers to avoid the tightness of bonding to a single caretaker that so often provides the ground of an entire neurotic system."[15] I totally agree.

While the guilt-gurus tell us that children need to "attach" to their parents, I take the opposite point of view. The less attachment to any one person, the more security. Closeness, intimacy, love, caring, trust--yes. But attachment, no. I can't think of anything more threatening than to think there is only one person in the world who could take care of you. There is no question in my mind that multiple caregivers create in children a feeling of trust that there are *many* people there for them with whom to feel closeness, intimacy, love, caring, and trust. It makes perfect sense. Forcing a child to have so much dependence on the mother has an element of cruelty, not safety, about it. Certainly, in prior times, children were never put into this untenable position. There were always a circle of arms to hold them and many voices to comfort them.

And there's more. A number of studies show that children fare much better in many things when they are exposed to more than one caregiver. Again, this makes perfect sense. Lois Braverman points out that in studies of working women, there is compelling data compiled by social scientists that shows that . . .

> Children are not harmed by maternal employment. Neither their intelligence, their independence, their self-esteem, their school functioning, their sex-role concept, nor their ability to make relationships with others are impaired as a result of their mother's work.[16]

This has been demonstrated in studies with infants, preschoolers, elementary school children, and adolescents.[17]

Children with multiple caregivers have greater interpersonal skills, are more flexible, accepting of new people and situations, more independent . . . and all the other attributes associated with someone who doesn't have the anxiety of separation seen with children too attached to one single person. Joan Peters points to some more evidence:

> A recent British report comparing 100,000 children of employed mothers with the general population demonstrated that children with mothers in offices and factories have higher reading scores than children with mothers at home. A 14-university American study found that children in high-quality daycare from one-month-old on have better language and cognitive ability than children at home. Alison Clarke-Stewart's work on daycare argued that if children have good daycare, they have greater confidence and social skills than children of mothers-at-home. These and other similar studies suggest that mothers-at-home is not necessarily the most beneficial arrangement for children.

Her conclusion?

> Children flourish with multiple attachments. Far from depriving them of full-time mothers, maternal employment creates an opportunity for children to form other close connections—not only with their fathers but with a network of caring adults who can both diffuse and reinforce maternal love, relieving it of the isolation, self-abnegation, and involution that too frequently have given it unhappy and sometimes tragic dimensions.[18]

A powerful statement. The guilt-gurus will tell you that children need lots of attention and by working or doing other things you enjoy doing, you are shortchanging them. I could make the argument that you are shortchanging your children by not exposing them to multiple caregivers who can offer a much richer expanse of experience and learning.

I think you get the picture. Can something happen to a child while he or she is with an alternate caregiver? Of course. Something can *also* happen when children are in the care of parents, or at school, or at a friend's house, or sleeping in their cribs. In my parents' house with my mother, my father, my ex-husband and myself present, my son wandered into my parents' bathroom and downed a bottle of pills that my father, who was not used to having toddlers around, had left on the vanity. My son had to be rushed to the hospital to have his stomach pumped. A night none of us will ever forget!

We can't protect our children from everything unless we tie them to the bedposts. And even then, stuff happens. We have to stop hanging on too tightly for fear something can happen to our children. It will or it won't. We do our very best and then we live with the unflappable surety that whatever happens in our lives or in the lives of our children, we will find a way of handling it in an empowering way. In this kind of thinking, and only in this kind of thinking, lies the pathway to ultimate peace of mind.

Endnotes

[1]Clinton, Hillary Rodham. *It Takes a Village: And Other Lessons Children Teach Us*. Simon and Schuster, New York, 1996, p. 12.

[2]Bartlett, Jane. *Will You Be Mother?: Women Who Choose to Say No*. New York University Press, New York, 1994, pp. 65-66. (Originally published by Virago Press, London, 1994.)

[3]Maushart, Susan. *The Mask of Motherhood*. Random House, Australia, NSW Australia, 1997, pp. 160-161.

[4]Ibid., p. 164.

[5]Ibid., p. 162.

[6]This makes sense, as childcare workers usually have much-needed relief at the end of the day. Sources: *Current Trends in Child Abuse Reporting and Fatalities: The Results of the 1997 Annual Fifty State Survey*. Principal researcher, Ching-Tung Wang, Ph.D., director, Deborah Daro, D.S.W. Prepared by the Center on Child Abuse Prevention Research, a program of the National Committee to Prevent Child Abuse, Working Paper Number 808, available through the NCPCA, 200 S. Michigan Avenue, 17th Floor, Chicago, IL 60604-2404. And *Child Maltreatment 1996: Reports from the States to the National Child Abuse and Neglect Data System* (Washington, DC: US Government Printing Office, 1998) from the National Clearinghouse on Child Abuse and Neglect Information, PO Box 1182, Washington, DC 20013-1182.

[7]The estimates of abuse perpetrated by mothers rather than fathers for children under the age of eight range from 65 percent to 83 percent. After the age of eight, men exceed women in child abuse largely in the form of sexual abuse. Some sources to investigate if you are interested are: The US Department of Health and Human Services. *Child Maltreatment 1996: Reports from the States to the National Child Abuse and Neglect Data System* (Washington, DC: US Government Printing Office, 1998) and the National Clearinghouse on Child Abuse and Neglect Information, PO Box 1182, Washington, DC 20013-1182. I suspect similar findings would be found in all Western societies where the structure of the family is the same as the United States.

[8]Radl, Shirley L. *Mother's Day Is Over*. Charterhouse, New York, 1973, p. 63.

[9]This isn't to say that working mothers and fathers don't commit violent acts . . . they certainly do and in large numbers. But when parents—working or

not—have breaks from the unrelenting demands of their children, the likelihood of violence is greatly reduced.

[10]In 1996, 1,185 child abuse and neglect-related fatalities were confirmed by Child Protective Service (CPS) agencies. Based on these numbers, more than three children die each day as a result of child abuse or neglect. Since 1985, the rate of child-abuse fatalities has increased by 34 percent. (Wang and Daro, 1998). Again, in the majority of cases, women are the perpetrators.

[11]Swigart, Jane. *The Myth of the Bad Mother: The Emotional Realities of Mothering.* Doubleday, New York, (London), 1991, p. 38.

[12]Miller, Angelyn. *The Enabler: When Helping Harms the Ones You Love.* Ballantine Books, New York, 1988, p. 7. The term "enabler" was originally used to describe those who helped alcoholics remain alcoholics by letting them get away with their objectionable behavior. She is using it in the context of parents doing too much for their children.

[13]Ibid., p. 37.

[14]As found in Eyer, Diane. *Motherguilt: How Our Culture Blames Mothers for What's Wrong with Society.* Random House, New York, 1996, p. 57.

[15]As found in Peters, Joan K. *When Mothers Work: Loving Our Children Without Sacrificing Our Selves.* Hodder Headline Australia, 1998, p. 219.

[16]Braverman, Lois. "Beyond the Myth of Motherhood," in *Women in Families: A Framework for Family Therapy*, edited by Monica McGoldrick, Carol M. Anderson, and Froma Walsh, W. W. Norton & Company, Inc., New York, London, 1989, p. 233.

[17]Ibid., p. 233.

[18]Peters. Ibid., p. 4.

9

THERE'S NO PLACE LIKE WORK

It is impossible for a mother to love her children twenty-four hours a day.

Milton R. Sapirstein[1]

I have a strong belief in the equality of men and women. Just as women should have the right to go off to work if they so choose, I believe that men should have the right to stay home with the children, if they so choose. Whenever I make this argument, there are some men and women who look at me as though I am crazy and ask, "Why would they want to?" Of course, there are others who definitely *would* want to, but for many parents, there's no place like work. And in the end, this may be a very good thing. Why? Because, as I discussed in the last chapter . . . in large doses, mothers and their children may not be good for each other's health!

Given this reality, how lucky for mothers today that working is an acceptable option. It wasn't so long ago that a mother's place was definitely in the home. Picking up a briefcase and going off to work was clearly an unacceptable thing for a mother to do, except in times of dire financial need.

Then, because of the strength of the women's movement, society witnessed a liberating swing of the pendulum freeing women to enter the workplace. Finally women had true choice. That's the good news. The bad news is that the guilt-gurus are now doing their very best to reverse the swing of the pendulum and send moms, willing or not, back into the home. Their three main weapons? Guilt, guilt, and guilt. Oh, the destructive power of guilt!

There is no question in my mind that the guilt-gurus are wrong. A woman's following through on her desire to work is important for the well-being of all concerned . . . mother, father, child, and yes, even society at large. And here are a few reasons why this is so.

Of course, financial necessity

Many women *must* work to bring enough money into the household. In a strange way, these are the lucky ones: how can you feel guilt when you are putting food into the mouths of those adorable little faces? These women even receive a degree of empathy from society at large. "Well, she *has to* work." I have to add that for our guilt-gurus to suggest that women hurt their children when they work (which has *never* been proven to be true) is extremely cruel in light of the fact that so many women *must* work. Thankfully, I doubt that many of these women pay much attention to the guilt-gurus. After all, "you got to do what you got to do!" Of course, some women who must work yearn to quit their jobs so that they can be home with their children. And many who have had the opportunity to do so ultimately realize that there really is no place like work and they return to the workplace.

To better enjoy parenthood

One woman summed it up wisely when she said that her work gives her a sense of self instead of her self being swallowed up by the needs of her children. When she was a full-time parent, she couldn't wait to get away from her kids . . . now she looks forward to seeing them at the end of the day. There is no question in my mind that with a full, rich life, most women come home feeling more tender and loving toward their children.

To "get a life"

No child can give a parent a life. And once the umbilical cord is cut, no parent can give a child a life. It doesn't work that way. Everyone needs their own rich, full, rewarding lives based on their own needs and desires. And, if you think about it, the needs and desires of parent and child rarely coincide. One woman said it beautifully:

> I love being with my kids and I can have a great time for a limited time. It's exhausting but always entertaining. I enjoy it. I love seeing things through their eyes. I love the closeness. I love explaining vocabulary. But I have to have a balance. I couldn't do that every day. I couldn't stay home and love that every day. I don't think they'd love staying with me all day. They love play-school and enjoy being with their friends. I see how much fun they have elsewhere and I feel great about that. On the other hand, I see mothers who feel hurt about that. They've made their children their entire world. I see that a lot, even with intelligent, talented, creative women. I see them smothering their children and feeling badly if their child says they would rather play with his or her friends. Or if the child says something mean to them. I think these women really need to get a life.

As I pointed out in the last chapter, when we make our children our life, what an emotionally charged cocoon we create for ourselves . . . and what a burden we place upon our kids.

To save our sanity

I have heard it jokingly said that if children don't drive you to drink, they certainly will drive you to work. And for many of us women, this joke has a ring of truth. We have created wonderful careers for ourselves simply because we needed to get out of the house. One woman I know became a gardener; one went back to school and became a lawyer; one became a dress designer; one became a graphic designer; and I went off to get my doctorate in psychology. You may think only women with exciting careers love the state of work. Not so. One woman I interviewed would rather clean houses than stay home with her children all day . . . and she does. She said that scrubbing floors definitely beats a day at home with her demanding kids. It seems to me that most women need a life outside the world of their children to save their sanity—even those with the LBP genes!

To keep our dignity

I believe that in our society, even the most liberated among us women still have a hidden or not so hidden desire to be taken care of by Prince Charming. (It's hard to let go of those fairy-tales, isn't it?) Thankfully, most women also know that to be taken care of is to remain in a child-like state that truly has many disadvantages . . . a loss of confidence, independence, power, equality, and self-respect, to name a few. At some level, it is a blow to many women's dignity to depend on someone else for money. Some women are totally comfortable in this situation, and that is fine. Others have a great deal of trouble with it. One woman said that when she stopped working, the whole power structure of the relationship changed as she felt an element of real or imagined subservience creeping in. This feeling got her back into the workplace—fast!

A housewife phoned a radio talk-show and asked the host psychologist how she could get more money from her husband. I gasped as the psychologist told her to try asking for money in baby-talk, and she would get anything she wanted. Then I heard the housewife say, "You know you're right. When my kids pull that with him, they get anything they want." Yes, fathers do love their kids, don't they? But it isn't necessarily good for us and our self-esteem to remain a child forever.

To protect ourselves and our families

Today, women finally have a choice about whether they want to work or not—or do they? Women must take their heads out of the sand and realize:

It isn't noble for women to take care of others while not being able to take care of themselves.

I believe that any woman (or man) who can't take care of herself financially puts herself and her family in a clear and present danger. Even if a woman truly enjoys being at home, she needs to be aware that for unexpected reasons, she may be called upon to earn a living. And she would be foolish not to be prepared to work if she is called upon to do so. Divorce, a husband's death, illness, or loss of his job can create intense financial difficulty and need. I always advise women at home to "get thee to evening courses" or whatever it takes to be prepared to work if necessary. A greater insurance policy, one can never buy.

To bring men into the parenthood picture

I have seen it happen time and again that when children are born, many women leave the workplace which by definition puts pressure on men to spend more time in the workplace. The result? The women get close to their children and the men are shadow figures who pop in once in a while for dinner and a goodnight kiss. As I said earlier, we live in a lopsided world. We need a revisioning in the roles of both men and women; men need to get more involved and women, less involved. Fathers contribute much to their children's lives and many fathers yearn for greater closeness with their children.

To make our marriages stronger

There is no question in my mind that many marriages have a better chance of succeeding and are stronger with both parents working. Working mothers are free of the resentment many stay-at-home mothers feel, and which causes great friction in the relationship. Instead of these women waving goodbye to their husbands going off to work each morning, they now both go off to work waving goodbye to the baby sitter. Also, men are now beginning to admit that they are relieved not to have to shoulder all the financial responsibility for the family. It is a great strain, indeed. Few women willingly take on that responsibility unless circumstances mandate that they must. I know. I have polled many women on this subject and have had no takers. And, as you saw in the last chapter, in many families, everyone's life can be enriched as a result of both parents working . . . including the baby's.

Thankfully, more and more men are doing their part in the home (whether they want to or not) making it easier for working women and making it better for their relationships. In 1989, it was reported that when both parents worked, men did only about 20 percent of the work around the house, spending 17 minutes doing housework and 12 minutes a day doing childcare.[2] (How's that for detail?) Times have changed and it is now reported that women still do more than men, but not that much more . . . about 55 percent of the housework, which includes cleaning, paying bills, shopping, and cooking. However, it is pointed out that, on the average, men still work at jobs longer than women.[3] So we can't be too critical of men. It is hopeful that in the not too distant future, a real flow of respect and co-operation will make the jobs of both men and women at work and at home a little easier.

To fulfill our great potential

The world gains something wonderful when a child is born—a potential for great things. The world also loses something when a child is born—a potential for great things. The latter speaks, not to those women who can be and are fulfilled by raising their children, but to the many women who stifle their calling, who kill their potential contribution to this world by becoming martyrs and staying home with the children.

As you will see in a later chapter, I believe we are all meant to follow our "calling" whether that calling is to be a writer, a doctor, a scientist, a teacher, or whatever. And absolutely, for some, that calling is to be a stay-at-home mom. Yet for the rest of us, when we don't expand into all that we want to be, or at least aim ourselves in that direction, we can't help but live *longingly* ever after . . . and at some level, we may even end up resenting the very children we have given up so much to love. Women are filled with strivings, hopes, goals, dreams, and the desire to succeed in their chosen field. And because women have so much to contribute to this world, if it is what they so desire, it is important that they have a chance at success. The world definitely needs their contributions.

For the best reason of all . . . it makes them happy

Surveys have consistently shown that employed women are happier, healthier, and feel more valued *even at home*, than women who are full-time homemakers. In fact, I know of no study that doesn't show that the happiest women, the happiest families, are those where women are as fulfilled as the other members of the family are fulfilled.

No matter the level of the job, whether high or low on the totem pole, women find many things to love about work . . . the company of adults, mental stimulation, self-esteem, money, an uninterrupted lunch hour, talks around the coffee machine, and, as one mother said, "no one pulling on my leg when I'm sitting on the toilet." Simple things. Such important things. Work is a place where most of the time people are rational, life is rational. And having rational time in your day can be so helpful in coming home to deal with one's children, who often are not rational.

And what about the kids? I believe that when children have happy mothers, it can't help but add to their happiness as well. What child would want to live in a home where a mother's depression and resentment cloud the atmosphere? One woman went back to work with a deep understanding that, "If I'm this miserable, my child can't be happy."

These are just a few reasons why many women need and want to work. And so they should. But this is not the whole story. It is important for women to be cognizant of some very important realities. While childfree women have made many advances in terms of the equality equation at home and at work, there remains one little glitch that needs to be reckoned with:

Equal becomes unequal as soon as a child enters the picture.

When women become mothers, the oppressive weight of custom steps in to obliterate a lot of the opportunity we have created for ourselves in recent years. As we become the primary caretakers of our children, society dictates that we either stop working or work in a greatly diminished capacity. This, by definition, creates a huge inequity in the workforce. Fathers go forward and mothers retreat. *This isn't good or bad, it just is . . . until we change it.* This is an important thing to know before we jump into parenthood.

The less ambitious among us who enjoy work may find this inequity perfectly acceptable once the columns on the balance sheet are counted. These women will willingly give up some work identity and success to be more available to their children. However, the very ambitious among us may want to forgo having children until a time when true co-parenting exists and the idea of mother as primary caretaker becomes a relic of the past. Until then, mothers will, in many cases, remain in an inferior position when it comes to their relationship to work.

Many career-minded women have found this out too late. They become very disheartened as they watch their dreams fall away once they become mothers. They find themselves forced to compromise, scale down, refuse promotions, work part-time, enter the "mommy track" or quit their jobs altogether to be more available to their children. They know they will end up far below the level of what their great potential would have predicted under normal circumstances. Women complain that some employers don't even like to hire mothers. If a child is sick, on vacation, in trouble in school, and so on, who has to run off and deal with it? Usually, Mother . . . which, of course, creates hardships for employers.

When women ultimately *demand* that men are included in the parenting process, you will see a shift in the prejudices of the workplace. For now, the prejudice against hiring or advancing mothers definitely exists. Our society is structured to give child-free women equal opportunity, but not necessarily mothers.

In addition to diminished opportunity at work, mothers experience what Monica McGoldrick calls "role overload,"[4] particularly divorced women who have custody of their children. Again, until women *demand* that men get involved in the process—which would be great for all concerned—women will continue to walk around a little hunchbacked from the burden placed upon their shoulders. Interestingly, even with all this overload, most women wouldn't give up their jobs because of the many rewards they derive from them. Being a working mom has intense difficulties, to be sure, but the fact that so many women feel "Thank God it's Monday" speaks volumes.

As time goes by, let's hope the face of child-rearing will change so that there is more equality in both work *and* parenting. In the end, the task of creating this change belongs largely to mothers. We have to give up our place as "most important" in a child's life and share it with others; we have to *demand* that men pitch in their 50 percent of *all* child-rearing tasks; we have to *demand* that our children do their part in helping around the house, even at a young age (knowing they make a difference will raise their self-esteem considerably); we have to learn how to give up some of the control; we have to be politically active to ensure that our society provides enough good alternative care for all children; we have to be willing to be criticized as we plow ahead into new territory; and we have to be willing to say "No, I don't want children," if we really and truly don't want to have them. The task of getting women into the workplace rested on the power of women, and while there is still more work to be done in that arena, we have succeeded—

in a very short time—beyond our wildest dreams. The task of creating equal opportunities for mothers now rests on the power of mothers, and I know that when we see our goals clearly before us, we will once again succeed beyond our wildest dreams.

Before I end this chapter, let me stand on my soapbox for a moment longer and discuss some things that have been on my mind for a long time:

First, I find it interesting that we approve of women's working, or women's doing anything else, only if we determine it is good for the children. *Where is it written that women can't do something simply for their own good . . . because it makes them happy?* Is it only men and children who are entitled to do things to make themselves happy? Why do we have to apologize, defend, make excuses, justify, and create rationalizations for seeking a rich life away from our children?

At what point in history did women's needs become so unimportant?

Maybe the time has come for women to acknowledge their right to work simply because they want to . . . *even if the children don't like it!* Maybe women have to learn how to say, "So what if they don't like it; *I like it*!" Maybe children just have to learn to adjust to their mother's needs . . . explore their own lives . . . become more independent . . . know they will survive . . . help in the running of the household. Is this so bad? No, I think it's great for children to understand that their mothers are people too and have their own needs. There are too many children running around today who only take, take, take.

This does not, of course, mean I am encouraging mothers to do things that would obviously be harmful or cruel to the child. I am talking about *responsibly* taking care of the legitimate needs of the child as she responsibly takes care of her own needs.

As we need to teach ourselves that we can handle whatever life hands us, we have to trust that our children will handle whatever life hands them. To have that trust in our children is to hand them perhaps the best gift we can ever offer.

It always concerns me how ashamed mothers are to admit that they have personal ambitions when they have children. Have we been so brainwashed that we think only men and children have a right to expand to be the best that they can be? And what does this say to our daughters? Can we look them in the eye and say, "Dream on, little girl, but remember when you grow up and have kids, you can throw those dreams out the window"? Do we really want to say that? Do we really want to allow a situation where our daughters are "less than" their husbands and children when they grow up? If not, *why do we allow it for ourselves*?

I believe that both women and men have an equal right to follow their own dreams and to pursue and experience their own incredible genius and magnificence. And I defy anyone, even the guilt-gurus, to say it isn't so . . . especially when so many studies can be cited that explode the myths of maternal bonding, deprivation and the like as nothing more than scientific fictions.

I have noticed that women are called "selfish" when they want to follow their dreams. I think it is time for women to become *more* selfish and demand of both husbands and children more equal participation in the household. The idea that women's desires and needs are not important offends me terribly . . . as it should all men and women out there.

It's time that we stopped being victims and took responsibility for creating rich full lives for ourselves without a feeling of guilt, but with a feeling of pride in all that we have to give to the world. What stops many of us from taking the steps we need to take is our need to be seen as The Good Mother. When things are done only for the sake of what people will think, The Good Mother, in the end, invariably becomes The Bad Mother. Women have to stop worrying about what everyone else thinks and begin focusing on their own needs and purpose in life, as well as their children's.

It is a strange comfort to know in advance that no matter what we do, we will be criticized, often by other women. Knowing this in advance allows us to be psychologically prepared. If we stay at home, we will be criticized. If we go to work, we will be criticized. If we decide not to have children, we will be criticized. And, I say, *so what*! We can handle criticism. As long as we stand up tall and do what is right for who we are as mothers, women, and human beings, we can withstand—and even laugh at—the criticism. We have to guiltlessly embrace the advances we have made and refuse to retreat. As I said earlier, I lived through a time when a women's place was in the home. And, for many of us for whom parenting was not our calling, what a prison that home became. Women have fought hard to get out of the house; let us not relinquish our right to stay out.

As I stated earlier, there are ominous signs that the pendulum is swinging back to the old cliché that "Mother's place is in the home." For example, I recently heard the most astonishing interchange on a television talk show. A pregnant woman running for political office in the state of Massachusetts was castigated by her male opponent *because she was going to be working after the birth of her child.* I am hopeful that the people in Massachusetts were outraged at such a prejudiced remark against women. And that's exactly what it is . . . prejudice. Can you imagine castigating a man because he was going to be working after the birth of his child? Certainly we are learning that a father's participation is just as important as his wife's (despite the guilt-gurus' protestation to the contrary)! Her answer was a lot more restrained than mine would have been. She calmly and respectfully told him, "It's none of anyone's business how I plan to raise my child." End of story. If we could all have such calm confidence in our right to live our life the way we want to live it with the trust our children will be just fine, it would be liberating, indeed.

I have heard the question asked, "Why *have* children if you don't want to be with them?" I have never understood this question. It is a question that could only be asked in our irrationally child-centered world. In another time, another place, children were only a part of a much bigger life; they were *never* our whole life. Nothing should be our whole life! Nowhere is it written that the purpose of having children is to be with them *all* the time. It is to enjoy what children can bring into our lives and, more importantly, *it is to offer life to a new being.* The latter is perhaps the true purpose of it all . . . to offer life to a new being. But giving life to a new being doesn't mean we are meant to stifle our own lives. It means that *in the process of following our own dreams, we encourage our children to be independent beings who can follow their own dreams.* Isn't that what it's all about? I love this passage in *The Prophet* by Kahlil Gibran:

> Your children are not your children.
> They are the sons and daughters of Life's longing for itself.
> They come through you but not from you
> And though they are with you yet they belong not to you.[5]

No, they don't belong to us; nor do we belong to them. It isn't about bonding, attaching, and stifling. A separateness of each body, mind and soul is what we need to strive for in order to end the dysfunctional nature of so many families today. And, indeed, for many, there's no place like work to accomplish this very important goal for all concerned.

Endnotes

[1]Sapirstein, Milton R. Quoted in *Child: Quotations About the Delight, Wonder, and Mystery of Being a Child.* Edited by Helen Handley and Andra Samelson, Penguin Books, New York, 1988, p. 53.

[2]These statistics are taken from *The Second Shift: Working Parents and the Revolution at Home* by Arlie Hochschild and Anne Machung (Avon, New York, 1989). Cited in "The Improv Mom" by Susan Seliger in *Working Mother*, September 1997, pp. 34-40.

[3]Seliger also cites the work of Rosalind Barnett, senior scholar in residence at the Murray Research Center at Radcliffe college and co-author of *She Works/He Works* (HarperCollins). Barnett says about 55 percent of the housework is done by women which includes cleaning, paying bills, shopping, and cooking. Barnett also says that women put in 3.7 hours a day, while men put in 3 hours a day. However, she points out, men, on average, work longer hours than women -- 48.5 hours per week versus 42 hours for the women. So it evens out.

[4]McGoldrick, Monica. "Women Through the Family Life Cycle." In *Women in Families: A Framework for Family Therapy*. Edited by Monica McGoldrick, Carol M. Anderson, and Froma Walsh. W. W. Norton and Company, Inc., New York, 1989, p. 201.

[5]Gibran, Kahlil. *The Prophet*. p. 17. Published by Phone Media, Sydney, Australia. Fax No. '(61-2) 9948 6362. Distributed in the USA by Seven Hills Book Distributors, Cincinnati, (800) 545-2005. Fax: (513) 381-0753. Distributed in Australia by HarperCollins Publishers, Sydney. Cover and illustrations by Aubrey Beardsley. Originally published in 1923.

PART III

SHOULD WE . . .
SHOULDN'T WE . . .
WHY DID WE?

10

SO WHY DO WE DO IT?

We longed for the patter of little feet, so we got a dog. It was cheaper than a baby and it had more feet.
Rita Rudner

One would think that the answer to the question, "Why do we have children?" would be very simple: "We adore children and are willing to sacrifice whatever it takes to raise one or two or more." When I asked many people this question in the writing of this book, this was rarely the response I got. I thought you would enjoy my sharing some of the responses I actually did get. They point out how unprepared many of us actually are to raise our children and show how ill-conceived (pardon the pun) their reasons for having children are. If you already have children, you will probably recognize yourself in one or more of the following answers. Before you start yelling at me, I must point out that this doesn't mean that, despite our ill-considered reasons to have children, we ultimately won't adore the whole process, but these answers certainly do give us something to think (and laugh) about. If you don't have any children, you will definitely learn from what you read!

WHY DO PEOPLE HAVE CHILDREN?

Irresponsible sex

"It was an accident." Whoops! This item speaks for itself. Not a promising beginning for a new life. Often the least able are given the huge responsibility that raising a child entails. Irwin Matus suggests that:

> Rather than a blessing, it is more sensible to attribute this irony to a god with a rather wicked sense of humor.[1]

For some, abortion is a solution; for others, it is a no-no. And for the latter, it is the beginning of a journey many would have been better off not traveling. While an unexpected pregnancy can be a delightful gift to some, it can be a disaster for others . . . and to the children they bring into this world.

Pressure by parents to make them grandparents

I think that parents want to be grandparents for one or both of the following reasons:

- Having a grandchild is parenting in a way that many would have preferred right from the beginning: in very short spurts, whenever they were in the mood, with the option of giving the children back, especially when they were behaving like brats.
- *A little touch of vengeance, perhaps?* Thinking back, it was only when my mother was terribly angry at me that she would storm out of my room saying, "I hope you grow up and have children just like yourself!" When my children were behaving at their absolute worst, I would think, *"Well, Mom, you got your wish!"* Indeed, many parents want their children to become parents themselves so they can understand how difficult the process is . . . and at last to appreciate all the love and effort put into raising them.

In any case, pleasing your parents is not a great reason to have a child. It might be too painful if they inform you they never want to baby-sit!

Pressure from society

Oh, the need to conform! Not wanting a child is still seen as an oddity and certainly we don't want to be seen as odd. A person not wanting a child is looked upon as strange, selfish, and/or lacking in something spiritually and morally correct. Not wanting a child goes against the grain of something sacrosanct.

We need to be strong. We need to take a stand. We need to think for ourselves. It doesn't serve us well to become embroiled in irrational pressure from society. We need to be sure that if we decide to have a child, it is a wise choice on our part; and we need to be sure that if we decide not to have a child, it is a wise choice on our part.

Wise choices come from looking carefully within ourselves, not from the mandates and expectations of society.

It is also very important to notice that society is generally negligent in supporting the needs of parents. It provides too few child-care centers and other amenities to help parents along the rocky road of raising their children. Why be pressured by a system that talks about family values and acts like Oliver Twist?

All our friends are having kids

Everyone wants to join the crowd. But having a child just to join the crowd is foolish. There are other choices. First you can make new friends—which you might want to do anyway since new parents can become very boring, indeed, because of their need to focus on the world of children. Or you can help your friends out—they need all the help they can get. The more you baby-sit, the better able you will be to determine whether you are cut out for parenthood or not, and if so, when.

To manipulate a man into marriage
Yes, some women actually get pregnant in order to snag their men. Whoops, again! Talk about biting off your nose to spite your face! Why would you strap yourself with a lifelong commitment to a child in order to snag a man who probably will never truly be yours—not if he didn't want to be yours to begin with. And we know what kids can do to a relationship. Not good. So using pregnancy to snag a man definitely is not a well-thought-out course of action.

To make a marriage complete
Given all of the trade-ins we are required to make when a child is born, "completion" is hardly the right word; "depletion" is more like it. As I explained earlier, children can take away so much of what already completes the package. For those with the Loving-Being-A-Parent (LBP) genes, the "new addition" can certainly make up for the losses. But for those without those LBP genes, the losses are staggeringly dramatic. Some of the happiest families I know consist simply of two people who love each other enormously and want to spend the rest of their lives together.

To heal a relationship
The *last* thing you want to do to heal a troubled relationship is to have a child. Save your time and energy and phone your divorce attorneys immediately. This marriage is doomed. Again, common sense tells us that a marriage has to be incredibly strong to withstand the assault that accompanies the birth of a child. What is needed to heal a relationship is a focus on loving each other, not a focus on caring for a helpless being who keeps you from focusing on loving each other.

To prove I can be the parent my parents weren't
I don't really understand this kind of reasoning, but I've heard it from a few people. Certainly it is not advisable to "use" a child to prove something festering within ourselves from a long, long time ago. In any case, it probably won't work. Those who have tried to be the

parents their parents weren't have been sadly disappointed—mostly in themselves. James Kunen, a product of the Sixties tells us:

> We knew that when we became parents, with our '60s spontaneity and spirituality intact, our kids would want to be just like us . . . Our children turned out like us after all. But we are not who we thought we'd be.[2]

And, in the end, it's just possible that our parents weren't who we thought they were either.

To create something to be proud of
I often look at teenage boys and girls with orange hair, baggy pants, earrings winding up their earlobes and in their belly-buttons and an obvious attitude of disdain to all adults that inhabit the planet. I say to myself, *"Boy, I bet their parents are really proud of them!"* One woman said of her less-than-something-to-be-proud-of-kind-of daughter, *"Who is this child? I can't believe she came from my loins."* I know many parents who are incredibly proud of their children, and with good reason, but *there aren't any guarantees.* In any case, if you want something to be proud of (and something that would cost a lot less money), buy a new car. At least a car comes with a guarantee.

It is a way of assuring immortality
It's not a good idea to think of children as a continuation of who we are. We may give birth to children, but they are their own people. When we think of children as our legacy, so many of our needs and expectations get in the way and we set ourselves up for a great deal of disappointment. For immortality, I think I'd rather leave a building. There are no guarantees how children will turn out; but how a building will turn out is pretty much under our control. Children are too chancy.

We've bought into the hype that parenting is the height of fulfillment
With parents, friends, and society telling us how great parenting is, how can we resist? In truth, it *is* the height of fulfillment for those

with the LBP genes; but for the rest of us it is hard, hard, hard. We need to look inward to find what gives us true fulfillment and not buy into the hype.

Religion tells us it is our God-given responsibility
Religion tells us to be fruitful and multiply. Considering the population crisis in today's world, I wonder if God was referring to fruits and vegetables instead of children. Perhaps our religious leaders have misinterpreted the message. In any case, in today's world of environmental depletion caused largely by over-population, I don't think adding to the problem is a good idea. Helping the children that already exist is probably more in line with what God had in mind.

We don't want to miss the experience
One man told me he was happy he had children because he would have always wondered what he missed if he didn't have them. It never occurred to him to wonder what he missed *because he did have them!* In the end, either way, we miss an experience; either way, we gain an experience. They are just different experiences.

To have someone take care of us when we are old
Oh, it happens sometimes, but I wouldn't count on it. Research tells us that children can be very poor caretakers where parents are concerned. Older folks living with their children aren't usually happy and when in nursing homes, children don't visit enough. People who have frequent contact with the elderly will tell you that those who have never relied on children to take care of them fare best of all. They are better at reaching out to establish good friendships. On a more dire note, I found a recent statistic telling us that, in the US, there are well over a million reported cases annually of abuse of elderly parents.[3] Even if our children are, thankfully, not the abusing kind, I don't think it is wise to depend on them to take care of us when we are old. One woman laughed when she said:

> I would hate to rely on my kids when I get old. If we were all in a life-boat together, they'd want me to row!

For you beautiful children out there who have knocked yourself out for your parents, God Bless You!

A desire to have someone love us unconditionally

I recently heard a Hollywood star comment that the joy he gets from his young ones comes from the unconditional love they give him. He really doesn't understand. As I discussed earlier, children are needy. It is impossible for needy people to love unconditionally; their needs get in the way. Oh, yes, their hugs and kisses and wonderful smiles of welcome when we come through the door are delicious and definitely look like unconditional love. But how does he explain the times they treat him horribly? The terrible twos and tantrum threes, for example? If this is what unconditional love looks like, I can do without it! One woman lamented:

> If I were married to someone who treated me the way my children treated me at various times throughout their lives, I certainly would have gotten a divorce. In fact, the man I divorced treated me much better than my kids!

I doubt that unconditional love exists anywhere, but if it does, I wouldn't depend on it coming from our children. To me, love is a give and take. Children are great at taking; they balk at giving. Again, to establish a more stable and dependable kind of love, we are better off developing a strong circle of friends and a glorious relationship with our mate (if we have one)—all of whom are more likely to be there for us when we need them.

A cop-out for having to face the big bad world out there

Some full-time moms confess that staying at home with their children offered a welcome excuse for not testing themselves in the big wide world of work. One woman said:

> I was a parent because I didn't know what else to be. I had a fear of growing up. Of becoming my own person. I've loved being a parent, but I know I've also hidden behind that veil of parenthood. It's a safe role even though it is a difficult role.

She realizes how dependent she is on her husband's income and it frightens her. But, now that the children are grown, she is still too fearful to "grow up" and test herself in the world out there. But she's working on it.

A way to stop working for those who don't like to work
One woman told me:

> I didn't like working. A baby gave me an excuse to quit my job and stay home.

I asked, *"Why didn't you just stay home?"* Her answer was that she would have felt too guilty having her husband work while she was doing nothing. Guess what happened. It didn't take her long to learn that parenting was much more difficult than working. And back to work she went. Now she feels guilty leaving her children to go to work. But, she feels that for the sake of her sanity, there is no other choice.

It gives one an identity
Monica McGoldrick tells us that "identity" in psychological history is defined as "having a sense of self apart from one's family."[4] Having children doesn't give us an identity—an identity crisis perhaps, but not an identity. One parent of two teenage children said, *"I know the children will soon be out of the house, and who am I then?"* Identity doesn't come from anything external; it comes from us looking within and discovering and honoring the depth and breadth of who we are as human beings.

To carry on the family name
Unless one is royalty, and even then, what is the big deal about the family name? And if you have only girls, are you going to convince

them never to change their names when they get married? Good luck! I have a made-up name. I made it up after I divorced my first husband. A new name for a new life. It's not my father's name, nor my ex-husband's name—it's *my* name. I like that arrangement. And when I married my present husband, he certainly didn't expect me to give up the name I gave myself. Or how about this? When a man and woman wed, they should pick a totally new name that both of them love—*their* name. Hyphenated names are too comical and cumbersome and since usually only the women hyphenate their names, it is also sexist. I definitely think we should think about letting this idea of our children carrying on the family name go down in history as a silly idea.

A primal instinct

One father said:

> Having children has to be blamed on a biological urge as it is totally irrational to willingly bring someone into your life who alters it in such a tremendous way. No person in their right mind would take on such a responsibility. Running a country is easier than raising a kid.

On the surface, what he says makes sense, but as I said in an earlier chapter, a primal instinct to have children doesn't seem to exist . . . or at least is overridden by society's fashion of the day. I believe that if more people really understood what they were getting into, the idea of primal instinct would go down the drain.

To find oneself

One woman stated that her kids were her life. What a limited life and what a burden to place on a kid! In order to be "found," we must understand that we are more than our kids, and for that matter, we are more than our jobs, our relationships, our friends, and all the other pieces that make up our life. The only way we can truly find ourselves is to realize that we are meaningful beings who have much to contribute to this world in a multitude of ways. And what a magnificent "finding" that is!

To make one feel whole
Similarly, if you need a child to make you feel whole, this implies you now feel incomplete. Trust me when I tell you that a person who feels incomplete handles children a lot less effectively than one who feels complete. The former has a tendency to hang on for dear life; the latter encourages a child to blossom and grow into a healthy, independent human being. A whole person doesn't "need" to have a child; he or she may "choose" to have a child. A world of difference. To be sure, it is better to attain a feeling of wholeness *before* a child is born.

To be needed
It would be wonderful if everyone in the world understood that they don't need children to be needed. *The world needs all of us in many, many ways.* For example, it needs us to help the homeless, our elders, the environment, and a multitude of other neglected areas in our midst. Once we realize that we are needed *everywhere,* we may choose to have a child because we adore caring for children, but not because we need a child to feel needed.

The biological clock is ticking
This thinking goes, *"I better have a child now before it's too late."* It's possible that if you have one now, *just because the biological clock is ticking,* it certainly will be too late—too late to change your mind! If you are lucky enough to be someone with the LBP genes, you will have made a wise decision. If you don't have those essential genes for enjoying parenthood, you certainly would have been better off waiting until it was too late!

To expand the mind
Having a child can expand the mind in many wonderful directions. It can also expand the mind in directions you would prefer not to

have it expanded! And it can also contract the mind. Certainly parenting narrows our options considerably as you learned earlier in the book. In fact, for many it is the end of seeking and exploring. Yes, children can expand our minds, but so can college, travel, politics, career, friends, books, computers, and all the other rich potentials for adventures that this world provides. There are many things that can expand our minds and it is a wise person who chooses those avenues that are most fulfilling and enjoyable for who he or she is as a human being. This choice may include children; it may not.

It's the thing you do

When I had my children, people didn't *decide* to have children; it was an automatic . . . the thing you did. "Should we have children?" was a question never asked. Hopefully, this mentality is now changing and people are realizing that we do have a choice. It's not "a thing you do," it is a thing you *choose* to do . . . or not do. And the world will be a lot happier and healthier when more people realize that not having children can be for some as happy and healthy an option as having children is for others.

Unrealistic expectations

This quote says it all:

> Of course I wanted to be a mother one day, but I would be so different from any mother because *I was a booming meteor of a woman with a life, for god's sake!*

Five months after the birth of her child:

> My God! What is this? I've been sitting on this couch for five months. I smell bad, I can't fit into my jeans, and I haven't showered for days. It's too much of a hassle to leave the house with her because all she wants to do is poop, pee, and eat, and every time I do leave I feel

> compelled to spend money that I don't have because I'm not working! Aaaakk! What the hell is going on here?[5]

Need I add more?

To overcome loneliness
To overcome loneliness, one needs to learn how to be happily alone, and at the same time have a wonderful group of friends and colleagues with whom to share our lives. Children are not remedies for loneliness. They are not great companions until they are older . . . and sometimes not even then. Stay-at-home moms are often the loneliest people of all. A return to work often signifies the end of loneliness.

Because my spouse wanted to
Knowing what I now know, it is hard to imagine having a child to please my spouse. I have seen the results of such a sacrifice and what I have seen isn't pretty. If a decision to have a child isn't mutual, resentment rules. Certainly, the decision to have a child is something that has to be agreed upon before one says, "I do." Of course, there are those who are pleased with their decision to please their spouse; others, however, rue the day they didn't say no.

To have "our" baby
It seems so romantic, doesn't it? "Our baby." Some feel that the creation of a child is living proof of the love a couple shares. This is definitely a myth that could backfire. As you have already learned, a child too often causes us to express anything but love for our spouse. To me living proof of the love a couple shares is demonstrated, not by the creation of a baby, but by the way they treat each other. Living proof lies in the caring, sharing, thanking, and appreciating that we give our mates—whether we have children or not. There are many people who have "our baby," and then behave very badly toward each other.

I want it all

I treasure a remark a dear professor once told me . . .

> You can have anything you want in life; but you can't have everything you want.

One choice precludes another and it is the measure of a wise person to create a beautiful life based on any decisions he or she makes . . . whether those decisions include children or not. To me, being happy with our choices *is* having it all.

A deep love and respect for life

This reason is on the right track emotionally, but, in today's world, doesn't the choice of *not* having a child also demonstrate a deep love and respect for life? As we are becoming painfully aware, the growing population is making it harder and harder for "life" to exist on this planet. There are many other ways to show a deep love and respect for life. Adopt. Be a mentor. Feed. Clothe. There is so much to do with the "life" already here that it staggers the imagination.

You have searched your soul and have decided you are ready to commit to parenthood

Unfortunately, until you are a parent, there is no way to be sure you will love the process of parenting; that is, there is no way of knowing if you have the LBP genes. But if the majority of the following statements are true for you, then you have a better chance than most to enjoy the state of parenthood:

- Even though your life is now good, you are ready to trade your present life for a different one.
- You have spent a great deal of time with babies and have decided you absolutely love spending time with and taking care of them.
- You've already experienced many things in life you always wanted to experience, such as education, travel, and work.

- You have become a responsible adult, that is, you are ready to become the "giver."
- You are financially responsible.
- You can afford some type of help with the baby or have a relative or other support system to help you out.
- You are okay with putting certain aspects of your relationship and other areas of your life on the back burner until the child grows up.
- You understand that the parenting process may be very difficult.
- You understand that your child may turn out nothing like you ever expected or wanted. You know you are raising your child "for better or for worse."
- You have a great deal of patience.
- If need be, you are ready to take 100 percent responsibility for your child, including financial responsibility. This is important. Divorce, death, and disappearance are always a possibility when it comes to our mates. "You and me and baby makes three" could become "me and baby makes two." And we always need to be ready, willing, and able to do it all on our own.

How would you rate yourself as a potential parent given this criteria? Of course, until you actually have a child, you can't be sure. But, by definition, the greater "fit" you have with those qualities that make parenthood rewarding, the more likely it is that you will enjoy the process.

I know I've missed a few, but this is a pretty extensive and representative list of reasons why people have children. Judge for yourself. It would seem that the last two I cited are truly valid reasons. The others appear to be ill-informed and irrational. However, and this is important to understand:

It is totally possible to have children for all the "wrong" reasons and still have a great time raising them. And it is totally possible to have children for all the "right" reasons and not enjoy parenthood at all.

I've known those who had children for all the "wrong" reasons and who were not, on the face of it, equipped to bring them up in a healthy way. Yet they succeeded beyond all odds and found loving parts of themselves they never knew existed. And I've known those who've had children for all the "right" reasons and for whom child-rearing turned out to be a very unsatisfactory experience for all concerned. I think it is safe to say that only one thing is guaranteed, and that is . . . it's all so chancy!

Before ending this chapter, I'd like to explore one question that has always baffled me:

Why do people have more than one child?

A very good question, especially when so many people admit to finding the parenting experience so difficult! One perfectly valid reason is that there are those who absolutely love the experience of parenting and want as many kids around as they can have. Here are some other, not-so-good reasons:

One woman said her first child was a girl and she wanted to have a boy. As fate would have it, she had another girl . . . and another . . . and another. Finally a friend said to her, "Why don't you just accept the fact that there are no boys up there for you," and she finally stopped trying.

One woman kept having children because she loved babies so much. She didn't consider the fact that babies grow up. If parents waited until the children were teenagers before giving them a sibling, I bet we would have a lot of only children around! The teen years make some previously devoted and adoring parents sorry they ever had kids to begin with.

One couple said they had more than one because of their fear of something happening to their first. As if one child can replace another!

One couple had more than one because their first was delicious. Unfortunately, the second didn't taste so good. Ironically, another couple had more than one because their first was so horrible. They figured they missed something and the second had to be better. Maybe yes, maybe no! Chancy!

One woman had four children. She said she left her first child with her first husband because she felt she couldn't handle him. Later she had three more to prove she really could be a good mother. She has, indeed, proven that to herself, but she said:

> It was important for me to feel okay about myself. I know if I had felt better about myself to begin with, I wouldn't have made the decision to have more.

Thankfully for her children, she has enjoyed raising them and, from all observations, is a caring mother. I was surprised and dismayed at how many women felt they needed children to feel okay about themselves.

One woman said the following about having more than one child:

> I figured I messed up the rest of my life with the first. What's the difference if there's two? Of course, I didn't realize how much more difficult two was than one!

Another who had a child very quickly after the first said:

> I thought I would have them close together to get the bad stuff over quickly. I didn't know the bad stuff never ends! And now I've compounded the problem.

And the list of reasons goes on.

I know that when my children were born, all of us "good parents" felt we *must* provide siblings for our children. It wasn't a question of *should I?;* it was a question of *When should I?* Many people still feel that way today. It has become part of the collective unconscious to believe that children must have siblings or they will turn out to be selfish, spoiled, lonely, horrible, at a terrible disadvantage, or all of the above—another destructive myth we have bought into. Let me set the record straight.

Single children are not necessarily at a disadvantage at all!

In fact, recent studies suggest that only children are equal in most traits and *often at an advantage* in other traits! Here is what these recent studies say:

Only children are equal in maturity, citizenship, flexibility, self-control, generosity, leadership and contentment. They are ahead in self-esteem and motivation to achieve, educational achievement and cognitive test scores.[6] They suffer no apparent social problems and are more likely to enjoy solitary activities such as reading and painting.[7] They have a more positive outlook because they don't have meddling brothers or sisters to fend off all the time. They are more likely to build positive relationships with their families than are children with siblings.[8] They do better in educational aspects because they receive more personal attention and more resources than children from larger families. They also become more "socially sophisticated" at reaching out to others and they are more likely to gain a greater sense of independence.[9] The only down side was that those with siblings develop thicker skins from frequent teasing and squabbling.[10] (Have you ever been around siblings who are always teasing and squabbling? Who needs that?)

At this point, I can hear the cry of, *"Now you tell me!"* from unhappy parents out there who bought into the "children need a sibling" myth. One wonders why this information hasn't been shouted from the rooftops! Why are we led to believe we must have more than one? Of course just a single trip to Disneyland watching families with multiple children should give us all the clues we could ever need. But when one is so immersed in mythology, one is blind to the obvious.

Juggling all of the tasks for one child is difficult; for more than one it can be tortuous. Elaine St. James tells it like it is:

> You've just arrived home after a grueling afternoon at work. You retrieved your two-year-old from the baby sitter and your seven-year-old from her dance class, but it completely slipped your mind that you were supposed to pick up your ten-year-old after his softball game. How could you forget your son's game? When the phone rings, you run to answer it, hoping it's Tommy saying he's got a ride home. No such luck—it's the fifth-grade teacher: Tommy hasn't been turning in his homework. You search frantically for a pencil to write down the missing assignments, but all you can find is a broken crayon. Call-waiting beeps; you put the teacher on hold to find out the carpool for tomorrow has fallen through. As you get back to the teacher, your toddler begins to whine. He's hungry, but you can't even think about cooking before you clean up the breakfast mess everyone left. Your seven-year-old picks this moment to show you the routine she learned today, and asks if you like it. No, do you really, really like it, or are you just saying that? When your husband walks in, you skip the greeting and simply bark at him to pick Tommy up from softball.[11]

Joni Hilton gives us a similar story. She calls those with more than one child "the new homeless" for obvious reasons—they are never home.

> You drive the kids to school, run errands, take the baby to Mommy and Me class, stop by the library, post office and dry cleaners, pick up one child, take him to violin, pick up the other, take him to scouts, go back and get the first child, take him to a birthday party, get the scouts boy and take him to soccer, pick up the birthday child, take him . . .[12]

Maureen Green tells us:

> After the second child, married life becomes family life with a vengeance. "The second child can be the point where a woman feels she has disappeared from view," says one

> counsellor. "The overwork, the running of two children's schedules, being at the beck and call of two babies, is self-annihilating."[13]

If the above is not enough, consider the fact that while some siblings adore one another, as I adore my sister, some siblings can't stand one another. Again, chancy. One woman told me she hasn't spoken to her brother in six years. She thinks he is a horrible person . . . and always has been. Certainly she isn't alone for her dislike of her sibling. Paraphrasing a woman who wrote to an Agony Aunt:

> I know my son loves his brother but you wouldn't know it in terms of how badly he treats him. He calls him horrible names and even tells him he hates him. I feel so badly for the little one. He must think his brother really does hate him.

I hope I can break it gently to this naïve woman, *at some level, his brother does hate him!* This may change as the years go by, but for this moment in time, love is not what big brother feels.

Siblings can even be dangerous to one another. I remember my father telling me about the day his mother walked in their front gate and saw my father dangling a sheet filled with a heavy object from the second-story window. She said, "Leon, what have you got in the sheet?" He replied, "Sam." (Sam, of course, being his brother!) I can only imagine the racing of my grandmother's heart contrasted with the gentle, slow words she used to entice my father to carefully pull the bundle containing his brother back into the house.

Of course, some only children complain that they didn't have brothers or sisters for company or to dangle out of second-story windows. Obviously they haven't been exposed to the teasing and the squabbles and the divided attention of their parents. It's the old "grass is greener on the other side" syndrome. But they certainly are better off in many ways.

I hope I have convinced you to think twice before having a second child simply for the sake of providing a sibling for your first child. If you totally adore the process of parenting and love having children around, that's another story, but *you are now relieved of the burden of having to have a second child just for the sake of the first.* Hallelujah!

Now that you know some of the reasons why men and women choose to include children in their lives, let me introduce you to some courageous souls among us who have decided to say no to parenting. You will discover why they have made this often criticized decision . . . as if, by now, you didn't already know!

Endnotes

[1]Matus, Irwin. *Wrestling with Parenthood: Contemporary Dilemmas.* Gylantic Publishing, Littleton, Colorado, 1995, p. 13.

[2]Kunen, James S. "It Ain't Us Babe," in *Time,* September 1, 1997, p. 66.

[3]As reported in an editorial in the *Atlantic Inquirer* (V. 36, N. 14, p. 4, 1996) entitled "Parent Abuse."

[4]McGoldrick, Monica. "Women Through the Family Life Cycle," in *Women in Families: A Framework for Family Therapy.* Edited by Monica McGoldrick, Carol M. Anderson, and Froma Walsh. W. W, Norton and Company, Inc., 1989, p. 203.

[5]Wagner, Laurie. *Expectations: Thirty Women Talk About Becoming a Mother.* Chronicle Books, San Francisco, 1998, pp. 12-13.

[6]Psychologist Toni Falbo, a professor at the University of Texas at Austin, reviewed 141 studies comparing only children to those with siblings. Found in "Only Children: Well Enough Alone," by Martin Lasden, in *Hippocrates,* March/April, 1988, pp. 30-32.

[7]John Claudy of the American Institute for Research in Palo Alto, California compiled personality profiles of 4,000 high-school students and then followed the students for 11 years. He expected the only children to develop at least a few more psychological problems than their peers. Instead, the only children did no worse when measured against any standard of competence and actually fared slightly better in educational achievement and cognitive test scores. They also tended to marry slightly more educated spouses. But Claudy emphasizes, "It was the group's similarities, not their differences, that were most striking." Found in "Only Children: Well Enough Alone," by Martin Lasden, in *Hippocrates,* March/April, 1988, pp. 30-32.

[8]Reported by Helen Cleminshaw, an only child who became a professor of child and family development at the University of Akron. Found in "Only Children: Well Enough Alone," by Martin Lasden, in *Hippocrates,* March/April, 1988, pp. 30-32.

[9]Brophy, Beth. "It Doesn't Hurt to Be Alone: Debunking the Myths About Only Children." *U.S. News and World Report,* March 6, 1989, p. 54.

[10]Psychologist Gloria Kamenske of the National Institute of Child Health and Human Development in Bethesda, Maryland, cites studies she has funded and

concludes that in not a single study have "onlies" been shown to have any disadvantage. Found in "Only Children: Well Enough Alone," by Martin Lasden, in *Hippocrates*, March/April, 1988, pp. 30-32.

[11]St. James, Elaine. "How to Simplify Family Life," in *Ladies' Home Journal*, September 1997, p.98.

[12]Hilton, Joni. *Guilt-Free Motherhood: How to Raise Great Kids and Have Fun Doing It*. Covenant Communications, Inc., American Fork, Utah, 1996, p. 90.

[13]Green, Maureen. *Marriage*. Fontana Paperbacks, Great Britain, 1984, p. 147.

11

SO WHY *DON'T* WE DO IT?

Children should be seen and not had!

Joey Adams

More and more couples are agreeing with Joey Adams! They have looked into the mirror and asked, "Mirror, mirror on the wall, is parenthood really for me?" And the answer that has come back to them has been, "No way!" Those who fit into this category seem to have risen above the "horseradish" of our conditioning and have seen that, for them, a rich, satisfying, and wonderful life did not have to include children; in fact, they have determined that their lives would be better off without them. Bravo for their courage at a time when it is politically incorrect to choose a childfree life!

Just as there are many reasons people decide to have children, there are many reasons people decide *not* to have children. Here are a few:

- Some know instinctively that they are not endowed with those all-important LBP genes.
- Some have decided that their preferred lifestyles were not compatible with children.

- Some have decided that experiences other than raising a child are more important in their lives: their career, their relationship, their personal time, their freedom, their privacy, travel, and so on.
- Some looked around at the lives of their friends who had children and didn't like what they saw.
- Some decided they didn't want the responsibility and worry and expense that comes with the territory of raising a child.
- Some said they really didn't like kids very much and had no desire to have one in their lives.
- Some said they really do love kids, but wouldn't want to have one full-time. They love playing aunt or uncle, but they wouldn't want to be mother or father.
- Some felt that because they were so involved in a career which they adored, a child wouldn't receive the attention it deserved.
- Some had an independent streak and didn't want to fulfill themselves through someone else, but through their own achievements, experiences, and day-to-day adventures of life.
- Some realize they are not interested in the things that interest children and feel they would be cheating themselves out of a beautiful life . . . and their children out of an interested parent.
- Some feel this is a lousy world into which to bring a child.
- Some are really concerned about overpopulation and what it does to the environment . . . and have decided to do their part in not making it any worse.

For all of the above reasons and others I haven't mentioned, those who say No to children, have decided that the losses incurred in having a child outweigh the benefits. Childfree living for them is the better way to go. The question arises:

Can couples be happy without children?

Of course. In some cases, more so. I have read a number of research reports about childfree women (those who are childfree out of choice) and these studies have concluded that they are not sad and unfulfilled as the myth of society would have us believe; in fact, they are happy, energetic, and very satisfied with their lives. Knowing what you already know about children and the changes in lifestyle they represent, all of this shouldn't come as any surprise. All of the childfree men and women I spoke to (those who are childfree out of choice) have never regretted their decision and feel they are at a distinct advantage in many ways to those who have children.

Again, I can hear the shouts from parents who had children because they thought parent-people were happier than childfree people, *"Now you tell me!"* Again, why hasn't this information been shouted from the rooftops? We can now see how the conspiracy of silence keeps so many truths about parenting from our ears. Because of this conspiracy, the critical mass has not been reached in our society for it to be "normal" for a man and woman to say "NO" to parenting. Obviously, collective beliefs are hard to change. As a result, it takes great strength for an individual to say, "No, I don't want that."

I love the courage of Denise Castañon who wrote an essay in the *Los Angeles Times*, entitled "I Don't Want Kids, Period."[1] At the time of her writing the essay, she was a 21-year-old student at the University of Southern California majoring in journalism and political science. She said that people were incredulous when she stated that she did not want children. "Oh, you don't mean it!" was a common reply. She says she does really mean it. She doesn't like kids very much. She never saw them as a part of her life. She won't marry a man who wants them. She said, "People call me selfish wanting to have life on my terms." I ask you, on whose terms should we want our life to be about?

Think about this: couples who don't want children are sometimes labeled "selfish." Does this make any sense to you in a world of over-population? In fact, one could argue that in today's world it is selfish and irresponsible to have children! Jane Bartlett states:

> "The fuse of the population bomb has already been ignited and the consequences of the explosion for the future of the world will be a great deal more devastating than any nuclear holocaust," warns Prince Philip, who is president of the Worldwide Fund for Nature International. The statistics are frightening: the world population has reached 5.5 billion and is set to double by the year 2050.[2]

This is no longer a time to be fruitful and multiply when it comes to people. It is a time to be fruitful in other ways and repair the damage we have already done to this planet.

Also, why is it so terrible to be selfish when it comes to deciding how we want to live our lives? How else should we be? One brave woman told me she gave up a wonderful man simply because he had custody of his young kids. She said,

> As we did things together with the kids, I realized that being a mother was not for me. I don't want to play lifeguard at the beach, or make their meals, or pick up after them and on and on and on. It's just not me! I know now that I have to find a man who doesn't have or want children. I feel very strongly about that.

Here is one case where selfishness, if that's what you want to call it, is a blessing to all concerned.

One childfree couple told me that the intrusion of other people's opinions was something they were always encountering. But not wanting the intrusion of a child in their life was stronger than the intrusion of other people's opinions. Unfortunately, many couples succumb to the pressure to produce when they really don't want to have a child. Our films, our religions, our parents, our friends . . .

all are against our saying NO to kids. They haven't yet learned that children aren't for everyone.

To counteract the intense pressure put upon childfree individuals, a number of organizations have been created to give support to the beleaguered who don't want to have kids. Here are two examples:

- The British Organization of Non-Parents (BON).[3] Their stated goals are to 1) eliminate the cultural and media bias against non-parents; 2) challenge the social tendency to glorify and romanticize parenthood; 3) call for responsible parenthood by dispelling myths and emphasizing the realities involved in child-raising and 4) provide social contacts and activities for its members. They state that there is nothing wrong in honestly stating that having children is not your ideal way of life. There is, however, something very wrong in having a child you don't really want.
- The ChildFree Network. This is also a support and educational group for those who don't want to have babies. It was organized by Leslie Lafayette, author of *Why Don't You Have Kids?: Living a Full Life Without Parenthood.*[4] She talks about how important it was to her (and to me) to use the term "childfree" rather than "childless" since the latter emphasizes a lack. (Great distinction!) She feels those who choose not to or who can't have children should not feel "less" anything. They can make wonderful, full lives for themselves.[5] The ChildFree Network lobbies for the rights of non-parents in areas such as taxation, the workplace, and other areas where the childfree feel discriminated against. The Network also wants a more realistic picture of parenthood with all its demands and responsibilities to be portrayed by the media, schools, and parents.[6]

It appears that organizations like this are greatly needed to bolster the resolve of men and women to stick to their guns when they know parenting is not for them. Thankfully, more and more are listening to their hearts instead of the pressure being put upon them by parents and friends, and deciding to say, "No, I don't want to bring any children into this world. I don't want the responsibility of caring for children. I want to do other things with my life." Their clarity is refreshing. And their numbers are rising. Precise statistics are difficult to find, but, as I said earlier, I have seen estimates that from 16 to 25 percent of couples are deciding not to have children.

To break society's negativity toward non-parents, Irwin Matus suggests that perhaps they should be honored:

> Individuals who understand and accept their shortcomings for parenthood are to be congratulated for choosing not to have children. Indeed, why not accord them honor? To Mother's Day in May and Father's Day in June add Non-parent's Day in July. Why not a Non-parent of the Year Award?[7]

I like this idea! For many people, saying NO to having a child is a very positive decision. For the world's over-population problem, saying *no* to having a child is also a very positive decision.

Before I end this chapter, let me say a word about those who want children and cannot have them. You will notice that some react to this news with an understandable disappointment, a passing sadness, but they know they can go on and create a beautiful life for themselves—children or no children. And they do. A very healthy response to an unfulfilled expectation. Some adopt and some decide to enjoy their life without children.

This is not the case for many others, who experience desperation and a wide variety of other negative emotions. Some seek treatment for their infertility and, for many, this is very difficult and demoralizing. Matthew Mervyn Jones tells of one study which reported that the trauma of seeking treatment to have a baby left one in five men and women feeling suicidal. And more than 90 percent in another study experienced frustration, depression, and isolation. Couples reported feeling "empty, unwhole, angry, fearful, bitter, and lonely."[8] My heart goes out to them. The pain they feel is enormous.

Why the desperation? The reasons are varied and often have to do with a deep inner need. Some have an expectation that a child will somehow fill their painful sense of emptiness, loneliness, and lack of purpose. Of course, if they were to have a child, the chances are they would be greatly disappointed. It is rare that the birth of a child can fill these deep inner needs.

I had a friend many, many years ago who desperately wanted a child. Each month when her period began, she went into a deeply depressed state. Finally she became pregnant and was ecstatic. She had a wonderful son and soon became pregnant with another. Two small sons, a wonderful husband, plenty of money—and she became an alcoholic. Obviously, children were not the answer. I remember her husband sobbing as he asked me what he should do. (Thankfully, they had responsible caregivers minding the children at all times.) At the time, I had no answer. Ultimately, he divorced her and I lost track of them. I hope that one day she did find herself.

If we hold great expectations within our being that a child will fill all the empty spaces, the disappointment can't help but be enormous when, after the child is born, the emptiness and other painful emotions still remain.

Another reason some women are desperate to have a child is because they feel their value as a woman depends on their ability to procreate. Our society perpetuates the stigma attached to the "barren" woman. I find this insulting and we must be careful not to buy into it. We must all understand that, whether we have children or not, within each and every one of us are riches beyond our wildest dreams. It's just a matter of accessing all those riches . . . and then radiating them out to the world around us. This, as I see it, is a health-filled prescription for a beautiful life.

Thankfully, there are many resources in today's world for those who are stuck in their desperation to have children. In addition to professional help, there is an endless supply of books, tapes, and workshops geared to helping us find the strength, beauty, and wholeness within. I suggest that if you are someone who can't find a way out of your desperation, that you jump into these resources with vigor until you find the pathway to the best of who you are. The truth is that you are a beautiful person who has much to give to this world. Once you become aware of this reality, your desperation to have a child will certainly be transformed into a loving desire to help this world in a multitude of ways.

Ultimately, it is clear to me that whether we have children or not, our lives can be rich and full and wonderful. If it is not about the raising of children, it is about improving the world in our own way. I have known very fulfilled, loving individuals who have decided to have children and I have known very fulfilled, loving individuals who have decided not to have children—or who never were able to have children. They have done wonderful things with their lives, and feel very complete in who they are as human beings. In the end, we must realize that:

If we choose to have children it's just one pathway; if we can't or choose not to have children, it's just another pathway. And we would be wise to create a beautiful life on whichever pathway we find ourselves traveling.

Endnotes

[1]Castañon, Denise. "I Don't Want Kids. Period," in the *Los Angeles Times*, May 3, 1997, p. B7.

[2]Bartlett, Jane. *Will You Be Mother?: Women Who Choose to Say No*. New York University Press, New York, 1994, p. 230. (Originally published in the U.K. by Virago, London, 1994.)

[3]The address of BON at the time of this writing is BM Box 5866, London, WC1N 3XX, England.

[4]Lafayette, Leslie. *Why Don't You Have Kids?: Living a Full Life Without Parenthood*. Kensington Books, New York, 1995.

[5]Ibid., pp. 192-194.

[6]You can contact Leslie Layfayette by e-mail at cnetwork@aol.com. Her Web site address is www.childfreenetwork.com.

[7]Matus, Irwin. *Wrestling with Parenthood: Contemporary Dilemmas*. Gylantic Publishing Company, Littleton, Colorado, 1995, p. 130.

[8]Jones, Mathew Mervyn. "Heartbreak of Couples Desperate to Have a Baby," in the *Express*, June 14, 1997, p. 13.

12

IF ONE COULD DO IT OVER AGAIN . . .

The planned and wanted children of the world often wind up unwanted after they've been around awhile.

Shirley Radl[1]

You learn a lot at the doctor's office. Seeing a picture of his children sitting on his desk, I asked my doctor if he enjoyed raising them. He clasped his hands in a gesture of thanks and said, "Oh, I'm so lucky. My kids are great." I said, "That's not what I asked you. I asked you if you enjoyed raising them." He rolled his eyes and reluctantly confessed he was happy he didn't have to spend too much time with them. His wife did all the work of raising them.

Undaunted, I pressed on and asked how his wife felt about that. He hesitated but then was honest enough to admit that it upset her that he was out in the world and she was stuck at home. He said that he encouraged her to go out to work if she wanted to, but she felt guilty and chose to stay home. (There's that destructive guilt again.) I then asked the big question: "If you had it to do all over again, knowing what you know today, would you have had children?" He was silent for a few seconds and finally he shook his head from left to right and with a very quiet voice he said, "No." I am certain my doctor had never admitted this to anyone before.

As I was paying my bill at a restaurant, a pregnant woman walked by and my waitress muttered, "Poor thing." I laughed. I said, "I suppose you have children." She told me she had two children, one nineteen and one fifteen. I asked her the same question I had asked my doctor, "If you had it to do over again, knowing what you know today, would you have had children?" Without a moment's hesitation she said loudly and definitively, "No way!"

I began asking this question to many parents I met along the way, of course with the promise of anonymity. And many revealed this same "secret" that very few people openly talk about . . . *that had they known what they were getting into beforehand, they would not have had children.* Some qualified their answers. They said, "Once you hold your child in your arms and care for them for a while, it's hard to imagine them not being in your life." I then ask, "But what if you could reverse the hands of time and your child has not as yet even been conceived?" Stated this way, many more answered, "No, I wouldn't have done it." I understand why many would want to deny this deep and dark reality: they don't want to hurt their kids; nor do they want to be attacked for being a heretic!

While there were many who would say no to doing it again, there were, of course, many who are thrilled they had children despite the problems in raising them. They consider parenting one of the most fulfilling parts of their lives, and they have no regrets. Some would have been very happy raising just one child, and found the pain of parenting only manifested itself after the second birth. Yet others said they actually would have had more, if they could have. It was only the lack of time and/or money that stopped them.

The interesting question is: what makes parenthood feel so good to some and not so good to others? Here are a few answers:

The "fit" between a parent and a child

Recently I saw a very telling segment on a television show. It was all about how to pick a puppy. Here is the message of the "puppy expert" in a nutshell:

> All puppies are adorable, but if you want to enjoy your puppy, you have to pick one that fits your personality. There has to be a good people/puppy match. Never pick a puppy on the basis of how it looks. Some adorable puppies don't always warm up to their owners and can be tough to handle. Many owners have such a hard time that they give their adorable puppy away within the first year. Personality is the whole story. A puppy is a living being you are bringing into your life and home. And the better the fit, the bigger the joy and delight.

I'm sure you see where I am going with this. What happens when there is no good parent/child fit? The same thing that happens when there is no good people/puppy fit. A difficult time is had by all. The big difference is that there is no giving our children away . . . we're stuck for life! As you can imagine or already know, it's very frustrating to raise a child who doesn't fit with who you are as a human being—even if you have the LBP genes: You love quiet, your child loves loud. You love physical, your child loves cerebral. You love affectionate; your child loves playing it cool. One mother of a two-year-old lamented:

> My baby has my husband's genetic endowment, which is tons of energy, very macho, and a tendency to anger, a baby warrior. I'm trying to keep a baby warrior at home in a playpen. And it's hard. I'm the museum type. I love reading books. And other quiet activities. I've taken him to museums but he couldn't care less. He's much more fascinated running up and down the corridors. He's bored with me and I'm bored with him.

One wonderful television show is built around the humor inherent in a situation where there is no fit between parent and child, and that show is *Frasier*. Frasier and his brother Niles have diametrically opposed interests and tastes relative to their father's, and their interactions lead to great comedy. In real life, a poor fit isn't quite so funny; it's often very difficult. And closeness is hard to achieve when our personality is so different from our child's.

While some parents and children seem to glide through their years together, others hit a bumpy road seemingly from the minute they lay eyes on each other. Unfortunately, no guarantee comes with the package. Which egg and sperm happen to get together is definitely out of our control! Chancy! Chancy! Chancy! Too often we don't get the kind of child we want to love or need to love. Children come in their own little package. They are not putty in our hands to mold as we wish. They are their own people. So we may be born to parent . . . but not born to parent the child we have been given!

The child's temperament

Some kids are wonderful to be around and bring their parents a great deal of joy . . . even if the parents are missing those LBP genes. These parents might decide they would probably do it again. But some kids are brats from the minute they are born and nothing ever really changes. I've interviewed a number of people who admitted that there is at least one of their brood that they would have gladly returned if they had the chance. I appreciated their honesty. One woman said:

> I have a son who was just horrible, horrible bad luck. I can't believe I produced such a child. I can't say I love him.

She truly loved raising her first child, but hated raising her second. Another woman said . . .

> My daughter is someone I have nothing in common with. I don't like her. She's just a mean person. She will attack me for anything I say. Who needs it? I believe she was bad from the time she was born. I always dreaded taking her places. I think she wanted to purposely embarrass me.

> She's been this way from the minute she was born. Especially to me. I was going to have more kids, but now I'm sorry I even had this one.

The child's stage of development

When children are young, it's very hard to look into their adorable little faces and wish you hadn't had them. They are needy. You are their guardian. One feels, "How can I be so cruel as to wish I didn't have them?" Then comes the teenage years. Their faces aren't so adorable any more and they aren't so needy. In addition, they have gone from cuddly to various degrees of obnoxious. At this age, what is on the lips of many is, "Deliver me from this torture." Many parents of adolescents gladly admit that they wouldn't have had children had they known about the horrors of adolescence . . . and beyond. So much effort and so little satisfaction. One woman said:

> My husband and I worked very hard and gave our time, money, and energy to our son. We didn't deserve to be treated so badly . . . anger, disdain, and his surly mood. Would we do it again? No. Not if we knew what we were getting into.

And then there comes adulthood. Some children happily absolve themselves as they pull out of their teens and go off on their own. They become loving, caring, and appreciative of what their parents have sacrificed. Of course, this can make their parents once again happy that they were born. But some children remain forever difficult and their parents go through life wondering what it was all about.

The deep, deep love

There is another reason some parents responded that they would not go through the experience again. As I talked about in chapter 2, what many parents are least prepared for when they have children is how much they love and worry about them . . . and it is this very love that often makes having children so difficult. This love can be so intense, so painful, that it is overwhelming, especially in light of so many things that could go wrong from cradle to adolescence and beyond. Would they have chosen to feel this kind of love had they known in advance? The answer is no. For these people, it is a *terrible* love, not a rewarding love like one has for their loyal friend or their caring mate in a happy marriage.

Contrary to these unfortunates, there are the lucky parents who learn early in the game the secret of detaching and "letting go" so that their terrible love isn't so terrible any more. (Some clues as to how to do this can be found in the addendum.) These parents are capable of appreciating the love they have for their children. Instead of being a terrible love, it is a wonderful love.

The effect on the parents' own behavior
Some who would definitely do it over again were those who felt their children had actually saved their lives . . . yes, saved their lives. In their youth, they were self-consumed human beings high on drugs and alcohol. They feel that having children gave them focus, got them off drugs, and certainly made them grow up. They are grateful to their children for the sobering effect—literally and figuratively—they had on their lives. In a similar vein, one woman said that her child made her stop her anorexic behavior. Again, for the sake of her child, she had to grow up. One parent claimed her child was her lifeline to the part of herself that is the giving, caring adult.

Please understand that this does not mean that if someone is an addict, he or she should run out and have a child. Parenthood for some makes matters worse. Earlier in the book I talked about my friend who *became* an alcoholic after her children were born. Also, the above scenarios do not necessarily bode well for the child. Why? Some would argue that those coming off drugs or alcohol or anorexia nervosa need time to deal with many issues within their own being that created such negative choices. To jump into parenthood until these issues are dealt with is a bit chancy for all concerned.

One mother who is a recovering alcoholic said that it would have been awful for her and her child if she just came off alcohol and had to care for all of his demands. She was grateful for the four years of getting her act together before her child was born. But then again, who knows what's right and wrong? It's all chancy.

You see that there are many things that enter into the parenting picture that determine whether parenting feels good or whether it feels bad. In the end, I guess it's a matter of balance. When the good feelings exceed the bad feelings, yes, most of us would want to do it over again. When the bad feelings exceed the good feelings, no, most of us would not want to do it over again. When the good and bad equal out, we could go either way depending on the time of the day. It's really that simple.

As you saw through the reading of this book, there are many factors that dictate this delicate balance of feelings. And, hopefully, you have a better understanding of why some of us love the experience and why so many of us find ourselves in the "life-drainingly, wretchedly, miserably hard" category. Obviously one who has those LBP genes is a far better candidate to embrace such an extraordinary task that requires that we give up many parts of our life.

Hegel once said, "The birth of children is the death of parents." A bit of an exaggeration perhaps, but there is no question that many parents, particularly mothers, trade in their hopes and dreams for themselves and begin hoping and dreaming for their children instead. It is sad that our conspiracy of silence has not spelled out what a person gives up to become a parent. Usually when they find out, it is too late. Again, while many feel that the loss of or change in so many aspects of their life is worth it, many do not.

I've "joked" about those Loving-Being-a-Parent genes (LBP genes), or the lack thereof, throughout the book. You may be surprised to learn that scientists have actually found a nurturing gene in mice. Yes, it's true. It is called the fosB gene. They have discovered that if this gene is absent in mice, nurturing behavior is also absent. The mice will be normal in all respects, *but they will ignore their babies.* Normally female mice protect their babies, cuddle them, lick them, and feed them. If a mouse doesn't have this fosB gene, the females totally ignore their pups and the poor things eventually die.[2]

It's amazing but this same fosB gene is also present in human beings. Now don't get excited . . . its role has not been studied when it comes to nurturing. But who knows! Perhaps the presence or absence of this gene explains why some parents love parenting and some parents don't . . . why some parents would do it over again and why some wouldn't. Unfortunately, many explanations of mice behavior don't translate to human behavior. But it is an interesting theory, and we will have to wait to see if further research gives us any more answers to the puzzling question of why some love parenting and others do not.

Let's look at another interesting possibility—a similar, but more spiritual possibility—to explain the extreme differences in our responses to the parenting role. In chapter 5, I briefly explained John Hillman's theory that children come into this world with their own "calling" which determines what they love to do and who they shall become. Well, by definition, we, too, have come into this world with our own calling.

In his book, *The Soul's Code,* Hillman speaks of "calling" as an invisible mystery at the center of every one of us which addresses the life-affirming questions, "Who must I be?" "What must I do?" "What must I have?"[3] Each person's calling is different. Each person brings into this world a uniqueness that asks to be lived. Calling isn't about our genes, a physical part of our being. Calling is about a spiritual part of our being. And those of you who know my previous work know that I am a big proponent of body, mind . . . and spirit.

I find Hillman's theory to be very compelling. It offers an attractive explanation as to why human beings are so different in their interests and strivings. Some of us are drawn to science, some to art, some to sports, some to medicine, some to teaching . . . and yes, some to parenting. It is hard to deny the existence of some sort of calling. Following his theory to its logical conclusion, does it make any sense to believe that all people come into this world with a calling to love parenting? No more than it makes any sense to believe that all people come into this world with a calling to love soccer. Some love soccer; some don't. And no matter how hard the latter try, they can't make themselves love soccer. I love my kids, but I certainly didn't love the process of parenting, and all the attempts to convince myself otherwise were futile . . . just as futile as trying to convince myself I love soccer! Matus confirms this message I am bringing you. He says:

> There is no joy in procreation if parenting offers no emotional fulfillment. If having a child is not relevant to one's life agenda, the result can be unhappy and disastrous.[4]

For many reasons we may avoid the truth about our calling but, if we are lucky, truth wins out. In *Feel the Fear and Do It Anyway,* I talk about "the off-course-correct" model which has great relevance here:

> The trick in life is not to worry about making a wrong decision; it's learning when to correct! There are many inner clues that help you know when it is time to correct. The two most obvious are confusion and dissatisfaction. Ironically, these are considered negatives, instead of positives. I know it is hard to accept, but an upset in your life is beneficial, in that it tells you that you are off-course in some way and you need to find your way back to your particular path of clarity once again. Your confusion and dissatisfaction are telling you that you're off-track, and, as a friend once suggested to me, "If you don't change your direction, you're likely to end up where you're heading."[5]

Madeleine Albright, who holds the important job of America's Secretary of State, was someone who was off-course early in her life and ultimately "corrected" by paying attention to her calling. Her twins were born six weeks premature and they spent almost two months in the hospital. Feeling somewhat at a loss, she enrolled in an eight-week, eight-hour-a-day crash course in Russian to take her mind off things. When the twins were well enough to come home, she had to feed them very frequently. She said, "Then I kind of sat there during the day, feeding them, watching soap operas, and I thought, I didn't go to college to do this." Her course in Russian reminded her that she really liked to study, so she enrolled in graduate school at Columbia University in New York City. She thought of what she loved to do . . . study. And she did it. And the rest is history.[6] Her early experience mirrored mine in many respects.

Hillman's theory suggests that we constantly need to ask ourselves, "Does this feel right for who I am?" If yes, we go forward. If no, we change our course. The secret is to keep asking ourselves this question throughout our lives and making changes whenever necessary . . . whether it has to do with parenting or not. Hillman talks of intuition, whispers, hints, sudden urges, and oddities that disturb your life.[7] I would like to add "meaningful coincidences." These are all voices of the inner wisdom we naturally possess. And when we learn to quiet our body and mind and listen to the spiritual part of who we are, so many answers are revealed. When we have the understanding that each person comes in with a different calling and is unique, we can see . . .

There is no right or wrong reaction to parenting; there are only different reactions to parenting.

So for those of you out there who are feeling guilt about your particular reaction to parenting, you can now let go of your guilt. Your reaction speaks of your uniqueness, your calling—nothing more, nothing less. And no matter how anyone judges you, nothing will change this essential reality. It is always important to keep in mind that you are not alone if you dislike parenthood. So many of us adore our children, but really hate the process of parenting. We do what it takes . . . but we would really rather be doing something else.

I am sure many parents out there identify with my experience of parenting. There were parts I loved, like the physical closeness I had with my children. When they were babies, I loved snuggling my nose into their necks and feeling the softness at the back of their heads. And they were cute. And funny. And cuddly. And bright. And I loved to teach them about things I had learned about the world. *But* . . . my calling was definitely not parenting. I did the best I could do with what I was given. I kissed their hurts, fed, clothed, and bathed their bodies, went to all the parent-teacher meetings, nursed them when they were sick, planned the birthday parties, bought the yearly Halloween costumes, took them frequently to the museums, the theater, the movies, and read to them so many children's books that they knew how to read before they even started school. Did I love it? No, I didn't love it. Did I love my children? You bet I did. But there is nothing in the world that I presently know of which could have *made* me love parenting. Perhaps one day there will be a way of implanting those LBP genes into the brains of those of us who don't seem to have them. Until then, we'll just have to do the best we can.

As you see, love for your children is not enough to make you love parenthood. But the good news is:

You don't have to love parenthood to be a good parent!

That should be a big consolation to many great parents out there who definitely fit in this category. All we can do is our very best to honor our responsibilities to our children and then let go of the outcome—understanding that, whether we loved the process or not, our children will blame us for everything that goes wrong with their lives anyway!

It is hard for some of us to face the reality that we will never enjoy parenting the way others may. But finding our calling elsewhere makes up for the disappointment. That is why we can't give up our dreams. I know of many women who have given up their dreams to raise their children according to the dictates of the guilt-gurus. It isn't necessary; it isn't even wise.

I believe that people are put in this world to expand to the width and breadth and depth of who they are capable of becoming. Those with the LBP genes or the "calling" or the fosB genes—or whatever—truly can feel this sense of expansion in the raising of their children. Others cannot. Their sense of meaning and purpose is not satisfied in the taking care of a child. Their yearning is elsewhere. And it is the measure of a wise person to find out where that "elsewhere" is and make plans to get there any way he or she can. Many times when I have been off-course in my life, I remember the words of Rollo May that I learned many years ago:

> Every organism has one and only one central need in life—to fulfill it's own potentialities.

It is this very thought that sent me back to school and then off to work so many years ago. And it made all the difference in the world in terms of my being a fulfilled person . . . and certainly a better mother.

There are so many variables that go into the parent-child dynamic . . . most of which are out of our control. What these variables are will be debated for a long time to come. For now, our task is simply find a way of listening to the highest, yet deepest, part of who we are. Here we will find the answers as to where we need to go and what we need to do to keep us on our own personal track for a rich and wonderful life . . . whether we have children or not.

Endnotes

[1]Radl, Shirley L. *Mother's Day Is Over.* Charterhouse, New York, 1973, p. xi.

[2]"Gene in Mice Determines Maternal Behavior." Source: "In Tests of Mice, a Gene Seems to Hold Clues to the Nature of Nurturing," in the *New York Times*, July 26, 1996.

[3]Hillman, James. *The Soul's Code: In Search of Character and Calling.* Warner Books, New York, 1996.

[4]Matus, Irwin. *Wrestling with Parenthood: Contemporary Dilemmas.* Gylantic Publishing Company, Littleton, Colorado, 1995, p. 2.

[5]Jeffers, Susan. *Feel the Fear . . . and Do It Anyway.* Fawcett Columbine, New York, 1987, p. 127.

[6]"Lady of Steel and Silk: A Portrait of U.S. Secretary of State Madeline Albright," in *Hello* magazine, Number 509, May 16, 1998, p. 28.

[7]Hillman. Ibid., p. 10.

CONCLUSION

AND WHEN ALL IS SAID AND DONE

We weren't born to hold on to positions. Nor are we meant to be perfect. We are meant to flow in a world that is constantly moving beneath our feet.

Susan Jeffers[1]

There you have it. A picture of parenthood that you may have never seen before. In the preface, I promised to explode the myths about parents and kids. And that is what I have tried to do. It is my hope that I have played some part in breaking the conspiracy of silence that has gripped Western society for so long. It is also my hope that I have relieved some of the terrible guilt that has plagued parents for much too long a time. I thank profusely those who have given me their time, their thoughts, and their trust so they can play their part in breaking the conspiracy as well.

We need to stop glorifying parenthood; rather we need to paint it with the broad stroke of reality. As I watch parents with their children in the park, the market, a restaurant, or just walking down the street, I often pause, watch for a moment, and think to myself, "I know how hard it is and my heart goes out to you. And I pray that you have the courage to tell your truth to others who need to hear what you have to say." I can't think of anything more unjust than to withhold the truth from our own children, other parents who are suffering in silence, and would-be parents who haven't a clue as to what they are getting into.

When I find myself in the presence of young people, with or without children, one can almost see the black cloud of misinformation hanging over their heads. One young man said, "My father told me that anyone who doesn't have children will just dry up." That was a new one for me. I know childfree people who are having an admirably rich and "wet" life; dried-out they are not! Anyone locked in such societal beliefs is nothing but a prisoner of those beliefs.

Having said that, I know from my own experiences that, ultimately, all that we have already chosen in our life, or will choose in the future, can bring us great learning. If we have children, young or old, darlings or demons, we can learn how to make a wonderful life for ourselves. If we *don't* have children, we can also learn how to make a wonderful life for ourselves. There is no such thing as a "wrong" decision if we can learn and grow from it all. Those of you who are familiar with my previous books know I call this "saying *Yes* to life." And in the end, it's the measure of a very wise person who finds the unique opportunities for love, joy, caring, contribution, growth, and abundance inherent in all that life hands us.

This is our greatest challenge—an even greater challenge than raising a child! But what a gorgeous challenge it is, because with every step along the way we come closer and closer to that place within where only nourishing thoughts, feelings, and actions reside. And it is here that we discover that we can, indeed, create a heaven on earth no matter what is happening in our lives. As I said in *Feel the Fear And Do It Anyway,* "I trust we will meet along the way . . . if we haven't met already." And I greatly look forward to that.

From my heart to yours,

Susan Jeffers

Endnotes

[1]Jeffers, Susan. *End the Struggle and Dance with Life.* St. Martin's Press, New York, 1996, p. 207.

ADDENDUM

A SURVIVAL GUIDE!

Whatever the method, the purpose of quieting the mind is always the same—to step out of our own way and touch a Universal oneness with all things.
Susan Jeffers[1]

At the best of times, children can make us feel joyful, happy, proud, wonderful, loving, and every other positive emotion you can think of. *And at the worst of times*, children can make us feel sad, angry, frustrated, helpless, hurt, and every other negative emotion you can think of. For peace of mind, we must learn how to fully embrace the good times and deal with the bad times in an enriching way.

The following "survival" tools are some of my favorites to bring us that delicious sense of peace and clarity when it comes to our kids, or for that matter, when it comes to *all* situations in our lives. The purpose of each of these tools is to lift us into the most powerful and loving part of who we are. It is in this place that we are able to *react* to external events in a very positive way. (Understand that the only thing we can effectively control in this world *IS our reaction* to the world around us!) Used on a regular basis, these tools work wonders in our lives and it is very reassuring to know that they are always available to us when we need them.

I've presented the tools in "nutshell" form as they are not the primary focus of this book. For more explanations and details about these and other empowering tools, I direct you to my earlier books, particularly *Feel the Fear . . . And Do It Anyway, Feel the Fear . . . and Beyond,* and *End the Struggle and Dance with Life* . . . all of which were written to help you move from a position of pain to power in *any* area of your life. Wouldn't it be lovely to move from a position of pain to power when it comes to our children? Oh, yes! So here they are . . . a few of my favorites. Use them often and your chance of "survival" will certainly be much greater!

SURVIVAL TOOLS FOR CREATING HAPPIER PEOPLE

Build a rich, full life for yourself

No one thing in our lives should ever be the focus of *all* our attention, whether it be work, a relationship, or children. When we allow *anything* to be emotionally all-consuming, we are setting ourselves up for a great deal of fear, anger, resentment, frustration, and other negative emotions. When our lives are rich with meaningful experiences, loving people, and a sense of importance in the world, problems in one area of our lives, such as with our children, cannot wipe us out.

Let me give you a very telling visual demonstration of this principle. When we make children the total emotional focus of our lives, our "life-space" looks like the following:

Life-Space

Given this excessive focus on our children, think how wiped out we would feel whenever trouble of any kind is brewing in their lives or in our relationships with them. Not a healthy situation. On the contrary, it is a recipe for over-protection, obsessive concern, and negative emotions such as fear, anger, confusion. Not a happy parenting picture.

It's time to change the scene. Look at the following "life-space" which portrays a very different picture:

Life-Space

RELATIONSHIP	CAREER	CHILDREN
CONTRIBUTION TO COMMUNITY	SPIRITUAL GROWTH	FRIENDS
PERSONAL GROWTH	ALONE TIME	PLAY TIME

Here you have a life-space filled with many riches and opportunities. Here children are a very important part of your life, *but they are not your whole life.* There is so much more. Seen in this way, you have a child, but your life consists of *so much more* than your child. And, if things are not going well in the CHILDREN category, of course it causes distress, but not the kind of distress it would cause if children were your only emotional source of purpose and fulfillment. So a good beginning to creating a rich, full life for yourself is to create your own nine-boxed grid of life, similar to the above, that includes the nine components closest to your heart . . . thus creating a visual sense of the richness of your life.

"But, Susan," you might be thinking, "I already have other things in my life—my family, my friends, my husband, and so on—but it is only my children that really matter to me." Obviously, a sign of an out-of-balance perspective on life! If this is true for you, what you have neglected to do is to give other areas of your life the emotional importance they deserve. When you are able to do this, you will then be able to disperse the disproportionate importance given to only one area of your life—your children. Family *is* important. Friends *are* important. Your spouse *is* important. Contribution to the community *is* important. And so on. To help you put more conscious attention in all areas of your life, it is important to do the following:

Commit 100 percent to *all* areas of your life realizing that you count in each of these areas (you really do!).

Some of us really don't understand our importance to others around us and to the community at large. If this is true for you, it is important to play the "act-as-if-you-were-important" game. How do you do this? In each area of your nine-boxed grid, ask yourself a crucial question, "If I were really important here, what would I be doing?" Make a list. And then, little-by-little, begin doing everything on your list.

For example, "If I were really important in the community, what would I be doing?" Make a list and begin doing each item on the list—one step at a time. "If I were really important to my friends, what would I be doing for and with them." Again, make that list and begin doing each item on the list—one step at a time. And so on. Why should we do this? Because when we "act-as-if" we really are important, we ultimately "live into" the truth of our importance.

In *Feel the Fear . . . and Beyond,* I present a "Daily Power Planner" that helps you incorporate *each* of these categories into your everyday life so that you begin to see that your life is rich, full, rewarding, and meaningful—despite what is happening in the CHILDREN category. A wonderful discovery!

Note: This is not a formula for creating more responsibilities for yourself. This is a formula for a change of attitude in order to create a feeling of richness in your life. Little-by-little, step-by-step, as you shift your *emotional* focus in order to create more balance, you learn to appreciate the richness of your *whole* life, not just one aspect of it. When this happens, no one thing in your life can wipe you out, including your children.

Cut the cord . . . over and over again

As I said in the above section, a healthy concern for and about our children is a very good thing, but we must take care not to create an unhealthy dependency such that our entire sense of well-being is tied to that of our children. This kind of dependency creates a desperate need to control everything they do and everything that happens in their lives. This is, of course, a crazy-making need since total control of anything is impossible. As I said earlier, the only thing you can effectively control is your *reaction* to it all.

The following is a very effective exercise for helping us cut that imaginary cord of dependency that destroys our peace of mind. It is to be used whenever we find ourselves obsessing about anything having to do with our children.

CUT-THE-CORD EXERCISE

Close your eyes. Relax your body. In your mind's eye, see your child standing in front of you. Now imagine a strong cord holding the two of you together. Try moving around and imagine your child moving around as well. You can't help but notice that when one moves, the other has to move. Keep moving around and notice the discomfort, pain, and sense of imprisonment this attachment creates. Not a picture of a healthy parent/child relationship.

Now, in your mind's eye, see yourself picking up a strong pair of scissors and then decisively cutting the cord that binds. The very instant you cut that cord, take a deep, deep breath, feeling the immediate sense of relief, freedom, and peace this simple act allows you to feel. Once again, in your mind's eye, move around. This time you notice that your child is not forced to move with you. And you notice that when your child moves, you are free to stand on your own—tall and whole. With this simple mental act, you've set the both of you free.

Understand that many people have a great deal of trouble doing this exercise. (You may be one of them!) Even in their mind's eye, they are frightened to cut that cord, particularly when their children are young. A parent's fear about anything negative happening in their child's life keeps them holding on for dear life, trying to protect and control. This is a common experience and very understandable, indeed. It can be explained by a parent's lack of trust in themselves, their children, and what I love to call the "Grand Design" . . . that mysterious life scheme out there that can sometimes take over when we have made other plans. As you begin incorporating tools of trust into your life, such as those in this section, cutting the cord becomes easier and easier.

Cutting the cord, whether our children are young or old, symbolically means that we are allowing our children to explore their own path of self-discovery and the discovery of the world around them. And it means that we, as parents, are allowing ourselves to enjoy our lives without unhealthy attachment to the drama in our children's lives. *Of course*, on their journey from infancy to adulthood, we must do our very best to keep our children emotionally sound and physically safe. But there is so much in both arenas that we simply can't control.

So, as we are gripped with worry about something happening relative to our children, this wonderful visualization lets us know that we can do only so much, and then, for our own peace of mind and for the effective handling of any problems our children face, we must learn how to cut that punishing cord. In so doing, we are trusting that our children will handle whatever happens in their lives . . . as we will. What better message can we send those that we love?

Practice affirmations of trust

"What are affirmations?" As I am using them here, affirmations are strong, positive statements that tell us that something is so. Said over and over again, these strong, positive statements give us a sense of inner strength. To help us more easily let go of our unhealthy attachment to our children, affirmations of trust serve us well. For example, there are three words that I have learned to habitually repeat to myself when I feel myself unhealthily tied to my children (or anyone or anything else). These three important words are, "I'll handle it!" This affirmation is a shortened version of, "Whatever happens in the life of my child (or children), I'll handle it!" Powerful! Say this affirmation with me now 10 times:

Whatever happens in the life of my child, I'll handle it.
Whatever happens in the life of my child, I'll handle it.
Whatever happens in the life of my child, I'll handle it.
Whatever happens in the life of my child, I'll handle it.
Whatever happens in the life of my child, I'll handle it.
Whatever happens in the life of my child, I'll handle it.
Whatever happens in the life of my child, I'll handle it.
Whatever happens in the life of my child, I'll handle it.
Whatever happens in the life of my child, I'll handle it.
Whatever happens in the life of my child, I'll handle it.

Hopefully, you are feeling a greater sense of peace. The interesting thing about positive affirmations is that, said over and over again, they have a wonderful effect on the body, *whether we believe them or not.* Yes, whether we believe them or not. Just the saying of the words sends a message to the subconscious part of our being and calms us down. Amazing! So whenever the "What if's" come up in your mind relative to your children, simply respond to yourself, "I'll handle it." For example:

What if: What if he (or she) has problems at school?
You: I'll handle it.
What if: What if he gets sick?
You: I'll handle it.
What if: What if he is unhappy?
You: I'll handle it.

I suggest that you put signs all around your home that read, "I'll handle it!" to reassure you whenever you are filled with worry or upset. As you say these reassuring words often enough about all aspects of your child's life, ultimately you are able to let go of your need to control the uncontrollable. And a feeling of relief is inevitable.

Another affirmation of trust is:

It's all happening perfectly.

This is a shortened version of:

My mind cannot see the larger picture, the Grand Design. I will simply trust that all things happen for a reason and I will learn and grow from whatever life brings me. Therefore, even if a certain situation is not going the way I want it to go,
it's all happening perfectly.[1]

Now that you know the longer meaning of "It's all happening perfectly," say it with me ten times:

It's all happening perfectly.
It's all happening perfectly.
It's all happening perfectly.
It's all happening perfectly.
It's all happening perfectly.
It's all happening perfectly.
It's all happening perfectly.
It's all happening perfectly.
It's all happening perfectly.
It's all happening perfectly.

I hope this affirmation gives you a feeling of peace. It is one of my favorites. The world could be falling down around me and in my head the words, "It's all happening perfectly" are ringing in my ears giving me a feeling that there is a reason for it all. And it is up to me to find a way to learn and grow from it all. A few other affirmations of trust are:

I let go and I trust.

I peacefully allow my life to unfold.

I peacefully allow the lives of my children to unfold.

Using such powerful affirmations on a daily basis can make a wonderful difference in your life.

Let go of expectations

We have so many expectations of our children and for them. For greater peace of mind, we have to let go of these expectations; that is, we have to reset our hearts. As I say in *Feel the Fear . . . and Beyond*,

> A heart that is set on something is rigid. Not knowing how to flow, it often gets broken. When we un-set our heart, we are free. When we let go of the outcome, we are free to rise, to "float" peacefully and gracefully to the highest part of who we are. If whatever we have so carefully visualized happens, so be it. If it doesn't happen, so be it. This is freedom in its highest sense! It is this mind-set that allows us to let go of fear and bring peace into our hearts.[2]

Of course, many of our expectations will be realized; others will not. That's just a fact of life. When we can let go of our expectations, it stands to reason we will have a greater sense of flow and ease in our lives. And obviously in this state of mind, the happier our lives will be and the more we will enjoy the state of parenthood.

First, it is important to identify the expectations we have for our children. There are expectations we need to let go of at each stage of our children's lives . . . whether they will be safe, healthy, attractive, happy, smart, popular, successful, loving to us, honest, drug-free, and so on. I suggest you begin a list of all the expectations you have about and for your children. Each day add to the list as new expectations pop into your mind . . . and they always will. A few examples:

I have an expectation that my child will have many friends.

I have an expectation that my child will be well-behaved.

I have an expectation that my child will always treat me with honor and respect.

I have an expectation that my child will never be involved with drugs.

I have an expectation that my child will be successful.

When you have made your long, long list of expectations relative to your children, *the next step is to let them go, release them, un-set your heart*. How do you do that?

After each of your expectations write the following:

. . . or whatever the Grand Design has in store for him (or her). I let go and trust we will both learn and grow from it all.

So your list of expectations now looks like this:

I have an expectation that my child will have many friends **. . . or whatever the Grand Design has in store for him. I let go and trust we will both learn and grow from it all.**

I have an expectation that my child will be well-behaved . . . **or whatever the Grand Design has in store for him. I let go and trust we will both learn and grow from it all.**

I have an expectation that my child will always treat me with honor and respect **. . . or whatever the Grand Design has in store for him. I let go and trust we will both learn and grow from it all.**

I have an expectation that my child will never be involved with drugs **. . . or whatever the Grand Design has in**

store for him. I let go and trust we will both learn and grow from it all.

I have an expectation that my child will be successful **. . . or whatever the Grand Design has in store for him. I let go and trust we will both learn and grow from it all.**

You see how this kind of thinking helps you cut that unhealthy cord. Again, even if you don't "trust," say it anyway. Your subconscious mind has a way of taking in the impact of the words you utter. Words about fear create fear. Words about trust create trust. Again, positive inner-talk is wonderful for body, mind, and soul.

Focus on the blessings

Whether we have kids or not, good things happen and bad things happen every day of our lives. But did you notice that most of us have a habit of focusing only on the bad and not the good? We need to learn how to reverse this process and train ourselves to focus more often on the good. Why should we do this? Because, when we notice the good, relative to our children, the bad has less of an impact on our well-being and the experience of parenting becomes more positive. Focusing on the good seems like it should be such an easy and happy thing to do. But we seem to be masochists at heart because we have a strong habit of focusing on the bad. To break this self-defeating habit, we need a daily reminder. Therefore, I suggest that: whatever their age (6 or 60), people should keep a daily journal of all their right actions and all that is right in their lives.

Here are some examples: "They didn't get into any trouble today," "They are breathing," "Bobby helped with the dishes," "Sally got a good mark on her paper," "Tom called today just to say hello."

What is beautiful about our commitment to recording these positive events is that we form the habit of constantly looking for such items so that we have something to put in our journal, even when things are at their worst with our children. Needless to say this is a big help in parent-child relationships . . . and our peace of mind. You want to include as many things that are "right" with your children as you can think of, even if they are silly. The more the merrier. You get the point. When we have committed to looking for the good, we come up with more than we would have imagined. Focusing on the blessings where children are involved fills us with a sense of abundance instead of scarcity. And this definitely improves our feelings about parenthood!

Say YES to Life

Those of you who have read my previous books know that I am a great believer in "saying YES to Life." This means nodding your head up and down, letting go of the resistance, and letting in the possibility for learning and growth that all situations, good or bad, allow us. When we approach all things with a great big YES in our hearts, we are able to find the blessing, find the strength we never thought we had, and all things wonderful. I have used this approach in my bout with breast cancer, my divorce from my first husband, and other difficult situations in my life.[3] The word YES gave me strength I never thought I had. And, of course, I used this wonderful word in the raising of my children, despite what was happening in their lives. The alternative to saying Yes is, of course, saying No. This means to resist, to struggle, and to paint yourself a victim. A no-win situation and a recipe for making a misery out of parenthood or anything else! So make a list of all that can go wrong in your life and the lives of your children. After each item, write:

I have the power to say YES to this. I will learn and grow from it all.

Little by little, you realize, you can, indeed, say Yes to it all . . . not only the good, but also the bad.

Enter the Land of Tears . . . often

Using positive tools does not mean putting ourselves in a state of denial about the pain in our lives. Children create a rainbow of feelings . . . from deep, deep sadness to great, great joy. Too many times, we stuff the bad feelings deep within our hearts, thereby deadening our experience of life, even our joy. I am convinced that unless one deals with the hurts along the way, one can never embrace the breathlessly astonishing moments of wonder that parenting can provide.

There is a lot of deep, deep pain that comes with the raising of children—no matter their age—and crying is a great healer. I, for one, did not cry enough when my children were younger. I deadened many parts of my being to cope with the vast array of feelings that were constantly flooding my being. While, in many ways, it was a great survival mechanism, there are many healthier and happier ways of dealing with the realities of parenting . . . and crying is one of them.

So I advise you to enter what I call the Land of Tears often, whether you are a man or a woman. (It is a myth that only weak men cry!) A word of caution: as you learned above, we can say YES to life or NO to life. We can also cry the tears of YES or the tears of NO. The tears of YES are not the tears of the victim. They are tears that trust that we will get to the other side of whatever problem we are facing. The tears of YES understand that the possibility for good lies within all the pain. The tears of NO, on the other hand, are the tears of the victim. "Why did this happen to poor me?" The tears of NO have absolutely no healing effect as they keep us locked in helplessness.

So when we enter the Land of Tears, it is important to take our attitude of YES with us. YES, this hurts, and YES, we will get to other side, and YES, we will learn and grow from it all. When crying tears of YES, we ultimately feel a weight lifted from our shoulders and find peace within our hearts.

If you find it difficult to cry, as many people in our culture do, study chapter 9 in *End the Struggle and Dance with Life*. Here you will learn how to access the Land of Tears, so that you can release the deep pain that lies within your heart. You will find that once the tears are all used up, it's as if a thousand pounds have been lifted from your shoulders and life seems ever so much lighter and more manageable once again.

Pray . . . a lot

I am not a *religious* person, but I consider myself to be a *spiritual* person. I feel a strong connection to what many call God, a Higher Power, the Universal Light, or whatever name one wants to give that wonderful force out there that can bring to us a great feeling of peace. I have created a prayer when I want to commune with this mysterious force and saying it always brings me peace. I offer it to you here. Notice that this prayer has no specific expectations that can create disappointment. It is a prayer of trust, gratitude, and purpose.

By the way, you may be interested to know that studies show that prayers work, *even if you don't believe in a Higher Power.* So I suggest you recite this prayer to yourself in the morning, before bedtime, and any time you find yourself troubled about anything to do with your children or anyone or anything else in your life. Here it is:

> I trust that no matter what happens in my life, it is for my highest good. And no matter what happens in the lives of those I love, it is for their highest good. From all things that are put before us, we shall become stronger and more loving people. I am grateful for all the beauty and opportunity you put into my life. And in all that I do, I shall seek to be a channel for your love.[4]

Study each sentence in this powerful prayer. When you put it all together, it can only be described as peaceful, beautiful, trusting, loving, empowering, and freeing. How sweet it is.

There you have it. A taste of some wonderful tools to bring you peace of mind.

- Build a rich life for yourself
- Cut the cord . . . over and over again
- Practice affirmations of trust
- Let go of expectations
- Focus on the blessings
- Say YES to Life
- Enter the Land of Tears . . . often
- Pray . . . a lot

With constant use, these wonderful tools can help you lighten up and derive much more pleasure from the parenting process. So begin, step-by-step, day-by-day, bringing these very effective tools into your daily life. How do I know they are so effective? Because over the years I have learned how to integrate them into my daily life. And they have made all the difference in the world.

Endnotes

[1]Jeffers, Susan. *End the Struggle and Dance with Life.* St. Martin's Press, New York, 1996, p. 171.

[2]Jeffers, Susan. *Feel the Fear . . . and Beyond.* Random House, 1998, pp. 39-40.

[3]Ibid., pp. 76-77.

[4]Ibid., chapter 3.

[5]Jeffers, Susan. *End the Struggle and Dance with Life*, Hodder Headline Australia, 1996, p. 181.

BIBLIOGRAPHY

*(**Note:** If you cannot find a book in the bookstore, ask if it can be ordered. If not, you may be able to order it through an Internet bookstore. Sometimes books go out of print and are no longer available through traditional sources. Not to worry. You may find out-of-print books at secondhand bookstores or on the Internet. In any case, you will always find another book to satisfy your needs. The world of books is abundant!)*

Alexander, Jenny. *Bullying.* Element Books Limited, Shaftesbury, Dorset or Boston, 1998.

Astrachan, Anthony. *How Men Feel: Their Response to Women's Demands for Equality and Power.* Doubleday, New York, 1988.

Badinter, Elisabeth. *The Myth of Motherhood.* Souvenir Press, London, 1980.

Barrett, Nina. *I Wish Someone Had Told Me: A Realistic Guide to Early Motherhood.* Academy Chicago Publishers, Chicago, Illinois, 1997.

Bartlett, Jane. *Will You Be Mother?: Women Who Choose to Say No.* Virago Press, London, 1994. (In America, New York University Press, New York, 1994.)

Bigelsen, Sylvia & Virginia McCullough. *When the Wrong Thing Is Right: How to Overcome Conventional Wisdom, Popular Opinion, and All the Lies Your Parents Told You!* MasterMedia Limited, New York, 1994.

Blau, Melinda. *Families Apart: Ten Keys to Successful Co-Parenting.* The Berkley Publishing Group, New York, 1993.

Bombeck, Erma. *Forever Erma.* Andrews and McMeel, Kansas City, 1996.

Bombeck, Erma. *I Lost Everything in the Post-Natal Depression.* Ballantine Books, New York, 1970.

Bombeck, Erma. *Motherhood: The Second Oldest Profession.* Dell Publishing, New York, 1983.

Bombeck, Erma & Bil Keane. *Just Wait Till You Have Children of Your Own!* Ballantine Books, 1972.

Clinton, Hillary. *It Takes a Village: And Other Lessons Children Teach Us.* Simon and Schuster, New York, 1996.

Cosby, Bill. *Fatherhood.* Bantam Books, New York, 1986.

Eyer, Diane E. *Mother-Infant Bonding: A Scientific Fiction.* Yale University Press, New Haven and London, 1992.

Eyer, Diane E. *Motherguilt: How Our Culture Blames Mothers for What's Wrong with Society.* Random House, New York, 1996.

Forward, Ph.D., Susan (with Donna Frazier). *Emotional Blackmail: When the People in Your Life Use Fear, Obligation, and Guilt to Manipulate You.* HarperCollins, New York, 1997.

Gibran, Kahlil. *The Prophet.* Published by Phone Media, Sydney, Australia. Fax: (61-2)9948 6362. Distributed in the USA by Seven Hills Book Distributors, Cincinnati, (800) 545-2005. Fax: (513) 381-0753. Cover and illustrations by Aubrey Beardsley. Originally published in 1923.

Giannetti, Charlene C. & Sagarese, Margaret. *The Roller-Coaster Years.* Broadway Books, New York, 1997.

Green, Maureen. *Marriage.* Fontana Paperbacks, Great Britain, 1984.

Handley, Helen and Andra Samelson, Editors. *Child.* Penguin Books, New York, 1990. (First published by Pushcart Press, 1988.)

Harder, Arlene. *Letting Go of Our Adult Children: When What We Do Is Never Enough.* Bob Adams, Inc., Holbrook, MA, 1994.

Hart, Dr. Archibald D. *Helping Children Survive Divorce.* Word Publishing, Dallas, 1996.

Herst, Charney with Lynette Padwa. *For Mothers of Difficult Daughters: How to Enrich and Repair the Bond of Adulthood.* Villard Books, New York, 1998.

Hickey, Mary C. and Salmans, Sandra. *The Working Mother's Guilt Guide: Whatever You're Doing, It Isn't Enough*. Penguin Books, New York, 1992.

Hillman, James. *The Soul's Code: In Search of Character and Calling.* Warner Books, 1997.

Hilton, Joni. *Guilt-Free Motherhood: How to Raise Great Kids and Have Fun Doing It!* Covenant Communications, Inc., American Fork, Utah, 1996.

Hochschild, Arlie. *The Time Bind: When Work Becomes Home and Home Becomes Work.* Owl Books, 1998.

Huff, Darrell. Illustrated by Irving Geis. *How to Lie with Statistics.* W. W. Norton & Company, New York, London, 1954. (Norton paperback reissue, 1993.)

Jeffers, Susan. *End the Struggle and Dance with Life: How to Build Yourself Up When the World Gets You Down.* St. Martin's Press, New York, 1996.

Jeffers, Susan. *Feel the Fear and Do It Anyway.* A Fawcett Columbine Book, Ballantine Books, New York, 1987.

Jeffers, Susan. *Feel the Fear . . . and Beyond: Dynamic Techniques for Doing It Anyway.* A Fawcett Columbine Book, Ballantine Books, New York, 1998.

Kabat-Zinn, Myla and Jon. *Everyday Blessings: The Inner Work of Mindful Parenting.* Hyperion, New York, 1997.

Kline, Christina Baker. *Child of Mine: Writers Talk About the First Year of Motherhood.* Hyperion Books, New York, 1997.

Lafayette, Leslie. *Why Don't You Have Kids?: Living a Full Life Without Parenthood.* Kensington Books, New York, 1995.

Lansky, Vicki. *Vicki Lansky's Divorce Book for Parents.* The Book Peddlers, Deephaven, MN, 1989, 1996.

Lerner, Harriet. *The Mother Dance: How Children Change Your Life.* HarperCollins, New York, 1998.

Levine, Katherine Gordy. *Parents Are People Too: An Emotional Fitness Program for Parents.* Penguin Books, New York, 1997.

Lindbergh, Anne Morrow. *Gift from the Sea.* Pantheon Books, New York, 1955.

Mason, Mary Ann. *From Father's Property to Children's Rights.* Columbia University Press, New York, 1994.

Matus, Irwin. *Wrestling with Parenthood: Contemporary Dilemmas.* Gylantic Publishing, Littleton, Colorado, 1995.

Maushart, Susan. *The Mask of Motherhood: How Mothering Changes Everything and Why We Pretend It Doesn't.* Random House, Australia, NSW Australia, 1997.

McGoldrick, Monica, Carol M. Anderson and Froma Walsh, Editors. *Women in Families: A Framework for Family Therapy.* Edited by W.W. Norton and Company, Inc., New York, 1991.

Miller, Angelyn. *The Enabler: When Helping Harms the Ones You Love.* Ballantine Books, 1988.

Peters, Joan K. *When Mothers Work: Loving Our Children Without Sacrificing Our Selves.* Addison-Wesley, Reading, Massachusetts, 1997.

Ponton, M.D., Lynn E. *The Romance of Risk: Why Teenagers Do the Things They Do.* HarperCollins, New York, 1997.

Radl, Shirley L. *Mother's Day Is Over.* Charterhouse, New York, 1973.

Riera, Michael Ph.D., *Uncommon Sense for Parents with Teenagers.* Celestial Arts, Berkeley, California, 1995.

Stevens, Barry. *Burst Out Laughing.* Celestial Arts, Berkeley, CA, 1984.

Swigart, Jane. *The Myth of the Bad Mother.* Doubleday, New York, 1991.

Viorst, Judith. *Necessary Losses.* Ballantine, New York, 1986.

Wagner, Laurie. *Expectations: Thirty Women Talk About Becoming a Mother.* Chronicle Books, San Francisco, 1998.

Warshak, Ph.D., Richard. *The Custody Revolution: The Father Factor and the Motherhood Mystique.* Poseidon Press, New York, 1992.

Zen to Go. Compiled and edited by Jon Winokur. New American Library, Penguin Books, New York and Canada, 1989.

OTHER BOOKS AND TAPES BY SUSAN JEFFERS

*Feel the Fear and Do It Anyway: How to Turn Your Fear and Indecision into Confidence and Action**

*Feel the Fear . . . and Beyond: Dynamic Techniques for Doing It Anyway**

*End the Struggle and Dance with Life: How to Build Yourself Up When the World Gets You Down**

*Dare to Connect: Reaching Out in Romance, Friendship and the Workplace**

*Opening Our Hearts to Men: Taking Charge of Our Lives and Creating a Love That Works**

Losing a Love . . . Finding a Love: Healing the Pain of a Broken Relationship

*Thoughts of Power and Love**

The Little Book of Confidence

The "Fear-Less" Series:

- *Inner Talk for a Confident Day**
- *Inner Talk for a Love That Works**
- *Inner Talk for Peace of Mind**

*AVAILABLE IN AUDIOTAPE

WORKSHOP AUDIOTAPES

The Art of Fearbusting

A Fearbusting Workshop

Flirting from the Heart

Opening Our Hearts to Each Other

Visit Susan's Web site at
www.susanjeffers.com

About the Author

SUSAN JEFFERS, PH.D. is considered one of the top self-help authors in the world. She has helped millions of people overcome their fears and move forward in life with confidence and love. Dr. Jeffers is also a leading expert in the field of relationships. And with *I'm Okay . . . You're a Brat!*, she applies her wisdom and experience to the field of parenthood. As well as being a best-selling author, she is a popular workshop leader, public speaker, and media personality. She lives with her husband, Mark Shelmerdine, in Los Angeles. Her Web site address is www.susanjeffers.com.

9 781580 632027

5325614R0

Made in the USA
Lexington, KY
27 April 2010